How to Publish Your PhD

by Catherine Pope

2021

First published in 2021 by Catherine Pope Limited.

Catherine Pope has asserted her right under the Copyright, Designs and Patents Act 1988 to be identified as the author of this work.

All rights reserved. The use of any part of this publication reproduced, transmitted in any form or by any means, electronic, mechanical, photocopying, recording, or otherwise, or stored in a retrieval system, without prior consent of the publisher, constitutes an infringement of the copyright law.

ISBN 978-1-8382429-3-0

Contents

Introduction	5
1. Establishing Your Purpose	20
2. Planning Your Project	58
3. Understanding Your Publishing Options	106
4. Creating Your Proposal	144
5. Writing Your Manuscript	188
6. Getting Ready for Submission	236
7. Publishing and Promoting Your Book	278
Conclusion	321
Resources	325
Acknowledgements	330
Index	333

Introduction

> "Learn from the mistakes of others. You can't live long enough to make them all yourself." — Eleanor Roosevelt (possibly)

You've passed your viva, you've changed your title to Dr on your bank cards. The next step is usually to turn your thesis into a monograph. Although there's no shortage of people urging you to get started, they're probably not falling over themselves to explain exactly how to go about it. Is it just a few tweaks here and there? Or are you going to have to rewrite every single word? What on earth is a monograph, anyway?

Writing a book *sounds* easy. After all, you've already produced a thesis. But this is a completely different project, with additional constraints, more stakeholders, and potentially a tighter deadline. It's not unusual for publishers to demand completed manuscripts within twelve months of signing the contract. That would be a tall order if you were working on it full-time. Now, though, you probably have a job and a range of other responsibilities.

Perhaps it feels overwhelming. In the olden days, i.e., 20

years ago, it wasn't unusual for PhD students to have a permanent job and a book contract before they'd even finished their thesis. Now you're expected to have published several books and hosted your own TV series before a university will consider you for a part-time hourly paid lectureship. But the publishing world has changed, even if academic conventions haven't yet caught up.

Those traditional pathways no longer exist. While that gives you more freedom to choose your own direction, it also means spending more time working out your next steps. You have to navigate through this new territory, while most of the maps still refer to the last century. And the publishing world has changed. Publishers are dealing with declining sales, huge technological change, and the impact of initiatives such as Open Access.

There's a lot to understand if you want to embark upon your writing adventure. In this book, I'll guide you through everything you need to know about academic publishing in the 21st century. It won't be an easy journey, but I promise it'll be honest, realistic, and enlightening. I'll accompany you as you establish your purpose and scope, plan your schedule, approach a publisher, and actually write your book. Although we'll focus on the monograph, much of what we'll cover will apply to other publication types, too. Along the way, I'll also give you ideas about alternatives to traditional publishing.

This is a practical book with lots of activities. I'm not looking to fill your head with heaps of jargon, theory, and historical context. Instead, I'll be asking you nosy and provocative questions to ensure you find a path that's right for you. You'll need a notebook and some sticky notes. Lots of sticky notes. One of the advantages of becoming an author is that you have an excuse to buy more stationery. Worksheets and further resources are also available at www.howtopublishyourphd.com. If you work through all the activities, your experience of writing a monograph will be much smoother than mine.

Why I'm Writing this Book

I graduated from the University of Sussex in 2014 with a PhD on Florence Marryat, a prolific Victorian writer who produced 68 novels and enjoyed a colourful personal life. My research showed her 'trashy' fiction was a vehicle for radical feminist ideas, designed to infiltrate the impressionable minds of her female readers (and possibly to frighten her male readers). Given the liveliness of the subject and a growing interest in her work, I imagined publishers would welcome a monograph.

I approached three publishers with my proposal. One responded with "no" after just five minutes. He was very kind about it. It would've been even kinder had he given the impression of having thought about it for at least an hour. The other two rejected it more slowly, but no less emphatically. These three rejections made me see the proposal through the publishers' eyes, which is what I should've done in the first place. Obscure Victorian writers make great PhD topics, but they have almost zero appeal for publishers. With an eye on markets, they're largely interested in household names like Charlotte Brontë and George Eliot.

Although I quietly fumed, I couldn't blame them, really. I run a small publishing press — Victorian Secrets[1] — which specialises in books from and about the nineteenth century. This gives me a good view from the inside. While it's a labour of love rather than a commercial enterprise, I need people to buy books. I don't pay myself a salary and we have no premises beyond a corner of my study. But there are still costs, such as printing, distribution, accountancy, software, and biscuits. And it takes time. Lots of time where I'm not earning anything from my day job as a writer, coach, and trainer. I've taken a risk on some obscure titles, some of which have paid off, but there are a few titles where sales are in single figures.

Having abandoned hope of getting my book published, a publisher *approached me*. They'd created a new series called Key Popular Women Writers and were looking for someone to contribute a volume on Florence Marryat. I'd met the series editors at several conferences, and they were familiar with my work. Although I needed to submit a formal proposal, it was more about demonstrating my capacity to write the book, rather than convincing them of the merits of the idea. Despite my familiarity with the publishing world, I made a number of mistakes with my monograph:

- It took a lot longer than anticipated, the project outlasting my energy and enthusiasm by a considerable margin. By the end, friends and colleagues were far more excited about the book than I was.
- The slow process meant my approach in places seems dated. Although it was published in 2020, much of the

....
1 There's no underwear, just the occasional Freudian slip.

material was written five years earlier, when the debates around race, gender, and sexuality were framed differently. Even Victorian Studies moves with the times.

- I had no say in the front cover, which looks like a 1970s textbook. This made me reluctant to promote it on social media. Given I run a press, I didn't want anyone thinking *I'd* chosen the design. I should've looked at the publisher's other covers.

- There's no ebook. Although I signed over the ebook rights, the publisher doesn't publish electronically. This limits both the market and accessibility. I'll say more about this in the section on Understanding Rights and Contracts.

- I would've been much happier writing a biography of Marryat, rather than literary criticism. This would've been harder to write (and infinitely harder to get a publisher), but it would've been more fulfilling. I went for the (slightly) easier option, rather than pursuing the book I really wanted to write.

On the bright side:

- The reviewers' reports provided valuable feedback on my manuscript. It would've been hard to get those insights through other channels. Well, one review was quite damning, but you can't please everyone. The series editors were also supportive and enthusiastic throughout.

- I enjoyed the cachet of having been published and my monograph went through a traditional peer review process. Although I'm not seeking an academic post, I never know when this might come in handy. It's like having a driver's license — even if you don't drive, it's sometimes useful for other purposes. For instance, with a book on your CV, you can get a blue badge on Twitter and join the Society of Authors.

- I didn't have to do all the production work myself or cover the costs of it. I could've self-published my book *much* more quickly, but I really would've been fed up with looking at the wretched thing by the time I'd written, proofread, and typeset it.

- I got a very good review in an academic journal, along with a clutch of lovely tweets and emails from researchers who'd bought a copy. I felt incredibly chuffed that these people had read my book thoroughly and taken the time to comment on it.

- I can now share my experience with you. As someone who has *been* published, *self*-published, and published other people's work, I have a dizzying 360-degree perspective.

So many of the pitfalls could have been avoided, had I been more alert. But which of us is alert when we've just finished a PhD and are desperately working out what to do next? With this book, I'm sharing the information and insights that would have helped me make better decisions. There are a few existing books that go into a lot of detail about the process of publishing your PhD. While they're all helpful, I didn't come across one that gave the complete picture, especially not for academics based in the UK. Above all, none seemed realistic about the amount of work involved and whether this was worthwhile. I hope to offer a different perspective.

Apart from my monograph, I've published several other pieces: book chapters with Routledge and Palgrave, an online annotated bibliography through Oxford University Press, and an introduction for Valancourt Books. I've also self-published three books, including the one you're reading right now. Even though I have considerable experience of writing and publishing, it's still a challenge. I promise to be realistic about the difficulties, rather than pretending it's easy. Isn't it annoying when authors do that? It's hard, but not impossible.

Who this Book is For

This book is primarily intended for researchers in the arts, humanities, and social sciences. Although STEM researchers might find the occasional morsel useful, publishing in those disciplines involves different conventions, timescales, and formats. Engineers and scientists, for instance, usually write journal articles, rather than monographs. The advice here isn't specific to any discipline, either. I know nothing about your topic. And I won't be bandying around terms like ontological and epistemological, mainly because I've never really understood what they mean. This book is all about the *practical* business of getting a publisher and managing a large writing project.

I'm imagining you're:
- Approaching the end of your PhD and considering your next steps.

- Recently liberated from your PhD and keen to get cracking with a book.
- Suddenly realising you finished your PhD a couple of years ago and really ought to have done something with it by now.

You're probably a first-time author, although even those of you with some publishing experience might benefit from a deeper understanding of the options available.

This book is aimed at people writing in English, within the Western academic tradition. Although this tradition could certainly do with some major disruption, doing so is likely to limit your chances of getting published. If you want to push the boundaries, then smaller presses or self-publishing are usually better options. We'll explore those options in Chapter Three.

My focus is also on the UK. Most publishing books focus on North America, so I'm addressing a gap. Most of my examples, therefore, refer exclusively to the UK Higher Education system and publishing landscape. While the advice here might be more broadly applicable, you should always investigate the conventions in your part of the world, or the country where you're seeking to get published.

A Note on Language, Terminology, and Geography

Throughout this book, I'll be referring to your *thesis* — the term generally used in the UK for the written element of the PhD. In the US, it's usually known as the *dissertation*. The

Americans are right on this one. The argument based on your research is the *thesis*, and the *dissertation* is the written document in which you explain it. Given I'm based in the UK, I'm going with *'thesis'*. Otherwise, I'll just forget and end up being inconsistent. I called the book *How to Publish Your PhD* to avoid the more cumbersome *How to Publish Your Thesis or Dissertation*. And my focus here is on writing a *monograph*, by which I mean a scholarly study of a single topic. I use British spelling because anything else just feels odd.

How to Use this Book

Although this book is focused on your turning your thesis into a monograph, hopefully you'll also learn a range of techniques to help you with future projects. Even if you don't become an academic, you're likely to pursue a career that demands the ability to communicate clearly and meet deadlines. Like any other big challenge, writing a book is all about breaking it down into more manageable chunks, setting realistic targets, and establishing your most effective processes.

I'm here to guide you through every stage so you can make informed decisions that are right for you. It's a lot of work, but with a realistic and comprehensive plan, you'll do it much faster and to a higher standard. You'll learn from my experiences (and mistakes) and those of writers I've coached over the last few years. Sometimes I'm a good example, often a terrible warning. Both are instructive.

You can either read this book from cover to cover or simply jump into the chapter that's most relevant for you. I've kept it concise to ensure you don't waste time that could be spent working on your book. Each chapter concludes with a summary of what we've covered, along with action points and a troubleshooting guide.

The path you take through this book depends both on you and on your publisher. At the proposal stage, some publishers will expect a couple of sample chapters, others just an outline. You might have a major writing project to complete even before you start putting together a proposal. As I explain in Chapter Four, it's a good idea to have written a large chunk of your book, even if the publisher doesn't need to see it yet. Here are some suggested paths:

- You're completely new to all of this and are unsure about what you want to do — start at the beginning, as the first three chapters will help clarify your aims and assess their feasibility.

- You've already identified the publisher you want to approach, and they require two sample chapters or a full manuscript — begin with Chapter Two to create a plan, then proceed to Chapter Five to start writing.

- You've already had your proposal accepted and now have to write the book — start with Chapter Five to create your writing process. If you don't have a clear sense of what you're doing, go back to the planning stage in Chapter Two.

You'll notice that only half the book is dedicated to actually writing your monograph. That's because preparation is key. You need to both work *on* your book and *in* your book and develop the ability to pivot between the two. Working *on* your book means managing the overall project: establishing aims, defining the scope, and measuring progress. Working *in* your book is the writing phase. With a tight plan in place, this writing phase will be *much* easier. There's a lot of foundational work that must be done before you can see any visible evidence of your book.

Although I'm here to help you publish your thesis, there's only so much I can do. In this book, I'm focusing on the fundamentals — the processes you need to create, deploy, and refine. The next layer is the conventions in your discipline. This is where you'll need to talk to your supervisors, friends, and colleagues to find out how this information applies in your particular context. It will vary enormously according to the type of research you're pursuing. And then finally, the very top layer is the specifics for *your* project. Your monograph is completely unique. This means you'll have to adapt what you've learned from me *and* other people to come up with a solution that's right for you. Nobody else can tell you precisely what you should do with your book.

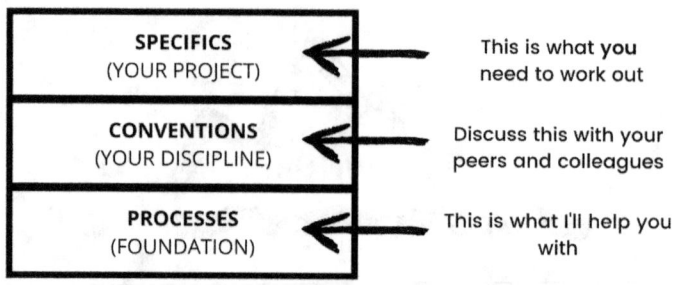

This book is arranged in seven chapters, each focused on a specific area of publishing your PhD:

In **Chapter One**, we'll start with *why*. By understanding your motivation for publishing your PhD, it'll help you decide whether this is a good use of your time. A sense of obligation probably won't be enough to propel you through the next couple of years. With a clear purpose, you can decide on the right format for your publication. Although we're focusing on monographs here, we'll consider alternatives, including journal articles and edited collections. I'll explain the main differences between a thesis and a monograph, also giving you an idea of how much work is involved. It's probably more than you think.

It might seem odd to plan your book before you've even written your proposal. However, this is essential for determining whether your book project is viable. In **Chapter Two,** I'll guide you through auditing your thesis, defining your scope, and mapping your book. I'll also explain the anatomy of a monograph so you understand exactly what you need to produce and how long it's likely to take you. We'll break your project down into 12-week sprints to help you stay on track.

The academic publishing world can be opaque to outsiders. In **Chapter Three,** I'll give you an overview of how publishing works in the 21st century, including the rapidly emerging force of Open Access. Depending on your career plans, this might be a route you need to pursue. You'll also discover how much you're likely to earn from your book (spoiler alert: not very much) and how much you need to *pay* to get published. Yes, there are costs involved, even with big publishers. And I'll guide you through the murky territory of contracts and copyright. I'm sure that's not making you quiver with anticipation, but a grasp of these areas means you'll avoid costly mistakes.

In **Chapter Four,** we'll investigate how to identify a suitable publisher. By doing your research, you'll greatly improve your chances of getting published. I'll share a process of assessing potential publishers and explain how you can make an informal approach. Then we'll get into the mechanics of writing a successful book proposal. Although a huge amount of work in itself, this document can save you time and result in a much better book. I'll also outline the typical publishing timeline and describe the various stages between submission and publication.

Once you have a contract, you'll need to get wiggling

with your writing. Like everything else these days, publishing is moving at a faster pace and you might have only twelve months to produce a full manuscript. In **Chapter Five**, I'll help you establish the right mindset, build a writing fortress, and stay on track. We'll dismantle the writing process so you can identify and overcome blocks to remove friction and boost your productivity.

With that elusive full draft complete, in **Chapter Six**, I'll provide clear guidance on getting it ready for submission. We'll work through my five-step editing programme to produce the best possible manuscript for your publisher. Although editing is an immense job, it's much easier (and more effective) with a plan to follow. I'll also help you understand how much support you're likely to get with editing and proofreading, and whether it's worth hiring a professional.

There's still a lot of work left to do, even after you've submitted your manuscript. In **Chapter Seven**, I'll explain how to interpret and implement reader's reports. Their feedback can be overwhelming at the end of a long and tiring project. I'll help you come up with a strategy for deciding how much extra work you want to do at this stage. I'll also clarify additional activities, such as checking proofs and compiling an index. Finally, we'll look at how to promote your book. Even if you're traditionally published, you'll be expected to do most of the marketing yourself.

None of the advice here is prescriptive. Please adopt (and adapt) anything that works for you and ignore what's not right for you or your project. Sometimes we just want someone to tell us exactly what to do. Although that feels like the easier path, it's often a less satisfying one. By considering all the options, you'll make a better long-term decision.

In whatever format you decide to publish your PhD, it's going to involve a big commitment in terms of time and energy. There are no quick wins. As we'll see, it often takes years for a book to go to press. It's important, then, to establish your motivation, which is what we'll do in the next chapter.

Are you ready? Let's get started.

Chapter 1: Establishing Your Purpose

"Find out who you are and do it on purpose."
Dolly Parton

Before plunging straight into this publishing adventure, it's important to establish your purpose. *Your* purpose and the purpose of *your book*. As you'll know from your PhD, any large writing project involves periods of despond and outright despair. Without a clear motive, it'll be hard to propel yourself through them. In this chapter, then, we'll start with the question of *why* you want to publish your PhD, before assessing the feasibility, and then addressing the practicalities. It's all about considering options and confronting realities.

PhD graduates want to publish their thesis for many reasons: to improve job prospects, to gain a wider readership, or simply because it's expected. All could be valid, but it's important to understand *your* motivation and whether it aligns with your life goals. Getting your book published is a truly satisfying experience and it might be key to finding your first job. However, it's a big commitment, too, sometimes taking longer than the actual PhD.

For some, writing a book (or even doing a PhD) is a means of delaying a more important and difficult decision, e.g., *what should I do with my life?* Although we have a lurking suspicion this pursuit might not lead where we'd hoped, at least it provides us with another clear goal. This is especially tempting when we've just finished a PhD. One potential outcome of reading this book is that you decide *against* publishing your PhD, at least for now. While that sounds defeatist, it's actually a positive outcome — you'll have made an *informed* decision.

As a coach, I get to ask tough questions, such as do you have time to write a book? Can you afford it? And is your thesis suitable for a monograph? Sitting with these uncomfortable thoughts for a little while will save future pain. By encouraging you to consider both your career and your publication strategy, you can decide whether this is the *right project* at the *right time.*

It's hard to make a good decision if you don't have all the information. I'll explain the different types of publication and how they might fit with your aspirations. Although I'll be focusing on monographs, you might decide to pursue a journal article or book chapter instead. At least for now.

Finally, we'll look at the differences between a thesis and a monograph. As you'll discover, they're very different beasts. By understanding exactly what's required, it'll be easier for you to decide whether this is a challenge you want to undertake. I'll also encourage you to identify some literary mascots to help you along the way.

We'll start with why ...

Starting with Why

In best-selling book *Start with Why*, Simon Sinek explains that when beginning a project, we dive straight into the *what* and the *how*. We thrash out the details, create complicated systems, and set ambitious targets. This is the dominion of our neocortex — the rational part of the brain. Although this area is vital for managing complexity, it's also slow to activate. The more responsive part of the brain is the limbic area, which governs our emotions. That's the bit you'll see on Twitter. If we satisfy this emotional area *first* by answering the *why* question, it's much easier to work out the *what* and the *how*. As we'll see in Chapter Five, this model is also useful in the writing itself.

For now, you get to be completely emotional. Make sure you have some tissues and biscuits handy.

Why do you want to publish your PhD?

I'd like you to spend some time reflecting on your motivation. The emphasis here is on getting all those thoughts out of your head in a non-judgemental way. If we try to rationalise those thoughts, we ignore the underlying emotions. And — whether we like it or not — those emotions drive us. Either talk to yourself (assuming you're on your own) or write down your responses. Not only do you have some notes to refer back to, it's also a good writing warm-up.

Ask yourself *why* and see what emerges. Be honest with yourself. It's fine to say, "I want the status of being a published author." Either use a bullet point list to capture all the reasons, or just respond to the question, "Why do I want to publish a book?" If you're writing your responses, there's absolutely no need for this to be polished.

Do you believe you have something to share? Something beyond what you've already said in your thesis? Could you build upon this contribution to either strengthen or extend those ideas, or to reach new audiences? Perhaps this is the first step of your publishing career that'll lead to further possibilities.

Or do you have a sense of unfinished business? Many of us begin our PhD with a vision of the final thesis — a grand Theory of Everything that takes our field by storm. When the viva comes around, though, we find ourselves desperately trying to account for the differences between that original vision and the document sitting in our lap. While the examination process provides an opportunity to correct some of those mistakes and strengthen a few of the arguments, we often remain fidgety. If only we could have another stab at it. Given what I now know, it would be *much* better. Turning your thesis into a monograph can provide this opportunity. As we'll see, the book form is less stuffy than the thesis, but it brings a different set of constraints.

Maybe it's validation you're craving? If you successfully pursue an academic career, your status is continually validated. Even if you don't publish much, you're an academic because you're teaching, attending conferences, and carrying out research. If you've decided against an academic career for whatever reason, publishing your thesis is a way of saying: "I might not be a lecturer, but I'm still a scholar. I have produced work of *publishable quality*."

Anyway, try to identify and record all those reasons. Then we can go a little deeper.

Going Deeper

If you're struggling to identify your motivation, try Cartesian Logic. Ask yourself the following questions (note the italics for the subtle differences between them):

- What *would* happen if you *did* publish your PhD? (e.g., status)
- What *would* happen if you *didn't* publish your PhD? (e.g., more time)
- What *wouldn't* happen if you *did* publish your PhD? (e.g., other books or projects)
- What *wouldn't* happen if you *didn't* publish your PhD? (e.g., an academic career)

If Cartesian logic is causing a brain spasm, try these questions instead:

- If you publish your PhD, what would change?
- If you publish your PhD, what would stay the same?

Finally, are you doing this for you or for other people? Extrinsic motivators really aren't that effective. They'll only get you so far. Unless you have a full-time coach nudging you at every stage, you need to find your own motivation. Consider what's worse: disappointing other people, or lumbering yourself with a huge unwanted project. And we often overestimate other people's disappointment. Sometimes they just want us to validate their own choices. Do what's right for you.

Developing Your Strategy

Assuming I haven't completely demolished your enthusiasm, let's think about your career strategy. While a 'career' now seems a delightfully quaint concept from the 1950s, it's good to have at least an idea of what you want to do next, even if that might be one of many jobs throughout your life. As a PhD graduate, there are lots of options open to you:

- Full-time, permanent (or tenured) academic.
- Teaching fellow (usually without research responsibilities).
- Part-time hourly paid lecturer (often doing all the unattractive teaching at short notice).
- Academic professional services, especially researcher development or research funding.
- Consultant.
- Academic publishing.
- Archives or museums.
- Charity.
- Policy wonk.
- Entrepreneur.
- Independent researcher.

Depending on what path you choose, different publishing options will be more appropriate. For instance, if you're pursuing a tenured academic position, traditionally published scholarly outputs are essential. This is typically how your worth as an academic is measured. For some disciplines, it's only the physical book, printed by a recognised publisher, that carries any weight. This is profoundly unfair, partly because it's so difficult to get a book published. But there's nothing to be gained from railing against the injustice of it all. Instead, devote your energy towards achieving that goal. When applying for academic jobs, you need to prove you're at least on the path to publication, for example by having a book under contract with a recognised press.

For teaching-based roles, an ambitious publishing strategy won't help (and may even hinder) you. In those situations, employers are more interested in your teaching experience. Unless you're hoping to pursue a research-based job while you teach, it might be worth putting your publishing plans on hold for the time being. Once you've done your teaching preparation (these roles are often heavily front-loaded), you'll have some more headspace for your book.

Moving down the list, museums and charities are likely to be interested in public engagement, so a well-tended and targeted social media presence could help you get a coveted role in this sector. For self-employment, it's generally better to publish work that's accessible by potential clients. Your clients are unlikely to buy an expensive monograph and it might take years to emerge from the presses, anyway. Trade journals or blogs might be more appropriate in this instance. However, a few peer-reviewed publications could add extra credibility. This also provides you with options, should you ever want to return to academia.

If you're becoming an independent researcher — either by choice, or through lack of alternatives — you need to think even more carefully. While it used to be odd to see monographs without institutional affiliations, it's now a far more common sight. Graduate employment is low and early career academics often have less time to write than independent scholars. They're frantically trying to keep on top of heavy teaching loads, mark endless essays, and secure a permanent position.

You might have the time to write a book, but is it a good use of that time? What will the book achieve for you? You might earn some credibility in certain quarters, but it's not the same as having an academic job. Attitudes are gradually shifting, but there's still a certain amount of snootiness around people perceived to be outside the academy. Given monographs are so closely pegged to academic career advancement, this might not be the right vehicle for you. If, for example, you're looking to become a TV historian, a blog or a more general book could be better for raising your profile.

I'm often asked whether you need an institutional affiliation to publish a monograph. Given the lack of academic positions, this is far less of a problem than it used to be. But publishers will want to know what connections you have. Are you presenting at conferences and participating in scholarly networks? They might require a reference from a tenured academic to confirm that you're still an active researcher. There could be a perception (not entirely misplaced) that independent scholars lack the funds to attend academic conferences and access to the latest research. We'll look at some of the costs of writing a book in a moment.

How, then, does the book fit into your overall career strategy? And what's the *opportunity* cost? If you spend all your free time over the next three years working on a book, what *aren't* you doing? That could include gaining vocational qualifications, writing a novel, or just indulging in some feckless hedonism. If you're anything like me, you'll want to pursue far more projects than could ever be achieved, even within several lifetimes. Annoyingly, we have to be selective.

Publishing Strategy

Alongside your career strategy, you'll also need a publishing strategy. That might sound impossibly grand, but give it some thought. Once you get started with writing, it's likely you'll see many other possibilities. You're not committing yourself to anything here, rather, you're thinking a couple of steps ahead to make sure you're not thwarting your future self. It's easy to think we have to seize every opportunity that arises. But there are always opportunities, if we're prepared to act on them.

For instance, it might be relatively straightforward to publish parts of your thesis as journal articles or book chapters. But does that mean you'll have less content for the book? As I'll explain in Chapter Two, publishers don't always allow you to reuse content. Although having published a journal article or two can help establish your author profile, make sure you haven't already given away your best ideas. There needs to be a reason to read your book, too. Given journal articles are more accessible and digestible, the book must offer something extra. Conference papers are a good way of road-testing your material without limiting your publishing options.

If you fancy yourself as a writer, don't be tempted to cram absolutely everything into this first book. When we're excited about our topic, we keep adding ideas and get distracted by shiny new thoughts. By resisting those urges, not only will you have a tighter narrative, but also you'll have some nuggets for future books. While theses can end up a fairly random collection of ideas, books require a much more coherent structure. We'll look at scope in Chapter Two and how to place some limits on your project.

Also consider whether your thesis is the right basis for your first book. Do you want to write a different book instead? Just because you have a thesis, it doesn't mean you have to do anything else with it. It'll still be available through your university's online repository. Don't feel under any obligation. As I mentioned earlier, you won't be able to propel yourself through this project if you're doing it for the wrong reasons. Instead, you could put your writing energy into another book. Equally, don't abandon your thesis just because writing another book feels easier. It won't be.

Of course, your publishing strategy won't necessarily work out, but having one in place makes success more likely. Pace yourself and don't try to do everything at once. A less ambitious book is more achievable and possibly easier to market, too. Most publishers aren't looking for earth-shattering ideas, rather a new perspective or insight on a topic of current interest. They'd much rather receive a proposal for a book that can be completed within a reasonable timeframe than one that takes twenty years to write. Don't sabotage yourself by thinking too big. You can build up gradually to writing the next *Sapiens*.

When's the Right Time?

Now you've considered your motivation and strategy, let's think about the right time to start publishing your PhD. As you'll discover, this is a substantial project and timing is crucial. You need to make sure you have enough resources — hours, headspace, and money — to keep going. Although you might be keen to get going ASAP, sometimes delaying can make sense. This gives you an opportunity to finish other projects and get yourself mentally prepared. If one of those 'other projects' happens to be finishing your PhD, timing is even more important.

Here are a few scenarios for you to consider.

You're Currently Finishing Your PhD

While working on this book, I spoke to a student who'd been advised by her supervisor to write a monograph *at the same time as her thesis*. Admittedly, this has a certain appeal: repurposing content on the fly and ending up with both a PhD *and* a publication is admirably efficient. However, I think it's inadvisable for three reasons:

- Finishing a PhD is bloody difficult! Pursuing another major project at the same time is going to consume too much energy and headspace.

- As we'll see at the end of this chapter, your thesis and book are intended for very different audiences and purposes. You can't hope to do justice to both simultaneously.
- It's almost impossible to get any perspective on your thesis until you've finished it. Once it's done, you'll get a peer review in the form of a viva. You need that validation and input before taking the next step.

Speaking of which, your viva is the perfect opportunity to get some feedback on those publishing prospects. Remember these caveats, though:

- Although your examiners will have many publications to their names, their experience of getting published will differ greatly from yours. Depending on their age, it might've been much easier to get a thesis published when they graduated. And, as more senior academics, they're more likely now to command the attention of publishers.
- Examiners often encourage PhD candidates to publish their thesis. This is because they're excited about the research, and also because this is seen as the next logical step. As career academics, they'll see a certain path for you. This path made sense until a decade or so ago, but now there are many more obstacles and opportunities for someone with a PhD. Your career strategy won't look like theirs.
- While your examiners will (quite rightly) think your

research is important, it's the *publisher* you need to convince. As I'll emphasise in Chapter Three, accepting a book proposal is a *business decision*. A publisher is primarily interested in selling books, not purely in disseminating the best ideas.

If you haven't yet finished your PhD, I'm not saying you shouldn't start *thinking* about your book. Indeed, this can be helpful for setting some limits on your thesis. It's often tempting to shove every idea we've ever had into the thesis. By planning longer term, you can earmark some of that content for future publications. This reduces your scope and makes for a tighter thesis. The PhD itself becomes part of your publishing strategy. The thesis could be the *foundation* of your book, but it's not actually a book.

Focus on the original contribution of your thesis, as that's going to help you both at the viva and with the book. And also work hard on the clarity of your writing. But don't be tempted to devote any time specifically to the book, even if a publisher approaches you. It'll delay your thesis submission and potentially mean you end up with neither a PhD nor a book. When you're stuck in the middle of endless thesis revisions, other projects are much more tempting. They seem far easier, mostly because you haven't yet discovered the inherent difficulties and obstacles. In some ways, a PhD is easier than a book. There's an obvious goal and the odds of succeeding are high. Whereas 90% of PhD candidates pass their viva, a far smaller number get their book proposal accepted.

In short, if you're still doing your PhD, this is your number one goal. Don't get distracted by the book. Once you've submitted that thesis, you'll probably have around three months before your viva. This is the perfect opportunity to consider your next steps. There'll be a gnawing gap in your life, and you'll suddenly have a lot more mental capacity. Now you can research publishers and understand what's required.

Unless you've been specifically advised otherwise, don't submit a book proposal until you've passed your viva. Publishers will see your PhD as a validation of your research project. Even if you have an excellent draft (which I'm sure you do), an editor cannot judge its *academic* merits. They're relying on your viva as a stamp of approval. While scholarly books are occasionally written by non-PhDs, these are always people with extensive backgrounds in research. Don't give publishers a reason to say "no" by getting excited and firing off a premature book proposal.

You've Just Finished Your PhD

If you've recently passed your viva, well done! If this was within the last few days or weeks, it's important to have a rest first. You don't want to leave it too long, but neither do you want to embark upon another big project before you've recovered properly. A rest is always a good idea under normal circumstances. These aren't normal circumstances, though. Even if you've not been directly affected by the pandemic — i.e., been ill yourself or lost loved ones — you'll have experienced stress. Although life is never certain, we've been forced to confront reality and adapt our lives radically. It's even more important, then, to take some time between finishing your PhD and beginning a monograph. You can't start a demanding project when you're exhausted.

You might be terrified about the job market. I've spoken to many PhD students recently who are so worried about what's coming *next*, they can't focus on what's happening *now*. It's still too early to tell what impact COVID will have on higher education and related sectors. While it's tempting to distract yourself by starting a demanding project, this might sap the energy you need for considering better options. Make sure you spend some time on your career and publishing strategy before making any firm decisions.

If you're publishing your PhD in the hope of getting an academic job, you'll need to establish the requirements in your field. These requirements vary enormously, so you'll need to establish what applies in your situation. Are prospective employers expecting:

- A published book, i.e., you can brandish a physical copy during the interview?
- A book that's gone to press, i.e., you have the proofs and publication is imminent?
- A book that's under contract, i.e., the publisher has seen the full manuscript and is committed to publishing it?
- A book that's under agreement, i.e., the publisher has accepted your proposal and you are currently writing the book. They're not necessarily under any obligation to publish the final manuscript. It'll be subject to readers' reports and various other checks. More on this in Chapter Seven.

Universities aren't always explicit about these requirements. You'll need to ask around through your network and get a sense of the publishing profiles and job descriptions of recent hires. In monograph-heavy areas, such as arts and humanities, it's reasonable to assume that the more progress you've made, the better.

If you need a published book or a completed manuscript, you'll have to move quickly. But make sure you're ready for the challenge.

You Finished Your PhD a While Ago

Maybe your PhD is a distant memory. Although you perhaps don't want an academic career, you'd nevertheless like to do something with that thesis, especially given how much effort you put into it. In this case, it's important to consider your commitments. Do you have any spare time? And how much of that time are you willing to spend on this project? I'll give you an idea of timescales in the next chapter. For now, though, it's about being realistic.

I'm assuming you're a motivated person with lots of ideas and interests. It's unlikely you're wondering what on earth to do with your day. You already have a full schedule. What are you going to stop doing to make time for your book project? If this is important, you can almost certainly find the hours. It needs to be important enough to make sacrifices, though. In some respects, a book project is even more pressured than a PhD. The timescales are often shorter and there's an editorial team setting deadlines and demanding changes.

If you have a full-time job, are you willing to spend most

of your weekends on the book? Would you be happy using your annual leave for visiting archives or checking proofs? Although there are some tasks that fit neatly into odd moments, you'll also need big chunks of time, especially at the beginning and end of your project. As you'll know from your PhD, you need *starting energy* and *finishing energy*. At the start, there's the mind-boggling stage where you're trying to fathom what on earth you're doing and get a sense of the scope; at the end, it's the seemingly endless slog of going over and over your drafts and ensuring they make sense to someone else.

Also consider how much headspace you've got. Even if you have the time, can you handle the pressure of another project right now? For me, working on this book provided focus and structure while I was dealing with health problems. It felt like something I could control, when everything — both personally and globally — seemed so terrifying and uncertain. As I was self-publishing it, though, there was absolutely no pressure for me to submit the manuscript to a deadline or provide updates to stakeholders. As such, the project fitted around my other commitments and energy levels. An external deadline would've added an unwelcome additional layer of stress.

If there's no career-based imperative for you to publish immediately, taking a break could ensure a more successful outcome. It's better to wait than to have to abandon your book. In the meantime, do something that's lower stakes, such as creating a blog for your topic or building your online academic networks.

Whatever your stage, think about how much time you're willing to give to this publishing venture. With big projects, there's always the risk they'll outlast our enthusiasm. That's what happened to me. From signing the contract, it was four years before my monograph went to press. It was hard to maintain my enthusiasm, especially when it took over a year to receive the readers' reports. I'd lost any sense of momentum and felt quite frustrated. I worked on many other non-academic projects during that hiatus, and it was hard to get back into that zone. If I'd known how long it was going to take, I wouldn't have done it.

There's no way of knowing at the outset exactly how long it'll take. Ask around to find out the typical timescales in your field. The shortest I've heard it six months, the longest seven years. Yes, seven! That's longer than many marriages. Then consider your own situation:

- Do you need a contract or a finished book before you apply for a job? If so, you'll need to hurry and find a publisher who's prepared to move at a similar pace.

- Do you have a small window of opportunity because of other commitments? Perhaps you have some time off before starting a new job, having a baby, or going travelling. Although you could probably manage a spot of editing alongside those life events, it's unlikely you'd get big chunks of time. What would be the consequences if it took much longer than expected? It almost certainly will.

- Do you have a lot of patience and don't mind how long it takes?

Can You Afford to Write a Book?

You don't just need time to write a book, you also need money — both to support yourself and to cover any research costs. It's rarely discussed explicitly, but you'll probably also have to pay towards the production of your book. This can include licensing fees for any images and also some editorial services, such as indexing and proofreading. I'll give you an idea of the specific publishing costs in Chapter Three, but it's a good idea to budget between £500-£1000. If that's alarmed you, don't worry. There are ways around it, but it'll mean compromising in some areas and potentially taking on tasks like indexing yourself.

You should be able to come up with a rough idea of the research costs yourself. These could include:

- Travel to archives or libraries (and possibly overnight accommodation).
- Books and journal articles for research (especially if you no longer have access to a university library).
- Photocopies or digitisation.
- Conference attendance.
- Equipment, software, and stationery.

If that's already looking prohibitively expensive, how could you reduce the costs? Maybe you can access material online, request scans, or get helpful friends to copy stuff for you. Even if you need to pay someone to copy a document for you, that could be significantly cheaper than travelling to the archive yourself. Academic Twitter is also very helpful in providing an underground network of research material.

I don't want to frighten you with the potential costs. However, as with any project, you need to understand the finances to ensure its feasibility.

Deciding on the Appropriate Publication Type

Although the focus in this book is on writing a monograph, we'll look at some of the other options available to you. This will help with your overall publishing strategy. If you decide on a different path, the later chapters on planning and writing will still be relevant. It's important to be clear on what's the right format for *you*, right *now*. If your goal is to publish a book, try everything within your power to do that first, then try Plan B, e.g., journal articles or book chapters. Cannibalising your thesis can compromise your chances of later publishing it as a monograph.

Here are some of the options.

Books

Monographs

A monograph is one of those words we think we know what it means, at least until someone asks us to explain it. Then we shuffle around nervously and change the subject. Generally speaking, a monograph is a scholarly work focused on a single topic and by one author. Or, it's a book that doesn't sell many copies. Due to their specialist nature, monographs typically shift around 200 copies. Yes, that's all. This is why they're so bloody expensive. I'll explain more about the woeful economics of scholarly publishing in Chapter Three.

Monographs are sometimes part of a series on a specific theme. This can be a good marketing wheeze, as libraries might be inclined to collect all the titles in the series. A series also provides opportunities for authors. Perhaps there's a forthcoming series with a gap into which your research fits. That's what happened to me. My book is part of the Key Popular Women Writers series. The publisher was keen to include a volume on Florence Marryat, and I just happened to have written my thesis on her. The potential disadvantage of contributing to a series is that you're often more constrained in terms of length, perspective, and style. The publisher will want all the volumes to fit together with an overarching theme.

The monograph is the primary scholarly format, at least in some disciplines. There are also a couple of other book formats for you to consider.

Trade

Trade publishing is for books aimed at a more general market. These titles are produced by mainstream publishers, such as Penguin Random House, and are found in bookstores. It's very unlikely you'll get a trade deal for your academic research, unless you're a media star like Professor Brian Cox or Dr Lucy Worsley. You'll probably need a few TV series before a big publisher will look upon you favourably. A few years ago, I was on a panel with an editor from Penguin. When discussing how to market books, he said: "Oh, we published this biography a couple of years ago and it only sold 30,000 copies. Complete disaster." That gives you an insight into their definition of success.

For smaller trade publishers, you'll at least need a significant social media presence. And it's a good idea to get an agent, too, as many publishers won't accept direct approaches from authors. Also, you need someone who understands the contracts and makes sure you get paid enough for your efforts. One researcher I spoke to received £1,000 for her first trade book when she handled the negotiations herself; with an agent on board, she got £50,000 for her next two-book deal. A good agent will know how best to exploit your intellectual property and help you with your overall publishing strategy. It's worth noting, though, that agents take 10-20% of your earnings in commission.

While £50,000 sounds like a lot, that's for at least two years' solid work and also needs to cover any research expenses, such as travel, books, and photocopying. And it's paid in instalments. You usually won't receive the final payment until the book goes to press. At least that stops you blowing it all on crisps in the first month. I know a few researchers who've enjoyed a reasonable income from publishing trade books. None of them, though, can live by writing alone. They also supplement those earnings with teaching, consultancy, and public speaking.

For trade books, you should consider how this fits into your career strategy. Although attitudes are slowly changing, there's a certain amount of snottiness towards trade books within academia. If you're looking to pursue an academic post either now or in the future, remember that a trade book might not carry much weight. I think this will change — after all, there's a big emphasis on public engagement now — but we can't be sure how fast.

If you're keen to pursue the trade route, consult the *Writers' and Artists' Yearbook* (www.writersandartists.co.uk). Here you'll find lots of advice and contact details for agents in different subject areas. Also, get yourself a copy of *Thinking Like Your Editor* by Susan Rabiner and Alfred Fortunato. They point out many of the potential pitfalls for academic authors, including our tendency to overestimate the likely interest in our topic. Because we're enthusiastic about it, we assume everyone else is equally excited.

Mini Monographs or Short Books

There's been a surge of mini-monographs, or short books, lately. They're usually less than 30,000 words and can be published in as little as twelve weeks. The disadvantage — at least to the publisher — is that the cover price is cheaper and therefore they need to shift them in much larger quantities. The speed and sales targets mean this format is best suited to current topics with broader appeal, such as cryptocurrencies or artificial intelligence. Examples of mini-monographs include OUP's Very Short Introductions, Palgrave Pivots, and Sage's Very Short, Fairly Interesting & Reasonably Cheap Series (that's really what it's called).

As with trade and textbooks, you'd need a relatively high profile for inclusion within a series like Very Short Introductions. Some of the other publishers might be more appropriate, but consider whether they serve your aims. If you're pursuing an academic career, a short book is unlikely to carry as much weight as a monograph.

Published Thesis

There are some presses that'll accept theses virtually unchanged. Their business model often relies on the thesis being embargoed and their ability to make it available ASAP at low cost. They're hoping that some inquisitive souls will stump up £100 to read the research before the embargo has been lifted. The costs to the press are minimal because they use print-on-demand technology and are not doing any editing or proofreading. Sometimes, they're also making a tidy profit by requiring you to pay a fee. Depending on the demand for your research, you might recover your costs and even pocket some royalties. But it's unlikely. This isn't the same as Open Access. In most cases, it's just exploitation.

This method has few merits, but might be appropriate if:

- You want your thesis to be available in book format with very little effort on your part.
- Your research is cutting-edge and will be useful to people in its current form.
- You want to earn some money from your thesis quickly (this is a very unlikely outcome, though!).

If you want to just get your thesis out there, I'd suggest self-publishing. It's a little more effort, but you'll retain control. I'll give you some pointers on those options in Chapter Three.

Journal Articles

Maybe you have a couple of standout chapters in your thesis

that are much stronger than the rest of it. In this case, you potentially have a choice between getting those other chapters up to standard, or publishing the best parts as journal articles. The main reason why editorial boards reject articles is because they lack a convincing argument and add nothing new. Make sure any pieces you repurpose have a good chance of success. In a book, you'll have a lot more space to build your argument and context; in a journal article, this must all be achieved in around 5,000 words.

If publishing journal articles is part of an academic career strategy, you need to place them in *right* titles. Unfortunately, there's been a boom in predatory journals. These dodgy outfits charge the author hundreds (sometimes thousands) of pounds and have absolutely no credibility. They're exploiting the murkiness around Open Access (see Chapter Three) and the imperative for publications. You can check out the credentials of journals on JournalSeek (www.journalseek.net), a free online service providing information on over 93,500 titles. Also visit Think Check Submit (www.thinkchecksubmit.org) for a wealth of good advice on finding trusted journals. Please don't give away your hard work to unscrupulous bandits.

If you really want or need to publish a book, don't be tempted by journal articles instead. Especially if you imagine this is the easier route. Big journals have three-year waiting lists and the peer review process in some disciplines also takes that long. You shouldn't submit your article to more than one journal at a time, either, so this could prove a protracted project. For anyone seeking a non-academic career, maybe trade journals or traditional media are more appropriate. Always consider your audience and where they consume their information.

Edited Collections

Edited collections are multi-author works, usually on a specific theme. Contributions comprise around 5-7,000 words. It's quite easy to get included in these collections, partly because editors sometimes struggle to secure contributions. But they don't necessarily carry much weight if you're pursuing an academic career. There's a lot of glory in editing a collection (your name is on the cover), but not so much in *contributing* a chapter.

Sometimes, you'll be invited to contribute a chapter based on a conference paper. While this sounds painless — after all, you've done most of the work — it's not always straightforward. It's flattering to be asked, but don't say yes right away. Ask yourself the following questions:

- Do you have time to write this chapter? How does it fit with your other commitments? Is the timescale realistic?
- Is there a proper project plan? Do you know when you'll be expected to submit your chapter and respond to peer review comments?
- Who are the editors? Are they well-known and respected within your field?
- Do you recognise the publisher? If not, look at some

of their publications. Are they good quality? Is there an index?

- How does this project fit with your publishing strategy?
- Does this compromise any other plans, such as writing a book? Will you be able to reuse that content?
- What are the publisher's terms? Will you get a copy of the book? (sometimes they'll try to fob you off with an ebook and a discount on a hard copy).

The editor(s) should've submitted a proposal for the collection to the publisher. Ask to see a copy. That'll help you understand the aims of the project and hopefully the proposed timeline, too.

My Experience with Edited Collections

I've contributed chapters to three edited collections. The first was straightforward and enjoyable. The editor — a friend of mine — approached me. I was given freedom to write the piece I wanted and there were minimal changes. It took a couple of years before the book went to press, but the editor was extremely proactive in dealing with the publisher and keeping everything going.

For the second collection, I was approached again, this time on the basis of a conference paper I'd given. This seemed to take forever. The editors rigidly enforced house style and insisted on the passive voice. This was frustrating because it no longer looked like my work and also it was at odds with what I teach in writing workshops — i.e. write like a human.

I should've requested and scrutinised the style guide before committing myself.

I was approached a third time, again on the basis of a conference paper. I duly turned it into a book chapter, then waited, and waited, and waited. Several years later, the editors popped up, asking for a completely different chapter. They wanted me to broaden the scope significantly and write in a more formal style. I declined. I've heard nothing since.

Is an Edited Collection Right for You?

Consider collections both within your career strategy *and* your publishing strategy. These collections are expensive. One book I contributed to costs £120. It was possibly my best piece of academic writing to date, but very few people will read it. The publishing contract stipulates that I can't share that work anywhere else. I was so excited about getting accepted, I didn't ponder the longer-term consequences.

If you're interested in *readers*, then journal articles are better than book chapters. The price of edited collections is often £60-£120, so individuals are unlikely to buy them. They'll sit in a few academic libraries. Journal articles are more widely available through online databases and scholars also share them covertly with people who don't have access.

Editing a Collection

Occasionally, someone tries to trick me into editing a collection ("This will be fun! It'll look really good on your CV! It's a fantastic opportunity!") Fortunately, I'm far too old to fall for that kind of flannel. Perhaps the experience can be best summarised by the title of an article on editing collections: 'Herding Cats'.[2] With edited collections, you have to be the project manager and oversee everyone else's content. You're probably contributing a chapter of your own, or at least writing the introduction, too. You'd need to put together the call for chapters, submit a proposal, and sort out contracts.

I've spoken to a few senior academics who've edited collections. Their bodies tense as they recall having to repeatedly chase contributors, rewrite terrible submissions, and deal with ever-extending timescales. However, I spoke to one younger academic who'd found this a mostly positive experience. Her main challenge was disruption caused by the pandemic, especially given the publisher wasn't prepared to budge on deadlines.

As with the other options, only plump for this route if you understand exactly what you're getting into and have the time to pursue it.

Understanding What's Required

Assuming you've decided to push ahead with a monograph, we need to think about what's required. There isn't a magic trick for transforming a thesis, it's a major feat that involves pulling apart and reimagining your work. It's not about 'finishing' or perfecting your thesis — this is a whole new project.

One the biggest mistakes I made was trying to turn my thesis into a book. Instead, I should have used my doctoral

---

2 Nederman, C.. "Herding Cats: The View from the Volume and Series Editor." *Journal of Scholarly Publishing* 36 (2005): 221-228.

research as the *basis* of the book. The structure needed to be totally different. Stop thinking of it as a thesis at all. It's now a book that includes some of your doctoral research. If you're still thinking of your project as a thesis, that will affect how you write it — the thesis language and apparatus will creep in. You're now an author, not a PhD candidate.

It feels like a big job to completely rewrite the book, but it's actually quicker (and more satisfying) than wrestling with the old format. Here are some of the key differences:

A thesis is:

- Part of an examination and designed to fulfil the requirements of the awarding institution.
- Intended for an audience of 2-3 examiners, who decide whether it makes an original and significant contribution to knowledge.
- Defensive in tone, as the author is proving their worth as an independent academic researcher.
- Reliant on rehearsing a wide range of scholarship to support the arguments.
- Archived and (usually) freely available once accepted.

A monograph is:

- Based on a business relationship between the author and publisher.
- Intended for a wider audience of hundreds (or hopefully thousands).

- Less defensive, as the author's status has been validated by a PhD.

- More authoritative, as the author has absorbed the scholarship in their field and is now contributing to it.

- Sold to individual and institutional buyers and then disseminated further.

The thesis is part of an examination — it's all about demonstrating what you know and why it's important. With a book, you're communicating ideas to a much wider audience. Your examiners are contractually obliged to read your thesis, even if it's clunky; nobody has to persevere with a shoddily presented book. In short, you can get away with writing in a thesis that won't be tolerated in a book.

Your future readers expect a pleasurable experience with a clear and logical structure that anticipates their needs. While this might feel daunting, there's a simple (if time consuming) method for learning this craft. Although you've undoubtedly read other people's monographs, you've probably just focused on extracting the information and arguments. Now you want to get acquainted with the mechanics of those books so you can understand why they work. And why sometimes they *don't*.

Choosing Your Literary Mascots

I want you to identify three monographs to accompany you during your writing project. These books will be your literary mascots. You can refer to them for inspiration or to discover the best way of presenting certain types of argument. Just because this book is published, though, it doesn't mean that's necessarily the best way. You might need to create a composite from those books to establish an approach that's right for you.

Your literary mascots might feature the following criteria:

- The author employs a similar methodology to you.
- The author writes in a style you enjoy. You're likely to be influenced by this style, so make sure it's one you want to emulate.
- They're a first-time author — this means it's more likely to have been based on a PhD and to follow a traditional structure.
- Published by a press you're targeting. This will give you a sense of that publisher's requirements and conventions. If you don't like how the book is laid out, perhaps this publisher isn't right for you.
- Published within the last two years. The publishing world moves quickly, so you need a sense of what they're publishing now, rather than what was favoured five or ten years ago.

Given the cost of monographs, you might be unable to afford your own copies. Browse through Open Research Library (www.openresearchlibrary.org) to see if you can find anything appropriate. Here, publishers make a small number of their titles freely available. Increasingly, university libraries also offer ebooks in PDF format. Even if you're no longer affiliated with an institution, you might find your login still works or that alumni are given access to specific resources.

Assessing Your Mascots

Once you have your three books, here's what you need to do. Read through each in turn, slowly, and with a notebook to hand. You're not reading for meaning. Instead, you're establishing:

- Number and length of chapters.
- Length of introduction and conclusion compared with chapters.
- Amount of space given to literature review and methodology.
- Balance between secondary literature and the author's own voice (e.g., how many block quotes are there?)
- Structure of chapters. Are there lots of sub-headings?
- Style — is it written in the passive voice, e.g., this book will argue, or does it display a more personal, engaging style?

Also see if you can find some reviews in journals.[3] Reviewers often comment on the structure, methodology, theoretical approach, and whether they believe it's successful. This is all helpful input for you. Drawing on the best elements of each book, build yourself a blueprint. Maybe this blueprint looks quite different from your thesis. Good! You now need to think about your book, not your thesis. While your thesis provides some of the research for this new project, your book has its own structure.

---
3 You can find free online book reviews at www.h-net.msu.edu.

BONUS ROUND: If you're feeling intrepid, track down the author's thesis. The biography or acknowledgements are likely to mention where they completed their PhD and you can then locate their institution's online repository. Alternatively, it might be available on the British Library's EThOS database (https://ethos.bl.uk) or Open Access Theses and Dissertations (https://oatd.org). The author would undoubtedly rather you just read the book, but comparing the two will give you a sense of that transition and how much work is involved. You can also see how long it took from PhD completion to the book appearing in print.

Now you've primed your brain with what's required, we can start planning your monograph in the next chapter.

Summary

As you'll have seen, publishing your PhD is a major undertaking. Before throwing yourself into this project, spend some time deliberating and establishing your motivation. Above all, don't feel pressured if you want to do something else. That's fine. If you definitely want to become an academic, publishing a monograph is probably unavoidable. Otherwise, choose your own path. While I'd love to see a photo of you beaming and holding a copy of your monograph, I'd be equally happy if this book helps you decide that publishing isn't right for you. My aim is to help you make *informed* decisions.

Remember, though, there's no such thing as a perfect decision, only the best decision you can make with the information currently available to you. Here some of the potential options, in ascending order of effort:

- Abandon your thesis altogether and pursue a different path.
- Find a way of publishing the thesis almost as-is (possibly through self-publishing).
- Publish a couple of the best chapters as articles or in edited collections.
- Substantially revise the thesis, improving the style, and find a publisher.
- Use elements of the thesis as a foundation for a book and augment them with substantial new material.
- Present the existing research through a new medium, such as a podcast, video, or blog.
- Use the skills you learned as a doctoral researcher to write a completely different book.

The average time between completing a thesis and the publication of a monograph is 5-7 years. It can be much faster, but it's a good idea to consider the worst-case scenario — would this still be a viable project for you? Think forward ten years. How would you feel if you hadn't published a book? Unfulfilled, indifferent, fidgety? If you've already exhausted your material or your enthusiasm, it'll be hard to sustain yourself. I don't think writing a book is any easier than doing a PhD. It (sometimes) takes less time because you've learned so many skills as a postgraduate researcher, but it's still a huge intellectual and psychological challenge.

ACTION POINTS

- If applicable, finish your PhD and any corrections!
- Ask yourself why — complete the exercise from the beginning of the chapter.
- Consider your career and publishing strategy and how this project fits within it.
- If you haven't done so already, apply for a thesis embargo. Or apply for an extension, if necessary and you're eligible.
- Decide on the most appropriate format for your publication, e.g., monograph, edited collection, journal articles.
- Identify and explore your literary mascots.

Please keep in mind your aims for this project. That worksheet you created earlier is going to remind you why this was a good idea. In the next chapter, we'll start pulling apart your thesis and hatching a plan. I'll see you there.

TROUBLESHOOTING

Everyone keeps telling me I should publish my thesis, but I'm not so sure

In this situation, it's worth considering *their* motivation. Why do they want you to publish your thesis? To validate their own choices? To ensure you suffer as they did? Are these people familiar with and understanding of your career strategy? Will they provide support and guidance to ensure you can finish this big project?

Cheerleaders are motivating during the visible parts of your challenge. But they won't be there every day, helping you crank out those words and endlessly revise them. During these moments, you'll need to draw on your own motivation. Do what's right for you.

I really want to publish my thesis, but I don't have time

If you can't give up any of your other commitments, then it's impossible for you to write a monograph now. There will be other opportunities in future. It's better to be realistic at this stage, rather than get partway through your book and realise you can't finish. You can't do everything (I know, I keep trying). It's all about priorities. In his book *Essentialism*, Greg McKeown explains how the meaning of *priority* has shifted:

> The word priority came into the English language in the 1400s. It was singular. It meant the very first or prior thing. It stayed singular for the next five hundred years. Only in the 1900s did we pluralise the term and start talking about priorities. Illogically, we reasoned that by changing the word we could bend reality. Somehow we would now be able to have multiple "first" things.

Competing priorities are a shortcut to procrastination and burnout. If you assign yourself another priority, you need to also let go of something else.

I want to write a book based on my thesis, but I don't like the idea of a monograph

Publishing a monograph certainly limits your readership and reach. However, it's hard as a first-time author to break into trade publishing. You'll probably have to spend much longer finding a publisher and turning your research into a format suitable for a general audience. It might be a good idea to treat a monograph as a stepping stone. Although it'll still be a lot of work, it's not such a big leap. You'll learn a huge amount about planning and writing a book. That'll make it easier for you to approach other formats. Also, trade publishers will know you're capable of producing a book-length work.

Chapter 2: Planning Your Project

"To achieve great things, two things are needed; a plan, and not quite enough time." – Leonard Bernstein

The last thing a publisher wants to see is a doctoral thesis. I know, because I've been sent quite a few in my time. A thesis is purely for the purposes of passing a viva so you can swish about and call yourself Dr. If you want to progress further in academia or related areas, you'll need to turn that raw material into other products. Your thesis is just a starting point.

Some publishers, such as Manchester University Press, state explicitly that they won't publish books *based on* theses, other than in exceptional cases. Even if a publisher does welcome thesis-based books, you'll still have to do a lot of work. As I mentioned in the previous chapter, you have to stop thinking of it as a thesis: it's now a book. To make this transition, you'll need to restructure, rewrite, and possibly carry out additional research. Both you and your thesis will undergo a transition. Just as you turned from a student into a researcher during your PhD, now you need to go from researcher to author. This is an important mindset shift.

You also need to be your own project manager. While your publisher provides some accountability, they're not going to check up on you every week or make sure you have enough snacks. You'll need the ability to work *in* your book (i.e., writing it) and *on* your book (i.e., stepping back and getting some perspective on the overall project). Even if you've already started rewriting your thesis, I'd recommend reading this chapter. When we get stuck with a project, the answer is almost always to revisit the planning stage. By the end of this chapter, you'll have a blueprint for your book and a schedule for writing it.

We'll start with taking a detailed look at your thesis. I know you probably don't want to do this, but it's important to get a realistic handle on its publication prospects. I'll guide you through a thesis audit to help you decide whether it has potential as a book, or might be better suited to shorter publications, such as journal articles. You'll identify chunks that can be retained or adapted, while quietly discarding those unfathomable digressions.

Having diligently sifted through your thesis, you can define your scope. Whereas theses tend to ramble, a monograph needs to be much more focused. We'll establish your subject, concept, and point of view. From there, you can start mapping your book to get a sense of your territory and also identify any gaps that need filling.

With a map in place, you'll start thinking of it as a book. I'll explain the typical structure of a monograph so you can see how everything fits together. By considering your structure and creating a word budget, you'll get a more realistic sense of how long it'll take you to complete the project. Having broken down the book into chunks, we'll do the same with your time. I'll introduce a technique called the 12-week sprint, a simple but effective way of establishing milestones and maintaining momentum

If you're already feeling tired, don't worry. I'll also emphasise the importance of setting limits. First, let's open that thesis ...

Auditing Your Thesis

The first (and unavoidable) step is to make an honest assessment of your thesis. Start by reading it from cover to cover. Don't dwell on your favourite parts or skim over the sticky bits that make no sense. You need to approach it with a reader's — rather than a creator's — eye. It's time to park your writer's ego temporarily. I think it's easiest to do this with a printed copy of your thesis. If you're reading on the screen, there's a temptation to make changes right away. For now, you're just *auditing*.

Take notes as you go along. Think back to when you were conducting your literature review, where you were noting the strengths, weaknesses, and usefulness of all those books and journal articles. Recall, too, what you found frustrating or irksome about some of that material. Try to be objective about your own work. Yes, it's hard! I still clearly remember my audit, even though it was five years ago. My main challenges were:

- Although my thesis passed first time and was praised by examiners for its style and coherence, it started unravelling when I reread it. Parts were confused. There were mistakes, contradictions, and bits that I couldn't fathom at all. What on earth had I been thinking?
- Indeed, my thinking had changed. I'd not been actively working on this area for a while, but those ideas had still been percolating at the back of my mind.
- I had new ideas and material to incorporate, too. And they didn't necessarily fit within the existing structure. Compared with material I'd written more than five years ago, they also looked glaringly shiny.
- I'd already used some of the strongest parts for book chapters so had some significant gaps to fill.

Here are some areas to keep in mind when auditing your thesis:

Relevance

Depending on how long ago you wrote your thesis, your field might've shifted. Is your material still relevant? It'll take at least another couple of years to publish your monograph — will your ideas seem dated by then? This usually happens over the course of a PhD, but it's likely to have been exacerbated by the impact of the pandemic. This has changed the landscape of some fields and also affected priorities. It's too early to speculate on the longer-term impact of COVID, but it's safe to say that everything is moving at a faster pace. If you're in the social sciences, your data might be superseded.

Would publishing a book mean redoing your fieldwork or conducting more interviews? Is this feasible?

If you find a lot has changed, don't despair. The purpose of your PhD was to train you to become a researcher. During those years, like me, you probably discovered lots of really bad ways of approaching a large research project. That hard-won experience is going to help you. Although you might have to pursue some entirely new research, you'll now have a stronger sense of how best to go about it. You're not starting from scratch this time.

Quality

As you're reacquainting yourself with your thesis, you need to consider what's of interest to your reader. Also, what's of interest to you? After all, you need to sustain that interest over several years while you rewrite, revise, and check your book. It might prove impossible to resuscitate moribund parts of your research, especially if you no longer have any enthusiasm for them. Ditching those dead bits will breathe life into your book. Of course, you'll need to replace them with something else, though, which demands a different type of energy.

If you're finding it impossible to judge your own work, look back at your examiners' reports, if you have them. Maybe you also have some feedback from your supervisors. Or peer reviewer comments from journal articles you published. Do they indicate the stronger areas of your research?

Purpose

As I'll tell you repeatedly, your thesis is part of an examination, it's not a book. Consequently, parts of it are no longer required. In your thesis, it's likely a large part of the introduction is devoted to a literature review. Or maybe you even dedicated an entire chapter to surveying the field. While your examiners needed to know exactly what material you interrogated, readers of your book just want you to get on with the story. Your monograph is still informed by that literature review, but you are no longer foregrounding it. That 30-page literature review might be distilled down to a couple of paragraphs.

The same goes for your methodology. For a thesis, the examiners need to see precisely how you reach your conclusions, with enough detail for them to recreate your process. Now you're no longer a student, it's assumed you know what you're doing (even if it doesn't feel like it). As with the literature review, you're likely to be distilling that information down to a much shorter section.

ACTIVITY

Go through your thesis with highlighters or coloured pens to flag the different areas, e.g., *retain*, *discard*, *adapt*. Don't get caught up in the sentences or words themselves — this is a top-level survey. You're not editing yet.

Do You Have Enough for a Book?

Monographs vary in length, but the average is 80,000 words. This can sometimes be shorter in social sciences and longer in more discursive humanities subjects such as history. Take a look at your literary mascots to get a sense of what's appropriate in your field. By the time you've removed the parts that aren't required for the monograph, there might be some substantial gaps.

With a book, you'll need a narrative that propels your reader from beginning to end. This might be how you wrote your thesis, anyway, but some theses are more a portfolio of ideas — those will need substantial work. What's missing from your book? Can you be bothered to fill those gaps? Sift through anything else you've written, such as journal articles, conference papers, or blog posts. Maybe there's some existing content you can redeploy.

If you can salvage parts of your thesis and augment them with new material, how will that work? Inevitably, those new parts will look shiny in comparison with something you wrote several years ago. Will you need to rewrite that original content? It's like painting one part of your house — this instantly makes the rest of it look rubbish. Based on your experience of doing a PhD, can you get a sense of how long this will take you? It's impossible to be precise, but you need to get a rough idea of the timescale.

Perhaps you've already published parts of your thesis. That's great! However, you'll need to establish whether those publishers will give permission for you to include this material in a monograph. Equally, your monograph publisher might not be too keen on your recycling journal articles. You'd need to make it clear that you're adding value, that this journal article isn't just a condensed version of the book.

Maybe you conclude your thesis can't be a book, for whatever reason. It lacks coherence and you don't have the time or energy to overhaul it. Although this might feel like defeat, it's better to find this out now, rather than after you've been working on it for months or years. There will definitely be elements you can use in different formats. Or, indeed, they might become the seed of a future book project. Keep an open mind.

Be honest with yourself, both in terms of your aspirations and what you can realistically achieve. If you find it impossible to pursue a book project right now, remember that this is "not yet," rather than "never". You can always come back it. Deciding not to publish your thesis isn't a failure. It's making a sensible decision that's right for you, rather than just doing what's expected. Don't delete everything, though: stash your notes so you can return to them.

If you've had enough of looking at your thesis, it's tempting to decide it's all rubbish and it would be much better to start something completely new. Analyse those thoughts carefully. In some cases, it's true, but writing an entirely different book is seldom easier. Perhaps you're feeling jaded about your research. If so, think back to why you were enthusiastic about it in the first place. Why was this important to you? What difference were you hoping to make to your field? Are these reasons still valid? You'll save yourself a lot of time if you can use your existing research.

With an honest assessment of your thesis, you can define your scope.

Defining Your Scope

Before you expand your thesis into a book, you need to be clear on the scope. Unless we establish these boundaries, it's easy to just keep adding ideas and blurring the focus. Your book needs a *subject*, a *concept*, and a *point of view*. The *subject* is the broad classification — in my case, that was Victorian women's writing. The *concept* is the broad aim, approach, or method — for me, that's examining fiction within its historical context. The *point of view* is your argument. My point of view was that Florence Marryat's novels were vehicles for radical feminist ideas.

The subject and concept don't need to be original, but your point of view *does*. You must bring something unique: your data, your insight, or your experience. Unless you're writing a textbook, this can't just be a synthesis. And you can't hedge your bets by adopting multiple points of view and remaining neutral. While it's important to consider all sides of an argument, you should always be clear where you stand. The book is the medium, and you're the message.

You need a clear argument, leading to a clear conclusion. This argument needs to be challenging, maybe even provocative. You're seeking an emotional response from your reader, so they want to read your book. It's the *why* question again. Nobody is short of reading material and most of us despair over how few books we can expect to finish in our lifetimes. We're unlikely to read a book that merely offers more of the same.

Identifying your point of view takes time. You might've discovered during your PhD that your argument emerges embarrassingly late in the process. Start by establishing your subject and concept, then your argument can develop. It might be obvious early on, or maybe it becomes visible when you peel away layers of writing at the editing stage.

Dealing with Interdisciplinarity

Very few projects *aren't* interdisciplinary these days, especially in the arts and humanities. Although interdisciplinarity can make for richer research, it presents three main problems in terms of publishing:

1) **Subject** — publishers tend to focus on subject-based lists, managed by editors with degrees or a background in those subjects. If you submit your book proposal on 'Charles Dickens and Artificial Intelligence', the editor might be unable to judge whether the AI elements are sound. Unless that press also has a computing department, there's no easy way for them to check, either. They're more likely to reject it as being beyond the scope of their list. They're thinking

about fit, both in terms of their own expertise and also the market.

2) **Editorial** — who do they get to review it? There might not be another academic with your exact expertise. They could send it to specialists in the respective areas, but whose opinion is going to carry most weight? Academics can be parochial. They might see their responsibility as repelling interlopers or reinforcing boundaries. Here you're giving yourself additional challenges: you need acceptance from two disciplines, rather than just one.

3) **Market** — publishers and librarians use a classification system, with commissioning and purchasing decisions made around those subject areas. While those editors and librarians might be personally excited by something completely new, they're representing an institution with its own priorities. Remember, your publisher is interested in who will *buy* the book. In the example of Charles Dickens and AI, scholars in the field of AI are unlikely to buy a monograph on Victorian literature. And many Victorianists would run a mile from a book about machine learning. Naturally, it would be good for both fields to learn from each other, but that's a struggle for another day.

I'm not suggesting that interdisciplinary books should be avoided, rather, you need to spend some time considering the implications. By ostensibly broadening the appeal of your book, you could be restricting its market: it becomes peripheral rather than core. And remember, your publisher is thinking about the *market*. It might be a case of deciding which is the *main* discipline and making this the focus. Don't make anyone struggle to understand what your book is about. Of course, there are some interdisciplinary areas that are now firmly established, such as medical humanities and digital humanities. Take time to understand the territory and where your book fits.

Mapping Your Book

When planning a book, you need to strike a balance between giving yourself enough structure to get started and also allowing space for your ideas to develop. You can't be too efficient, as that means limiting yourself. Your manuscript will almost certainly take on some odd shapes, but you can deal with that at the editing stage.

Here are two methods for you to consider:

- Establishing research questions.
- Assessing what you've got.

Establishing Research Questions

Maybe you already have a strong sense of your argument or point of view. If so, this could be a good method for you. Take that main argument and turn it into a research question — e.g. "Is Florence Marryat a feminist writer?" Next, break it down into smaller, more specific questions, if you don't already have them. Come up with as many as possible and write them on sticky notes. Then you can review them afterwards and see which stand out. Aim for between 6-8.

Now arrange those notes on a wall or window to identify a natural sequence or storyline. It might take you a little while to experiment. Eventually, you'll see something that looks right. Take a photo so you have a record of it.

Take each of those sticky notes and break them down further. Maybe there are specific angles to these research questions? Or nuances that you want to explore? If in doubt, try to think of three sub-ideas. Again, you can start by capturing all your ideas (even the shit ones), then whittling them down to the three best examples. Now add those notes to your map on the wall.

Assessing What You've Got

Don't worry if your research questions aren't yet clear. If that's the case, revisit your thesis audit. This time you're getting physical. Print a one-sided copy of your thesis, then go through and start cutting it into chunks (you might already have a marked-up version from the previous exercise). Make sure you label those chunks, if they don't have a page number. And also make a note for yourself to show what you need to do with the chunk, e.g., adapt, discard, retain. You can also add some more detailed notes on the reverse. Set anything marked *discard* to one side. Don't throw it away, though, as this material could be useful for plugging gaps later on.

If you have lots of different ideas in your thesis, you could devise a classification system for marking up those chunks, e.g., for a thematic project, it might be MED for medicine, REL for religion, LEG for legal. Then sort them into piles to see which are most prevalent. If there are just a couple of chunks in one pile, then perhaps that's an unimportant theme that can be discarded — it's just diluting or confusing the story. If there's an enormous pile for another subject, maybe that needs to be refined or broken down further. Rank these piles in order of importance. What's the main theme for your book? You can't have four main themes. Instead, you'd need one main theme, with three related sub-themes.

This is an unwieldy method, and you'll need lots of space. It can be helpful, though, for getting a stronger sense of a huge document. And it's good to approach your thesis in a non-linear way.

One you've mapped your book, step back and take a look. Is it reasonably balanced? Although you don't need a precise structure at this stage, you don't want one column with two sticky notes and another with ten. If a column is looking a bit sparse, could you brainstorm some additional material? Or consolidate that column with another? This isn't about creating the structure of your book yet; this is marking out the territory and achieving balance. You're giving some shape to your project.

Scoping and mapping ensures you don't get halfway through your book project before realising it lacks a concept and at least an emerging argument. At this stage, you could also show someone else your map (assuming it's legible) and ask them what they think it's about. You might need to either take a really good photo, or transplant it to an online tool like Trello, Miro, or Jamboard.

If you're struggling with mapping and scoping, consult your literary mascots. Can you get a sense of both their territory and structure? If you have time, try mapping them with sticky notes. This way, you can reverse-engineer books and understand why they're effective. There's no mystery around constructing a book — it's all about knowing your subject, concept, and point of view.

Deciding on a Structure

If you're lucky, the map you created also works as a book structure. As I explained, though, this is only the territory and won't necessarily form a narrative. You need to be prepared to experiment with different structures. If the main subject of your book is a person, a place, or an event, then a chronological approach is usually appropriate. With a broader subject, for example, examining ideas, genres, or phenomena, then a thematic approach is probably better.

For instance, if you were writing about the working practices of twentieth-century Irish authors, you could choose one of the following structures:

- Genre
- Chronology
- Author — e.g., one chapter per writer

In this example, one chapter per author looks neat and satisfying, but it might result in a repetitive structure. You'll be applying an identical approach to each author. Repetitive structures are acceptable in a thesis, but they're boring in a book. It might be better to divide it thematically, with chapters on the authors' style, routine, and themes.

For a chronological approach, you could start with a

timeline and apply it to your map. If you were writing a literary biography, you wouldn't simply chop it up into decades. The author's early and later years are likely to represent the largest portion of their life, but are perhaps less significant professionally. A decade might span several chapters.

Even if you don't employ a strictly chronological approach in your narrative, creating a timeline is helpful for you to refer to. The chronology provides your book with a backbone, then you can deviate from it occasionally for effect — for example, anticipating an event or looking back on it.

ACTIVITY

Revisit your map and see if you can organise the sticky notes into categories. Depending on your research, these categories might be based on people, places, novels, themes, or concepts. Or for chronological projects, work out an appropriate timeline. Experimenting means you're approaching your book from lots of different angles. This means it's more likely to be feasible. If later you suddenly discover your structure isn't working, you'll be better placed to adapt it. It gives you a 360-degree view, rather than just a linear one.

Finding Your Golden Thread

No less elusive than the Golden Fleece, the Golden Thread is the top prize for crafting a book. The Golden Thread is the central argument that holds your book together. Although you might have thematic chapters that almost work as stand-alone pieces, they should also be joined by this thread. The thread is a path your reader follows, providing coherence and enticement.

The Golden Thread can also be your main research question, which is linked by smaller questions you address in each chapter. If that's the technique you used earlier for mapping your book, you probably already have your Golden Thread. That's the main plot line, while all your smaller questions are sub-plots that are clearly linked to it. A thread should also hold everything together.

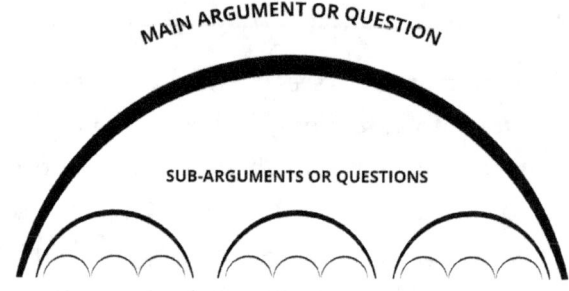

If you don't yet have this structure, don't put too much pressure on yourself to create a perfectly woven Golden Thread from the outset. At the planning and writing stage, it's enough to identify a few strands from which you can weave that thread. Then, at the editing stage, that thread will become more apparent as you remove all the loose threads and random fluffy bits.

If you're using a thematic or research question-based approach, then you don't need to do much more work at this stage. For those of you who aren't yet sure, consider these two approaches: *inductive* and *deductive*:

In **inductive** reasoning, you use a series of evidence to build up to a conclusion. With each additional piece of evidence, you narrow the topic and eliminate ambiguity. You take the reader with you and (hopefully) they reach the same conclusion as you. This is a democratic approach, as you're not trying to impose a viewpoint on them. You start small, building to a big conclusion.

This approach is good if your argument is more a patchwork of ideas that adds up to a conclusion. Your evidence is distributed throughout the book, then consolidated and amplified in the conclusion. You might think of yourself as Hercule Poirot, assembling everyone in the drawing room to reveal the murderer.

In **deductive** reasoning, you begin with your conclusion, then gradually unveil your evidence and reasoning. You start big, narrowing down on your evidence. Now you're playing the role of a defence barrister. If the reader is unconvinced by your opening statement, they might not stay for the verdict. With this approach, there's a risk the author (like a barrister) is selecting only the evidence that supports their case.

This approach is effective if you have a clear sense of your argument. There's a target you're aiming for, and you feel confident in making your case.

The Anatomy of a Monograph

Now you've mapped the *territory* and *arc* of your book, you can think about the *structure*. There's no such thing as a book template, but I'll outline the core elements of a monograph and explain their purpose. You're not going to start writing yet, but this section should help you understand what's required. You can then return to it later to apply structure during the writing and editing stage.

Typically, monographs follow an hourglass structure. You start broad by setting the wider context, then focus on individual research questions, themes, or concepts in each chapter. In the conclusion, you then broaden your scope again to situate your arguments within your field and to identify potential new directions.

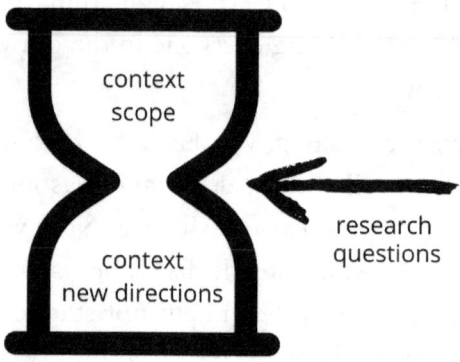

Let's explore the individual elements within that structure.

Introduction

I'm willing to bet the introduction was the toughest part of your thesis. Usually, we try to do this before we have a clear grasp of our project. After all, it's hard to introduce something you haven't yet written. I think it's better to *finish* the introduction last, but to start planning and drafting it early on. By having at least a framework in place, it'll make it easier for you to write the rest of the book. Also, it's helpful to establish the purpose of the introduction.

Firstly, the introduction piques your reader's curiosity and gives them a reason to continue. Your examiners were contractually obliged to read your thesis, but the casual reader is within their rights to toss your book aside. You're answering the *why* question again. In Chapter One, we considered why you wanted to write a book. Now, you're shifting perspective. Why is this important to your audience? You're setting the tone for the book and creating expectations in the reader's mind. We've all started books and completely forgotten we were reading them. Others, though, lurk in our minds and we want to know more. Admittedly, that's a hard trick to pull off. Think back, though, to those literary mascots. What devices did the authors employ to keep you reading?

A typical device is to challenge preconceptions or misconceptions. *You think you know this subject, but I'm going to show you something new.* This is creating a *knowledge gap*. Once we realise we don't understand something we thought we knew, our minds become receptive. We're desperate to fill that gap. In my monograph introduction, I started by relating an interview with Florence Marryat in which she is presented as a respectable grandmother, living in a cottage in Kensington. I then explained the reality: she lived in a much seedier part of town, with an actor 33 years her junior. She wasn't the archetypal Victorian woman.

Although you want to tantalise your readers, you

shouldn't withhold your overall argument or direction. Readers are far more likely to read your book if they know where it's going. They're trying to decide whether this publication is a good use of their time. Regardless of whether you're using the inductive or deductive flow, you need to be clear on the destination and *why* your reader should accompany you on the journey. They'll tolerate a certain amount of mystery with the inductive approach, but they need to feel confident it's worth the wait. You can't save all the revelations for the conclusion.

Here's a typical structure for an introduction.

- **Hook** — If possible, start with a story (remember, this is a book, not a thesis). As humans, we're hard-wired to engage with stories. Once the narrative has started, we want to know how it finishes. We crave that resolution.

- **Your big idea** — how does this story relate to your big idea, or your main research question? In my case, it was the contrast between how Marryat was obliged to present herself (respectable married woman) and the reality (co-habiting with an actor 33 years her junior). My overall argument was that the reality of Victorian women's lives differed greatly from how they're perceived in the 21st century.

- **Context** — what does your reader need to know to understand the rest of the book? This might include your underlying theory, or the historical, cultural, or political background. Unlike in a thesis, though, you're not required to justify your approach, merely to be clear on what it is. In my case, this was context on the legal position of wives in the nineteenth century, how this changed over Marryat's lifetime, and her position within that change. As I was arguing that Marryat was a radical feminist, I needed to establish those benchmarks. It can be difficult to gauge how much detail to include. Some of your readers will already be experts on some of the specifics; others will know very little. Keep this context as tight as possible. Then it's easy for newcomers to quickly digest the information and for experts to skip over it.

- **Chapter outlines** — a map of your book. This isn't exciting to write, but it's useful for your readers. Unfortunately, they won't all be reading it cover to cover. Instead, they'll be working out which are the most useful chapters. Hopefully, you'll already have some chapter outlines you can copy and paste from your proposal (see Chapter Four).

- **Final paragraph that sets the tone and pace.** This gets the reader back into the story after the outlines. Remind your reader of what they'll gain from your book, for example, filling that knowledge gap.

For now, you're not actually writing your introduction. Instead, you're using the elements above to think about the structure and requirements. Once you understand these elements, it'll be easier to plan your time and also you'll have a stronger sense of the book's purpose. Retrieve your literary mascots and assess the introductions. Could you create a composite blueprint to use in your own monograph?

Chapters

Chapters have become more important. Whereas in the olden days, we'd acquire and read an entire book, there are now other possibilities. Given the high cost of scholarly publications, libraries are now more likely to license individual chapters. This means those chapters need to work on their own *and* as part of the book. The main implication is that your chapter should be tight and focused.

Not everyone agrees, but I think chapters should be either digestible in one sitting or at least broken up into more manageable sections. Generally, book chapters are shorter than those in a thesis. I went from four chapters, each comprising 16,000 words, in my thesis, to seven chapters of 7,000 words in my monograph. Each became tightly focused on one specific topic. In the original thesis, each chapter has three main sub-sections; in the book, most of those sub-sections were promoted to their own chapter.

Also, chapters should be of roughly equal length to achieve a sense of balance. Otherwise, it gives the impression some chapters are more important than others, or that you've run out of things to say. Furthermore, rambling chapters are often concealing a shaky argument — the author hides the lack of meaning beneath a lot of waffle. A shorter chapter, meanwhile, benefits from a tight logic that's easy for the reader to follow.

Breaking it Down with Subsections

Subsections provide a more detailed map for your reader. They know where they are, where they've been, and where they're going. These subsection titles should be descriptive. If they just say 'Social Identity', this gives the reader very little information. If instead it's called 'Social Identity Theory and the Workplace', your reader knows exactly what's coming. Even better, frame it as a question: "How can Social Identity Theory reduce workplace bullying?" This then creates curiosity and a knowledge gap in the reader's mind.

> **TOP TIP**
>
> Even if you don't want to use questions as subheadings, you can employ them as prompts during the writing stage. It's much easier to answer a question than to respond to a vague heading. Maybe all you need to do afterwards is remove the question mark.

Subsections are also good for linking related but non-contiguous areas. That's not to say you can randomly fling ideas at your chapter; rather, it means you don't have to spend time creating an elegant segue between two paragraphs. If one chapter contains subsections, though, *all* the chapters should also contain subsections. Otherwise, it's a jarring change of format for your reader. Don't go overboard with subsections, either. However, used judiciously, they can make your book more usable and digestible. It also becomes easier for you to navigate around as you're writing it.

Creating Chapter Titles

Given the importance of chapters as standalone publications, their titles are now even more conspicuous. Chapter titles have become metadata that are used to classify and retrieve details about your book. Yes, this is adding yet another layer of complexity to your project.

Don't worry about getting your chapter titles absolutely right at the beginning, though. They'll no doubt change several times, and your publisher might also have suggestions based on their knowledge of the market and likely publication formats. For now, you at least want some working titles. Numbers aren't necessarily helpful, as you're likely to be mucking about with the narrative. You'll get into a complete pickle if you're obliged to remember that chapter 5 now comes before chapter 3.

For this book, I named my chapters *Purpose*, *Planning*, *Placing*, *Pitching*, *Producing*, *Polishing*, and *Publishing* while I was working on the manuscript. Although they're pithy, alliterative, and a reasonable reflection of what the chapters cover, these titles aren't descriptive enough for someone scanning the table of contents in a catalogue. However, they're convenient containers for me while I'm finalising my structure, and it doesn't matter if I move them around. I can decide on the final titles once everything's in place.

Here are a few guidelines on choosing chapter titles:

- Keep them short and to the point. Someone reading on a Kindle doesn't want to scroll through two pages just to read the title.

- Use a consistent format, e.g., if one chapter has a subtitle, they should all include subtitles.
- Avoid quotations, unless they're pivotal to the chapter, e.g., it's a quote that's central to your argument. Otherwise, quotes don't make good metadata.
- Use concrete, recognisable terms that reflect the chapter's content. Potential readers will scan the table of contents to see whether your book is relevant to them.

Deciding on Your Chapters

Maybe your mapping exercise from earlier revealed a coherent chapter structure. This is likely to be the case if you're adopting a thematic approach, or if you have an overarching research question with related smaller questions. Otherwise, you need to think about turning those sticky notes from your map into containers or chapters. Group together your sticky notes (or the digital equivalent) in different configurations. If you find you're making several major arguments in a chapter, perhaps it needs to be divided.

There are no hard and fast rules, but you probably want 6-8 chapters in an 80,000-word monograph. For longer books, you might want to group them into parts. This approach can be effective if you have three distinct main themes, each with clear sub-themes. Three chapters would be too few, as they'd each need to be incredibly long. Using parts could also work well if your book covers three distinct phases, e.g., before, during, after. These parts should be balanced, though — you don't want a part containing only one chapter.

Your chapters aren't set in stone at this stage. It might

feel like a lot of work if you need to move everything around once you've started writing, but it's not that difficult. And you'll end up with a better book which will be quicker to finish. Later, I'll explain how you can create building blocks of writing. Although you're assembling them as you write, you'll also move them around at the editing stage, when you have a clearer sense of where everything should go.

Structuring Your Chapter

The exact structure of your chapter depends on both your field and on your specific project. However, this outline offers a starting point both to keep it balanced and to ensure you've included all the necessary information.

1. **Start with why** — explain why the subject of this chapter is important. Earlier we looked at the *why* question in the context of your overall book, now you're thinking in terms of the current chapter. What gap are you filling? What misconception are you addressing? This gets your reader emotionally engaged.

2. **What** — having secured that emotional engagement, you can now explain *what* you're doing. You're going into more detail, giving some additional context for the why question. What does your reader need to know to understand the rest of the chapter? As you'll see, this mirrors the approach from your main Introduction. Now, though, you're focusing on a smaller concept.

3. **Linking** — explain how this chapter builds on the previous chapter and how it relates to the overall

argument of the book. This helps you achieve that elusive Golden Thread throughout your book. Also, it's easier and more satisfying for your reader to follow. They're unlikely to be reading your book in one sitting, so this serves as a reminder of your earlier arguments. And if they've only purchased or borrowed one chapter, this might tempt them to obtain the rest of your book.

4. **How** — explain how you've structured your chapter. Introduce the subsections and what you'll cover. This isn't especially exciting to write, but it helps readers gauge whether the chapter is relevant for their research. Also, it's a useful refresher for anyone who's read your book and has returned to seek specific information. Keep in mind both the *readability* and *usability* of your book.

5. **Hook** — as that last section was a bit boring, you might want to include an extra sentence at the end to remind them of the story. This creates momentum again.

6. **Body of your chapter** — maybe your research or your original thesis structure lends itself to an obvious layout. If not, Dr Pope's Rule of Three might help. Come up with three main points, ideas, or concepts you want to cover. Then break each of those down into three sub-points. As I'll explain later, you can assign word targets to each of these sections.

- Main point 1
    - Sub-point 1
    - Sub-point 2
    - Sub-point 3
- Main point 2
    - Sub-point 1
    - Sub-point 2
    - Sub-point 3
- Main point 3
    - Sub-point 1
    - Sub-point 2
    - Sub-point 3

7. Conclusion

- Summarise what you've said.
- Explain why it's important. Yes, you've said this already, but you want to engage your reader emotionally again so they remember what you've said.
- Relate it back to your overall argument again and then explain how this builds in the next chapter.

Whatever approach you use, break down the chapter into chunks and ensure it has a beginning, middle, and end. It's hard to write a chapter, but much easier to write *part* of a chapter. With identifiable chunks, you can make everything more manageable and navigable. Also, think about the opening and closing concepts — do they come full circle or achieve resolution? If you ask a question at the beginning, make sure you've answered it by the end. For structures with main and subsidiary questions, unpack them all systematically.

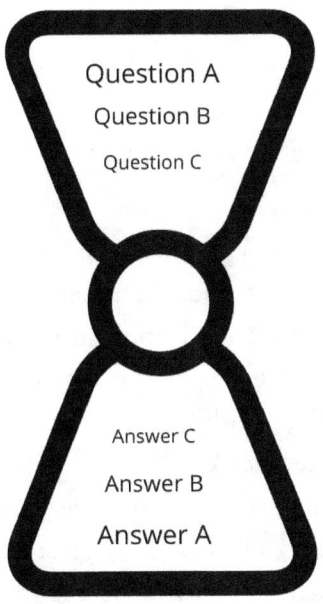

Maybe you're struggling to devise a structure for your chapter. This could suggest either that it lacks focus, or that it lacks weight and can be absorbed into another chapter. At the moment, don't worry too much about the precise mechanics of your chapter — that's for the writing and editing stage. For now, it's making sure you have scoped the chapter and ensured its feasibility.

Conclusion

Conclusions aren't the hardest part to write, but they're arguably the most boring. You've already said this stuff, why do you need to say it all over again? In a thesis, the conclusion partly serves to remind your examiners of that significant and original contribution to knowledge. It's a grand total, bringing together all the subtotals scattered throughout the other chapters. You still need this sense of resolution with the book, but it's less defensive. The basic model is: this is what I've said, this is why it's important, and here are the implications.

Your reader (and you) is probably quite tired by this point. They don't want you to suddenly shriek, "And here's another exciting idea!" And don't use devices such as, "unfortunately, there wasn't space to discuss x, y, z ....". Your reader might be seized with the fancy that x, y, and z would've made a much better book. Why on earth didn't the author write *that* book instead? Then you leave them with a sense of dissatisfaction. By all means, suggest paths for extending your research, but don't introduce the idea of a completely different path altogether.

Typically, the conclusion serves the following purposes:

- Summarises the arguments made throughout the book and relates them to the overarching argument.
- Addresses any questions posed in the introduction.
- Identifies new areas of research and potential applications for your ideas.

2: PLANNING YOUR PROJECT

Whenever possible, come full circle. This is satisfying and makes the book more memorable. For example, if your introduction starts with a story or anecdote, return to it in your conclusion. That helps your reader connect what they've learned. The final sentence is especially important. As with conference papers, people tend to pay more attention towards the end. Consider what thought you want to leave in the mind of your reader. You don't want them struggling to work out what you mean. We've all heard conference papers where the speaker concludes unsatisfactorily with, "err, well, that's it really". Don't fade out at the end, conclude with a clarion call or clear resolution.

There's no set length for a conclusion. Try not to think in terms of a word count, rather about addressing the required *elements*. Of course, you don't have infinite space. Consider your word limit and decide how much space you can allocate. It's probably easier to write something longer, then reduce it using the reverse outlining technique we'll see in Chapter Six. As we all know by now, it's much harder to write in a concise way. We have to get it out of our heads and impose order afterwards. If you do insist on my giving you a number, aim for no more than 5% of the book's overall word count for your conclusion.

As ever, consult your literary mascots to get a sense of what's appropriate in your field. How long are the conclusions? What elements do they include? Can you identify the devices employed by the author to achieve a sense of resolution?

Setting Some Limits

I have a friend who finished his PhD a couple of years before me, back in 2012. He was given a book contract soon afterwards, *but he's still working on his monograph.* Yes, it's coming up to a decade. Every time he painfully squeezes out a full draft, his publisher comes back with a few tiny comments. He then thinks, "Ooh, this is an excellent opportunity to completely rewrite several chapters and add a completely new one." Unless you have a tightly defined project, how do you know when you've done enough? Without limits, we just keep going. It's important to impose limits both in terms of scope and the amount of time you're going to spend on this project.

Allocating a Word Budget

Hopefully, you now have an overall map of your book, along with some chapter outlines. With those in place, you can allocate a word budget. Publishers usually stipulate strict word limits, so you need to be mindful of these numbers. If you don't have a sense of the likely range, you could instead use a percentage at this stage, e.g. you want the Introduction to be 10% of the overall word count.

Go through and start allocating your word budget. You might find this easiest to do in a spreadsheet, like this one:

	A	B	C	D	E	F	G	H	I
1	**Introduction**			**Chapter 1**			**Conclusion**		
2	Section 1	750		Section 1	500		Section 1	250	
3	Section 2	750		Section 2	750		Section 2	500	
4	Section 3	1250		Section 3	1250		Section 3	750	
5	Section 4	1000		Section 4	1250		Section 4	500	
6	Section 5	1000		Section 5	1250		Section 5	250	
7	Section 6	500		Section 6	500		Section 6	500	
8									
9	**TOTAL**	5250		**TOTAL**	5500		**TOTAL**	3850	
10									
11									
12	**GRAND TOTAL**			14,600					
13									

You want word counts for each chapter, and the sections within those chapters. Like balancing your finances, it'll take some experimentation and creative accounting. You're not committing yourself to these numbers — you always need room for flexibility — but this helps contain your project. There's no point in producing 2,000 words for a section that needs only 500. It'll make everything seem more manageable, too. You're not actually writing those sections yet or worrying about exactly what they'll look like. Instead, you're creating the space and allocating part of your word budget.

You'll now have a much more detailed map and project plan. No doubt you can spot gaps to be filled. In some cases, those gaps can be filled with existing material you'll redeploy from elsewhere; in others, though, you'll need to do some additional reading. Again, it's important to set limits.

Avoiding Readitis

If you've not heard of Readitis, it's a nasty condition affecting researchers at all stages. Hugh Kearns defines it as, "The belief that reading one more article will solve all your research problems and then you will be ready to write".[4] The problem is, you reach the end of that article, then it cites twelve more articles that look "really important". Those authors have also made helpful suggestions for further reading. Before you know it, those papers are popping up everywhere like bunnies.

Undoubtedly, you'll need to do some legitimate reading, either to plug gaps or to catch up on developments in your field. Unless you have a reading *plan*, though, it's easy to fall into the trap of reading until you feel like it's *enough*. It's never enough. Apart from this being exhausting and unproductive, your brain is then full of everyone else's ideas. There's no room for your own thoughts and your writing becomes an unwieldy synthesis. You lose your *point of view*, a vital ingredient of a monograph.

It's worth employing the Rule of Three again. When researching a topic, you first identify the three *best* sources — they might be journal articles, book chapters, or reference works. Start with the best and most recent scholarship and work backwards. The reason for this approach is that a new article might expose problems with earlier work, and also it could also provide some helpful summaries of other strong research. Maybe there are some annoyingly productive and

....
4 www.twitter.com/ithinkwellHugh/status/1439945038100840451

insightful people in your field. Start with their work, as they're likely to have been thorough and will save you a lot of time. You're not aiming to read everything, rather the best available scholarship.

Once you've digested those three sources, start writing about them. Inevitably, this draft will be patchy — that's OK. Now you can see the gaps and they tell you exactly what you need to read *next*. Take that first gap and identify the three best sources on that *specific* topic. And repeat. Rather than reading widely and randomly, you're always reading with a specific goal in mind. This reduces the amount of overall reading *and* improves the quality of your notes — you know precisely what you're seeking from that source. If you want to be really organised, you can create a list of questions that you need to answer. This might include broader questions, such as "do I agree with the author?" or specific points, such as "what did female mediums wear during séances?"

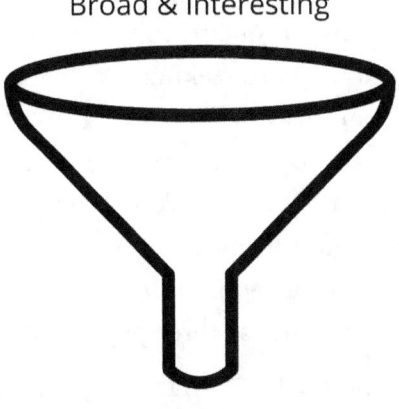

Broad & Interesting

Focused & Relevant

Make sure you're reading for *relevance*, not interest or potential. As you have an enquiring mind, *everything* is going to be interesting and also you'll probably notice nuggets for future projects. Going wide means you'll end up with too many notes and have a less focused reading session. It's much better to return to those sources another time with another set of specific questions. Key your eye on those research questions, like a cat watches a tin of tuna.

A technique I've adapted is SQ3R, which fortunately I've never needed to pronounce. It stands for:

- Survey
- Question
- Read
- Recite
- Review

First you skim-read or *survey* the publication to decide whether it's worth your time. With a general sense of it in your head, you can then formulate some *questions*. What's the specific information you're seeking? With your brain primed, you *read* slowly and carefully, making notes as you go. At the *recite* stage, you go through your notes to make sure you haven't missed anything. Then you *review* what you've got. Do you have enough information on this topic? If not, what are the gaps? And what will you read to fill those gaps? Of course, you can only choose three publications again.

Even if this approach isn't right for you, you'll need to set some limits on your reading. You don't want to try to read everything, then realise you've got two weeks left to actually write the book.

Managing Your Time

The idea of 'writing a book' suggests you sit at your computer, then all those thoughts emerge fully formed and appear on the screen in a continuous stream. In reality, there's a series of actions involved, some of which provoke a lot of swearing. I want you to start thinking about those actions now. Breaking it down in this way means you can plan much more effectively. We're also going to break down your time into more usable chunks.

If you were a full-time funded PhD student, you might've got used to having a lot of time at your disposal; or, at least, a great deal of flexibility. Anyone combining writing with either paid work or caring responsibilities needs to get used to using small chunks of time efficiently. Waiting for that fabled Clear Writing Day is just another form of procrastination. As if we needed one of those.

Consider how much time you can realistically commit. And also how much energy. Although I find it much easier to manage myself in middle age, I've also been confronted with my limitations. I can't push myself anymore. While a marathon session gets me ahead briefly, my body then shuts down for the next couple of days and I lie in bed fuming. You'll need to pace yourself. Also, you need to take into account the demands of different stages of your writing project.

You might've noticed from your PhD that you need *start-*

ing energy and *finishing energy*. Starting energy requires a huge burst of creativity and the ability to visualise your book — some of which we've done already. You're wrestling with this big idea and trying to set some limits on it. Once you've written a baggy first draft, you then need the energy to *finish* the project. By now, the excitement has faded. You're no longer making new discoveries or creating anything. It's the seemingly endless slog of knocking everything into shape. Going over and over this monster document, checking all the details, and quietly despairing. This part is all about perseverance in the face of monotony. Once you lose momentum, it's hard to get going again.

I think this type of project is dumbbell shaped. At the beginning, you've got that frenetic activity. Then you plod along in the middle. At the end, you've got another burst of activity in bringing it all together. At the beginning and end, you'll need to devote bigger chunks of time. At both these stages, you need to hold the entire project in your head. That's hard to do if you're snatching moments here and there. In the middle part, you're focusing on smaller blocks. Then it's much easier to fit those blocks around all your other commitments. In Chapter Five, we'll look at creating a writing routine that slots into your normal week.

ACTIVITY

Identify some big blocks of time at the beginning and end of your project. If you can't get any peace and quiet at home, could you go and stay somewhere else for a couple of days?

That's the high-level planning. Now we're going to break everything down into sprints.

Sprinting for Victory

Consider for a moment: what sounds longer, three months or twelve weeks?[5] When we have the illusion of time, we tend to dawdle. Even saying something is happening *next month* catapults it far into the future. I'm hoping you have at least three months before you need to submit your manuscript, as we're going to divide this project into 12-week sprints. The main aim of a sprint is to keep moving.

I'm a big fan of what Brian P. Moran and Michael Len-

---

5 Pedant's Corner: Yes, I know technically three months is a couple of days longer, but you get the point.

nington call the 12-Week Year.[6] Treating each quarter as though it's a full year enforces a lively momentum and establishes regular milestones. As they explain in their book, the deadline is always near enough that you can't lose sight of it. You're going to make every day, week, and month count. No more magical thinking, e.g. I'll definitely feel like writing *next week*. And a nice feature of the 12-week sprint is that you get a week off between these bursts of activity. This gives you time to step back from your project, reflect on how it's going, and also get some rest.

Planning Your Sprints

I'm basing this example on having a year to complete your book. I'll keep the maths simple so it's easy to adapt for shorter or longer timescales. Based on twelve months, you'd have four 12-week sprints. This is how you might use them:

Sprint 1 — Planning and scoping your book. This includes some of the activities we've already covered, such as auditing your thesis, mapping your chapters, defining your scope, and doing some additional research. This comprises 25% of your project time. If you've got only six months, you'll spend six weeks on this instead.

Sprints 2 and 3 — Writing your book. Unsurprisingly, this is the main activity and comprises 50% of your project. As we'll see in a moment, you'll be further breaking down these sprints.

---

6 They don't hyphenate 12-week in their book, so I'm snarkily correcting it here.

Sprint 4 — Editing your book. It might sound excessive to spend 25% your time on editing. If you're sceptical, take a peek at Chapter Six and see what's involved at this stage. Then have a lie down.

Maybe 50% doesn't seem enough for the writing. However, by planning effectively during the first sprint, you'll be making *much* better use of that time. And judicious editing in that final quarter will turn your baggy full draft into a manuscript of publishable quality.

Although you assign activities to each of the sprints that comprise your project, you only go into detail for the *first* sprint. In this example, you're just allocating the headline goals for sprints 2, 3, and 4. You're aiming to give yourself structure, but also to allow some flexibility. At this stage, you can't know exactly what's going to happen in six months' time. There's no way of controlling the future. Nevertheless, you want to make sure you've allocated some blocks of time to the main stages of writing and editing a book. You might need to adjust your course later, but you've got a better chance of staying on track if you've thought about it.

Now let's get stuck into that first sprint.

Applying Dr Pope's Rule of Three

Yes, I like rules. And I like threes. Now break your first sprint into three big goals. The nature of these goals depends on you and your project, but here's an example:

Sprint 1

- Auditing your thesis.
- Mapping your book.
- Completing additional reading.

Those are the headline goals for your 12-week sprint. Then you can break them down into smaller goals for each *week*. That instantly puts you on the hook, doesn't it? If you're anything like me, there were many weeks during your PhD when progress was imperceptible to the naked eye. With a tighter deadline and competing priorities, you can't afford to let things slip. That just stores up problems for your future self.

What might you be doing in each of those twelve weeks? Here's an example:

- Week 1 — Audit chapters 1 and 2 of thesis.
- Week 2 — Audit chapters 3 and 4 of thesis.
- Week 3 — Audit chapters 5 and 6 of thesis.
- Week 4 — Mapping book.
- Week 5 — Mapping book.
- Week 6 — Mapping book.
- Week 7 — Additional reading.
- Week 8 — Additional reading.
- Week 9 — Additional reading.
- Week 10 — Scoping.
- Week 11 — Creating chapter plan.
- Week 12 — Creating chapter plan.

This example isn't at all prescriptive, it's intended to give you an idea of the level of detail required. And to ensure you account for everything that needs to happen. Otherwise, you could easily spend the entire sprint just auditing our thesis. If we don't set limits, we keep going till it feels like enough. It never feels like enough.

Then you get even more detailed, creating three goals for each day or session you're working on your book. These smaller goals are very focused, for example:

- Auditing specific sections of your thesis chapter.
- Reading specific journal articles.
- Completing specific activities, e.g., adding references to Zotero.

The size of these goals needs to reflect how much time you have available. If you have only a couple of hours, you can't be too ambitious. And this might vary across the sprint and the entire project, too. Although sprints are designed to give you structure, they also need to reflect the realities of your life. When you have only a tiny amount of time, the goal needs to be correspondingly tiny. If you're working full time during the week, maybe you could still achieve a tiny goal each day, such as downloading some articles or adding references to Zotero. Above all, be specific with your goals, don't just resolve to "read some stuff". If you're mostly hitting those weekly goals, you'll know you're broadly on track. If you're struggling to maintain your momentum and hit those milestones, perhaps you need to lower your standards, limit your scope, or find a way of working more efficiently. That's what we'll consider in Chapter Five.

Summary

I've given you a lot of work already, and you've not even started writing the book yet. But spending time on the conceptual and planning stage is a worthwhile investment, because:

- You'll produce a much better book proposal.
- You'll identify potential problems before they arise.
- The writing process will be easier.

Setting limits is vital, too. This is a big project, and you're the project manager. As I mentioned earlier, you need the ability to work both *on* your book and *in* your book. That's to say, you have to step back and get the big picture. If you spend all your time *in* the book (i.e., writing it), you'll suffer scope creep and run out of time.

Don't think of this monograph as your final word on the subject. Even if you don't fancy writing another book afterwards (I wouldn't blame you), you'll undoubtedly publish journal articles or blog posts. Trying to cram everything into this project simply puts you under too much pressure and reduces the likelihood of you finishing before the end of the century. If the scope is unwieldy or the timescale seems impossible, it's a signal you need to simplify your plan.

Also, refer back to Chapter One to see how this book fits into your career or publishing strategy. How much time is it worth to you? Six months, a year, five years? What are the consequences if you've allowed six months, then it takes two years? If your book takes longer than you expect (which it will), you'll need to decide whether to allocate more time or to reduce the scope.

ACTION POINTS

- Audit your thesis to decide what you should retain, adapt, or discard.
- Establish your scope, so you're clear on subject, concept, and point of view.
- Map the territory of your book with sticky notes (or digital equivalent).
- Decide on your structure, e.g., chronological, thematic, etc.
- Create a chapter plan and allocate your word budget.
- Outline your sprints and identify your weekly goals for the first one.

Even if you decide not to write a monograph, these techniques will still help you with other projects. For those of you who remain undeterred, you need to acquaint yourself with the realities of academic publishing in the 21st century. I'll see you in the next chapter.

TROUBLESHOOTING

I really want to publish a monograph, but there's insufficient salvageable material from my thesis — it looks like Swiss cheese

Although those gaps look horrifying, filling them might involve less work than you think. Look back through your PhD notes, if you still have them. Are there any discarded bits you could redeploy? Also sift through old conference papers, blog posts, and journal articles.

If it's still looking meagre, could a different structure help? Experiment with the mapping techniques to see whether you can establish a better way of organising your material. Then it might be a case of expanding on what you already have, rather than having to come up with a lot of new ideas.

I've got too many ideas and am struggling to fit them all in

Don't! Keep it focused. Save those ideas and use them for journal articles or blog posts to publicise this book. Embracing too many ideas will make it harder for you at the editing stage and you'll be annoyed with your former self. Also, a meandering scope is less likely to appeal to either publishers or readers.

Use the mapping exercises to be clear on your territory and scope. You need to know what you're covering and also what you're *not* covering. Anything that doesn't fit belongs in another project.

I'm panicking that I don't have time to do everything

When we're stressed, we tend to focus on the problem and not the solution. Our brain screams, "Six months? I can't possibly complete this in six months!" and then refuses to co-operate. While we're unable to control exactly what happens over that time period, we can set ourselves goals and do our best each day to stay on track. Using the sprint methodology outlined earlier will help you account for everything that needs to happen, set milestones, and track progress. Focus on one task at a time, rather than worrying about what's going to happen later in the year.

Maintaining momentum is tough, but it'll give you a sense of control. Once you realise you're on track, you'll relax and maybe even enjoy yourself. If this drags on for too long, it'll occupy too much headspace and get in the way of other projects.

Chapter 3: Understanding Your Publishing Options

> "Publishing is a business. Writing may be art, but publishing, when all is said and done, comes down to dollars." Nicholas Sparks

You've probably spent a large chunk of your life trying to fathom the vagaries of academia. Once you start writing books, you also need to understand another world: publishing. As scholars, we're keen to establish a wide readership for our work. We seldom care about the logistics involved in making it available. We happily spend our time and money trundling around to conferences, writing blog posts, and endlessly revising journal articles. Publishers, though, are interested in *buyers* rather than readers. And not many people want to pay £60 for a book these days.

One of the fundamental problems is that academia still demands that graduates in some disciplines publish at least one monograph before they're offered a job. Publishers are under no obligation to publish these books, and the PhD process often produces theses that require a huge amount of work before they're fit for publication. While the odds of getting published are worsening, you can improve your chances significantly by understanding the academic publishing world and what they want from authors. These people are the gatekeepers between you and the next stage of your career strategy.

In this chapter, I'll give you an overview of academic publishing in the 21st century. By understanding some of the main challenges, you'll be better placed to navigate them. I'll also explain the growth of Open Access and how this might be a requirement for your monograph if you're pursuing an academic career.

You'll be giddy with excitement if your proposal is accepted, so I'll calm you down with a section on contracts, rights, and how little you can expect to earn from your book. As I'll explain, you might even have to cover some of the publishing costs. Maybe you'll decide the traditional publication routes aren't right for you. I'll outline the options for self-publishing and help you decide whether this is a good choice for your book. By thinking broadly at this stage, you're more likely to make good long-term decisions. It's easy to base our decisions on what worked ten years ago. But publishing in the 2020s is a very different world.

Academic Publishing in the 21st Century

The economics of academic publishing are sobering. Although we often hear of behemoths like Elsevier with their 8-figure turnover, many academic presses are running on tight margins. Even if they're part of a much larger and more profitable organisation, they'll have strict budgets and targets. Monographs — the sort that cost £60-120, are expected to sell around 200 copies. This modest target is sufficient to cover the direct costs, contribute to the running costs of the press, and provide a tiny profit. A few decades ago, publishers would've expected to sell copies in the *thousands*. Monographs are only viable now because some of the costs are lower — but they can't get *much* lower. Scholarly publishing isn't yet dead, but it's certainly in a critical condition.

The main problem is one of supply and demand. Many people (including you) want to write monographs; very few want to read them. Even fewer want to *buy* them. And publishers need buyers. Even if they're operating as part of a university, presses still have to support themselves financially, covering costs such as salaries, premises, and equipment. They aren't sitting around, twiddling their thumbs and hoping a manuscript will land on their desks. Most presses can only hope to publish around 5-10% of the books pitched to them. Some books won't live up to their potential — that's inevitable — but it's the editor's responsibility to minimise the number of duds. Given their heavy workloads, they don't have the time or energy to see past a sloppily presented proposal or a badly thought-through concept. It's your job to make the book viable, not theirs.

Presses are mainly expecting to sell monographs to libraries. They perhaps have a marketing list of a few hundred institutions who normally buy titles in specific areas. Libraries, though, are squeezed by budget cuts and sharp practice by journal publishers who hold them hostage by increasing subscriptions significantly every year. As universities rely on having access to the latest research, they're left with no choice but to cut the book budget. They work hard to serve students through inter-library loans and sharing books between institutions, but this is bad news for the publishers. They're publishing to a reliable but dwindling audience.

Of course, there's still a chance you'll be one of the winners in this game. It's important, though, to be realistic about your chances. Telling yourself, "I *have* to get published," or "someone *must* publish me," won't make it happen. Publishers don't have any responsibility for your career. You need to think about your book from the publisher's perspective. Step out of your role as author or creator for a moment. The editor may well agree that your research is important, but you need to convince them it's also *marketable*. This market-based model is precarious. We are reaching a point where universities will have to directly support the cost of monographs if they insist upon this format as a measure of academic success. Fortunately, they are starting to do this through Open Access and establishing their own presses. There remain problems with the model, though, as I'll explain in the next section.

While university presses don't have exactly the same financial pressures as their commercial counterparts, they still need to cover costs. Their staff are often on university salary scales, with sick pay, pensions, and other benefits. Unlike with commercial presses, though, there's no pressure for them to share profits with shareholders. This means any surplus goes back into producing books. There are exceptions on both sides, but I think university presses produce better quality books with higher production and editorial standards. Ethically, this can be a good choice, too. If we go with a large publisher who's simply seeking to maximise shareholder profits, then we're part of the problem. Naturally, though, you might not have the luxury of choice. In the next chapter, I'll walk you through the process of identifying potential publishers and deciding who to approach first. First, we need to get deeper into academic publishing and Open Access.

Open Access

Open Access (OA) is a complicated and often controversial space. On the one side are those who believe research should be freely available for all to read, especially if it's been publicly funded. On the other side sit publishers who incur the cost of editing, typesetting, and marketing the books. Between these two extremes lie many grey areas, hybrids, and other complexities. Here I'll attempt to unravel some of these complexities and suggest potential routes through it all. Ultimately, though, this is a very personal decision.

There are two main flavours of Open Access: green and gold.

Green OA is also referred to as *self-archiving*. Under this model, you can place a copy of your article or book in an online repository for anyone to read. Depending on the publisher, there might be restrictions on what version of your work can be shared and whether there's an embargo period before it's made publicly available.

Gold OA makes the final version of your publication freely and permanently available for everyone, immediately after publication. This is sometimes (not always accurately) referred to as the *author pays* model, as the publisher often expects payment in return for waiving the usual access restrictions. In some cases, this payment is more than £10,000. For me, this is the huge problem with Open Access: although it's fairer in terms of who can *access* scholarly research, it severely limits who can afford to *publish* it.

If we want high-quality research presented in convenient formats, somebody has to pay: either the publisher, the reader, or the author (or their institution). There's a persistent and unhelpful myth that e-publishing is free, as there are no physical materials or storage space required. Although the financial risks can certainly be lower, the same amount of effort does (or should) go into selecting, editing, and designing the book. Whereas print books usually appear in no more than two formats, ebooks might emerge as Kindle format, EPUB, PDF, or various other proprietary formats to suit the different online platforms. This involves significant investment in software and expertise to keep on top of it all.

Some OA initiatives — while laudable in making research freely available — rely on free labour from early career researchers who are doing all the editing, formatting, and tweaking on the basis that it'll look good on their CVs. Those publishing skills are only beneficial if there are also paid opportunities afterwards. There's nothing wrong with commercial presses, OA initiatives, or the various hybrids. The problem occurs when it's unclear who's paying and who's providing their labour for free. And also when large publishers are charging disproportionately high prices for books. One librarian complained on Twitter that they were expected to pay £1,200 for an ebook. It made more economic sense for them to buy several physical copies and repeatedly post them to students.

Open Access and Monographs

Open Access used to be only available for journal articles. Increasingly, though, you can now make monographs available ... at a cost. Many of the well-known publishers are offering a hybrid model. In return for a fee (known as a Book Processing Charge or BPC), they'll make your monograph available as a print edition for purchase and also for free online, either on their own website or on an aggregator site, such as Knowledge Unlatched (www.knowledgeunlatched.org). UCL Press, for instance, currently charges £5,000 to make your book OA. If that seems a bit steep, Liverpool, Manchester, and Cambridge University presses all require almost £10,000. And that excludes VAT. Palgrave (a commercial publisher) demands £11,000.

If this doesn't sound affordable, it's not meant to be. The price tag is aimed squarely at research bodies. Often, funded projects are required to produce published outputs and will have budgeted for such expenses. This means the route is largely denied to non-tenured academics or those without research funding. In some cases, too, I fear publishers are exploiting the ethical move towards Open Access. Given they're expecting to also sell print copies, £10,000 would leave them with a substantial profit. There's anecdotal evidence that OA increases print sales, as it gives readers a chance to try before they buy. I have nothing against publishers making a profit, but there's a lack of transparency here.

An exciting alternative model is offered by Open Book

Publishers (www.openbookpublishers.com). Their books are published in hardback, paperback and ebook editions that can be purchased, and they're also available to read or download for free from the website. OBP doesn't charge authors a fee, although they do sometimes ask them to contribute towards indexing and image processing costs. OBP is a not-for-profit social enterprise and makes its money from selling physical copies, applying for grants, and receiving donations. They're also transparent about the costs involved in producing a monograph. According to their website, it's around £5,000. This gives you an idea of whether those Book Processing Charges above are fair.

I'm not affiliated with Open Book Publishers and am not necessarily endorsing them. I believe, though, this offers a promising model for the future. Given universities are so reliant on scholarly publishing, they need to make more responsibility for keeping it sustainable. While the OA routes offered by some university presses are a good start, they severely restrict who can get published. Even if you don't want to approach OBP with your proposal, I'd recommend looking at their website. They include a wealth of information about the economics and mechanics of publishing.

Open Access might be a good option if:

- You want your research to be widely read.
- Your readers are outside academia and therefore lack access to university libraries and online journals.
- You want to challenge the traditional model of academic publishing.

The compromises, though, are:

- In some cases, you're relying on people doing the work for free and this might not match the standards of publishing professionals.
- You sometimes need to ensure those high standards by paying a BPC yourself.
- Making your work freely available might compromise future options, for example, seeking a traditional publisher or adapting the book into a different form. Always consider your publishing strategy before committing your future self.

Many of the people who advocate for OA publishing of monographs are in full-time paid jobs. Although they're undoubtedly writing in their own time, they can nevertheless rely on a predictable income and other benefits. They're also less likely to have to pay the costs of OA if their institution participates in one of the OA schemes or has its own press. If you're an independent scholar, do you really want to pay thousands of pounds so people can read your book for free? Maybe it increases your exposure and is worth the cost, but you're the one taking all the risk.

In short, I think Open Access is moving in the right direction, but it remains exclusionary and complicated, especially for those desperate to get their first academic job. However, if you're pursuing an academic career in the UK, you'll need to embrace OA and also another acronym: the REF.

Research Excellence Framework

The Research Excellence Framework (REF) aims to evaluate the quality and impact of the research published by British higher education institutions. By 'impact', it means having an effect beyond academia, e.g., societal change. As you might be thinking, most academic research is unlikely to have even a tiny impact on society. And, how on earth do you measure impact? Fortunately, the REF itself is beyond the scope of this book[7].

Under the terms of the last REF in 2021, full-time academic staff were expected to submit four published 'research output items' during the five-year assessment period, with no distinction made between books and journal articles. As you'll have grasped from these pages, writing a book takes a lot longer than a journal article. Yes, you could opt for four articles instead, but what if you're in a discipline that favours monographs? Could you write four books in five years? Maybe, with enough amphetamines and a tail wind.

The next REF is due in 2027. A consultation has taken place, but at time of writing (May 2021), no details are available. There is, however, a move towards Open Access with a suggestion that submissions (including monographs) should be available through OA, wherever possible. This is OK if your institution is willing to cover the five-figure Book Processing Charges, but presents problems for everyone else. While I can't suggest a solution — especially in the absence of the next REF's requirements — I would urge you to monitor

---
7 The phrase "beyond the scope of this book" is very useful for getting yourself out of a corner. You're welcome.

the situation, if it affects you. If OA becomes a vital part of both your publishing and career strategy, you'll need to familiarise yourself with the costs and processes involved. And who's going to cover those costs.

Anyway, unless you're already in an academic post or seriously considering one, this isn't something you need to worry about.

Understanding Rights and Contracts

Assuming a publisher says *yes*, you'll need to get acquainted with contracts. At the risk of stating the obvious, a publishing contract is a legal document. In signing this document, you're assuming certain responsibilities and giving up some rights. It's easy to get excited and apply your thumbprint before reading carefully. Contracts vary between publishers. Some are delightfully simple, others completely Byzantine (deliberately so). The amount of leverage you have depends on the size of the publisher and the value of your work to them.

The Authors Guild has provided a useful model contract on their website,[8] along with commentary to explain what everything means. Although it's not a specifically academic example, it'll alert you to some of the red flags and murky areas. Here are some of the main points to note:

Previous Publications

It is important to inform a prospective publisher if any part of your proposed book has been published elsewhere. Once you sign a contract, you will cede all rights to them, so they

---
8 https://go.authorsguild.org/contract_sections/1

don't want to suddenly discover the content is available in another publication. If you have published parts of your thesis as journal articles, for example, you might be unable to include them in a monograph without substantial revision. In the contract, you're often agreeing that the work hasn't been published in any other form. There's often flexibility here, but you need to have that conversation and obtain explicit consent.

Territories

Publishers often claim the right to publish your book *worldwide* or in *all territories*. While this sounds good — we want to be an international publishing phenomenon, obviously — it's often misleading. Just because publishers have the rights, it doesn't mean they'll necessarily *exercise* them. If you want your research to be available in sub-Saharan Africa, for instance, they probably won't be distributing there, but you won't be able to either. So, you need to think whether signing that contract makes it impossible for your research to reach its intended audience.

Experienced authors (especially those with agents) usually negotiate different deals in different territories. While you're probably not in a position to do this (yet), you can at least have a conversation with your publisher. They might agree that you can self-publish an edition in those countries beyond their distribution networks or perhaps there are some Open Access options.

Translation Rights

It's highly usual for academic publishers to translate works into other languages, partly because English has become the lingua franca for so many areas of academia. They're interested in the largest possible market. Even if they don't exercise translation rights, publishers are unlikely to cede them. Consider your research: is there any reason why you'd want to make it available to people in other languages? If you conducted an ethnography in a non-Anglophone country, perhaps you'd like to make that research available to the participants. Or maybe you were researching minority languages and want to contribute to the body of literature in that tongue. Some publishers will be supportive, while others will stubbornly enforce the contract. If this is important to you, work out which sort they are at the outset.

Formats

Along with all territories, publishers usually claim all *formats*, including *future* formats. It's vanishingly unlikely that your publisher will create an audio version of your book. Nevertheless, assigning themselves control over "all formats" means you can't do it either. Would you want to? Well, that depends. There's been a boom in audio books over the last couple of years, and they're currently outpacing ebooks. Some people find the audio format convenient, either so they can multitask, or because they have a condition that makes reading difficult. Think about your audience. Are they likely to require an audio book?

Although your publisher still won't create one for you, you might be able to reserve those rights for yourself. Creating an audio book is a time-consuming and expensive process, but it's becoming easier thanks to AI tools. If you even *suspect* that an audio book is a good idea, have that conversation with your publisher. For the best advice on the practicalities of producing an audio book, I recommend *Audio for Authors* by Joanna Penn.

The *all formats* clause is also a crafty way of dodging the need to be specific. Unless you have a very vivid imagination, it's difficult to guess what future formats might look like. My guess would be virtual reality or more immersive reading experiences. Maybe your book would lend itself to video games, or apps? If you think there's even the faintest chance of this happening, make sure it's clear in the contract. You don't want to discover there's a clause that awards all the proceeds of your app to the publisher.

Media Appearances

Given the proliferation of independent production companies, it's more likely now that your work might be used in television, film, or radio. Where fees are involved, make sure there's at least a 50/50 split with your publisher. I've known of authors who got paid absolutely nothing when their books were adapted for radio or TV.

You also need to be alert to podcasting rights. Although I've not yet heard of this happening in scholarly publishing, some trade publishers are rumoured to insist that authors can only appear on pre-approved podcasts.

Think long term! Don't give away rights you might need.

Deadline

Your contract stipulates the date by which you must submit your completed manuscript. Although there are no penalties for missing the deadline, the publisher usually then reserves the right to not publish it. Even if they're tolerant of tardiness, you might then miss a slot in the publishing schedule. Your publisher will be working simultaneously on several, maybe dozens, or even hundreds of titles. They need to allocate their team of typesetters, proofreaders, and editors across all those projects — so you might end up at the back of the queue. If you do sense you're going to miss the deadline, let your editor or contact know ASAP so you can negotiate a more realistic date. Then do everything in your power to stick to it.

Publishable Quality

Your contract will probably also state that the manuscript must be of publishable quality. There's no legal definition of what constitutes 'publishable'. This is literally a get-out clause in case your manuscript resembles a piggy's breakfast. I've had to invoke this clause a few times. In one case, the author submitted a manuscript that was painful to read. Every word seemed to be slightly wrong, although overall it made some kind of sense. I commenced a heavy edit, but it took me an entire week just to make the first chapter legible. I wasn't prepared to spend several months on it. I gave the author the opportunity to revise and resubmit, but version 2.0 wasn't appreciably better.

If you're a media personality, publishers will happily bankroll a team of editors and probably ghost writers; for monographs with tight margins, editors expect you to deliver something legible. They don't have the resources to turn that piggy's breakfast into a banquet. That's your job. Some publishers state in the contract that the author must bear the cost of any editorial work they deem necessary.

Word Count

If the contract says 60,000, under no circumstances submit 80,000 and hope for the best. Those additional pages bump up all the costs and may render the book financially unviable. In case you do overshoot massively, use the editing techniques in Chapter Six to make it tighter. The publisher is unlikely to mind if your completed manuscript is slightly shorter than advertised. However, if it looks unfinished or insubstantial, you'll be asked to do some more work.

Proofs

You're agreeing to check and return the proofs within a certain time period. Hopefully, your publisher will give you notice of when you're likely to receive the proofs. Make sure you've blocked out some time in your schedule. They may charge you for any subsequent changes that aren't printer's errors, so it's in your interests to be alert.

Copyright & libel

As author, you assume full responsibility for copyright infringement, libel, or any other illegal acts. If you include an image without permission, for example, the creator would sue you, not the publisher. No publisher is going to relieve you of that (potentially expensive) liability. When it comes to libel, some disciplines are safer than others. One of the best things about being a Victorianist is that everyone is dead.[9] If

---

9 You can't libel the dead. Mind you, the descendent of a Victorian author got very cross when I wrote about her great granny's adventurous sex life. I had to delete that bit.

you're writing about anyone who's still breathing, they might take exception to your words. Court cases are an expensive business, so litigation is a small risk. However, check everything thoroughly and don't say anything rude about tiny men with large bank balances. They don't like it.

I'll explain more about copyright later in the chapter.

Author copies

The contract will state the number of free copies you'll receive. I've always found academic publishers to be stingy and often I've needed to chase them repeatedly to get copies of my own work. One sent an email explaining they were giving us an electronic copy instead, claiming this was in some way more generous. If it's a monograph, you should hold out for at least two.

The contract is mainly there for the publisher's benefit — that's the power dynamic in this relationship. Question anything you're worried or unhappy about. One researcher told me her contract stated she was indemnifying the publisher against any legal action, even if it wasn't specifically related to her book. There's no way that would stand up in court, but it's unforgivable laziness on the part of the publisher. She successfully challenged it. Often, publishers use standard contracts and don't adapt them for specific circumstances. If you spot anything completely irrelevant or unnecessarily restrictive, politely seek clarification. They're not going to refuse to publish your book, simply because you query a clause. If they do, it suggests the publisher is scammy.

You can get contracts advice from the Society of Authors,

if you're a member. Otherwise, there's lots of useful (US-centric) information available through the Textbook & Academic Authors Association (www.taaonline.net).

In summary:

- Read the contract carefully.
- Question anything that's unclear or too restrictive.
- Make sure you understand and uphold your responsibilities as an author.

Royalties and Getting Paid

Estimates vary, but only around 10% of books sell more than 100 copies. In short, don't expect to get rich. As we saw at the beginning of the chapter, academic publishers are often operating on tight margins. While some authors will receive an advance from their publisher, this is becoming the exception rather than the rule. And this is an advance on your *projected royalties*. If the publisher predicts your book will sell 1,000 copies on which you'd get 50p each, they might offer you £500 upfront. Unless your book sales exceed that target of 1,000 copies, you won't receive a penny more — it just means you've 'earned out' your advance.

Royalties

If your proposal is accepted, you'll most likely be offered a royalty-only deal, typically 5-15% of *net receipts*. This means your percentage is based on what the publisher receives, once everyone else has been paid — e.g., the retailer, printer, distributor, and so on. It's not based on the cover price. For a book costing £30, this means you might get as little as 30p. More generous royalties are often based on thresholds — you'll only start receiving that money once a certain number of copies have been sold. Depending on production costs, the threshold could be set quite high, e.g., 500-1,000 copies, so your sales would need to be above average before you earned any money.

If you're working with a big commercial publisher and your book has a wide readership, it might be worth haggling, e.g., asking for a higher royalty if your book sells more than 1,000 copies. Don't push your luck, though — publishers will have a much better idea of the potential market.

You should receive a royalty statement each year, showing the number of copies sold and any money due to you. There's often a payment threshold, though, so don't book any holidays yet. Publishers don't want to make lots of tiny bank transfers, so you'll probably only receive a payout once you're owed more than £50.

A few publishers pay a flat fee — anything from £500 to £2,000 — and that's all you can expect to earn. While that looks like a welcome windfall, the hourly rate is still terrible. You might also have to pay some costs out of that money, such as indexing (see Chapter Seven). And you've signed over your rights in perpetuity. You'll never be able to make more money from that work.

Some publishers offer books as payment. Given the cost of monographs, this might actually constitute a decent hourly rate. It's only worthwhile, though, if they're books you'd want, anyway. Review the terms. Does the offer apply to the publisher's entire catalogue? Do you have to pay for shipping? Would the books be cheaper if you bought them elsewhere? You might be able to sell the books afterwards. You get a bit of cash, while another scholar gets a much-needed book at a more affordable price.

Other Income

There are a couple of ways to augment your meagre royalties.

The Authors' Licensing and Collecting Society (www.alcs.co.uk) is a British organisation dedicated to ensuring writers are fairly compensated for any of their works that are copied, broadcasted, or recorded. You've probably seen those stern notices on photocopiers that say you can only copy 5% of a book. If you want to copy more than that, you're supposed to pay a fee to the ALCS.

If you're registered as a creator with the ALCS, they collect the money from those honest souls on your behalf. This applies whether you've contributed a chapter to an edited collection or written an entire book. At time of writing, I have three publications registered with them, netting me around £50 a year. Admittedly, it's not life-changing, but it's enough for a bottle of gin and a new pair of slippers.

The Public Lending Right (www.bl.uk/plr/plr-payments) is a program that compensates authors for the potential loss of sales from their works being available in public libraries. If you join ALCS, you can ask them to share your details with the PLR.

All income you receive from your book(s) (including royalties and ALCS payments) is taxable and should be declared when you complete your tax return.

You're extremely unlikely to make more than a few hundred pounds from academic publishing. However, if landing a contract with a prestigious press leads you to a full-time position, then you indirectly make a good living from that book. Your rewards might be in the form of tenure or a promotion. Or perhaps your increased visibility results in consultancy work. Very few authors derive their sole income from writing. Those who make a good living often write 2-3 books *per year*. Some of them write one book *every month*. Yes, really!

Dealing with Copyright

The contract is partly an agreement to assign your Intellectual Property (IP) rights to a publisher. As a professional author, you need to get a grasp on copyright law from the other side, i.e., how you use other people's work. Now, copyright is a horribly complicated legal area. I'm not a copyright lawyer, otherwise I'd be sitting in a much fancier office. This section is intended as an overview to help you identify how copyright might affect your monograph. It doesn't constitute definitive advice, rather a starting point for you to establish what you need to do. As an author, it's your responsibility to check this stuff. Your contract will almost certainly state explicitly that you're liable for any copyright infringement.

As this book is aimed mainly at a UK readership, this guidance covers the UK only. Where copyright is concerned, it's the rules in your country that apply. It's more complicated if you're publishing your book in another country. In which case, find out what rules apply *there*. I'll link to some useful resources in the Bibliography. A book might be out of copyright in the US, but still protected in the UK.

When using other people's work, you need to establish:

- Who is the creator?
- Are they living or dead?
- If dead, *when* did they die?

In the UK, copyright applies for the life of the author or creator, plus 70 years. Virginia Woolf is fair game, having died in 1941; Agatha Christie doesn't emerge from copyright until 1st January 2046. If the work is still within copyright, you need to either seek permission to reproduce it or observe the principle of *fair dealing*.

Fair dealing is a legal term used to establish whether the use of copyrighted material is lawful. Unfortunately, there's no statutory definition of fair dealing, so it must be considered on a case-by-case basis. The key question is whether the work has been dealt with fairly and honestly. Some factors to take into account are:

- Has the use of this material affected the market for the original work? For instance, if you reproduced several poems by a living poet, you might cause them to lose revenue.
- Is the amount of material used reasonable and appropriate? Did you need to use a big chunk of someone else's book, or would a couple of paragraphs have sufficed?

It's usually straightforward to claim fair dealing for the purposes of academic research and criticism, provided you are mindful of those two factors. Song lyrics and poetry are most likely to cause problems. You should always check with the rights holder before reproducing those forms.

Obtaining Permissions for Text

For text, first identify the rights holder. If the book is still in print, then you need to approach the publisher. The author contract assigns the rights to the publisher, so *they* give permission. If the book is no longer in print (i.e. you can't order a new copy), it's likely those rights have reverted to the author. In this case, they would need to grant permission. If the author is still alive, you might be able to track them down through Twitter or a personal website. Otherwise, the University of Reading's WATCH (Writers and their Copyright Holders) database[10] is helpful for tracking down authors who are dead but still in copyright.

The PLS Clear website (www.plsclear.com) also provides some useful tools. Here you search for the book you want to reuse and then complete an online request form. Your request is automatically sent to the appropriate publisher. If the publisher says yes, you'll then pay any fees and download your license.

Before obtaining permissions, you'll need information such as the territories and formats in which your book will be published, along with the number of copies printed. Your publisher will advise you on these details.

---

10 www.reading.ac.uk/library/about-us/projects/lib-watch.aspx

Most larger publishers will have a permissions form you can use. This provides you with the format for obtaining the necessary rights and also ensures you fulfil the publisher's requirements. They need to know that you have clearance for any copyrighted material. If you don't receive a response from the rights holder, it's unlikely you'll be able to include the content. Lack of permissions can halt publication of your book. Publishers often have checklists that must be completed and there's no way around it. Don't be tempted to skip this process and hope for the best.

If you're concerned about copyright:

- Limit the amount you quote from other people's work. You're likely to be safe if it's just a couple of lines. Use as little as possible.
- Speak to your publisher. If it's a large press, they'll have permissions experts who can help you. Make sure you're upfront about any potential issues so there's time to resolve them. You don't want to have to delete large chunks of your book just before it goes to press.
- Speak to your university library. If you're still affiliated with an academic institution, there's probably a copyright expert in the library. They can offer advice and signpost further resources.

Copyright and Images

As with text, if the creator of an image is still living or died less than 70 years ago, it's still within copyright. There's an unwelcome layer of complexity here, too. Say you want to use a portrait of Henry VIII in your book. Although the artist Hans Holbein died nearly 500 years ago, you can't necessarily reproduce the image in your book. This is because the gallery can claim rights over the *reproduction*. You could go and take your own photo (assuming photography is allowed), but it's unlikely to be of a sufficiently high standard. Otherwise, you'll need to obtain permission and possibly pay a fee.

While fair dealing applies to images, it's less straightforward than with text. Rights holders could insist you can only use a low-resolution version of the image, which wouldn't be suitable for a book. Publishers, too, might be nervous of potential legal action. Although your contract protects them against legal action (that's all on you), it doesn't always protect them against the *consequences* of that action, e.g. needing to pulp copies of your book. They won't want to take any unnecessary risk. As the author is responsible both for seeking permission and paying any fees, the easiest route is for the publisher is simply to insist on you licensing all the images you use.

Just because an image is freely available online, it doesn't mean you can use it. You'll need to do some detective work and track down the creator and/or the owner of the reproduction. You especially want to avoid tangling with big image libraries like Getty, as they have the resources to identify and prosecute anyone who infringes their copyright. It's worth using Google Image Search to see whether the image is owned by a library. Even if the original creator is still alive, they might've sold the rights to an image library. In this case, you'd need permission from that library, rather than from the individual.

Some libraries and collectors will allow you to reproduce the image for free. Either they want to support scholarship, or to improve the visibility of their collections. You'll still need explicit permission, though, and they'll normally require you to include an image credit in a specific format, e.g. *Reproduced by kind permission of* .... . Other libraries will insist on a fee. This is usually to cover the costs of maintaining the collection or because you're dealing with a commercial enterprise. These fees can range from a nominal sum of £10, through to thousands of pounds. It's always worth negotiating on larger sums, but some organisations will be inflexible.

Your publisher will expect you to cover these costs yourself. If you can't afford the fees, you'll need to rethink the plan. One academic I spoke to was faced with a £2,000 bill to reproduce the images that were central to her argument. Although far from ideal, one workaround is to include QR codes in your text. Then readers can scan the code to view the online image alongside your text.[11]

When considering an image, ask yourself:

- Is this essential to my book?
- Will it work as a small monochrome image? (Colour is unlikely to be an option and full-page images are rare.)
- Can I obtain the necessary rights?

....
11   For instructions on creating a QR code, see https://www.qr-code-generator.com.

- Is it available in the appropriate resolution and format? Publishers usually want a resolution of at least 300dpi.

- Can I afford the costs?

Assuming you don't need that *specific* image, there are hundreds of repositories offering free options, including the Wellcome Collection, the Library of Congress, and the British Library. With public domain images, even though you don't require permission, it's polite to acknowledge the source. They've done the work of scanning, correcting, and hosting the image. Make sure you keep a list of any images you're using, along with the source and copyright status.

If you license an image, make sure you follow the terms exactly. I licensed an image from a gallery for the front cover of a book. I thought it would be nice to include a tiny version of the image on the title page, too. When the gallery spotted this, they invoiced me another £700. Ouch.

Calculating Author Costs

As you'll have seen in the previous section, it might *cost you* to publish your book, even if you're under contract with a traditional publisher. Even if you're not required to license any images, there are other potential costs, too:

- **Editing** — increasingly, some publishers are performing only a light edit of manuscripts. The contract might state it's the author's responsibility to manage and pay for more substantial editing. Check with your publisher to be clear on how much work they'll be doing. In Chapter Six, I'll explain the different types of editing so you'll be better placed to understand your responsibilities.

- **Proofreading** — although proofreading would appear to be a standard part of the editorial process, it's less commonly done by publishers these days. For instance, my contract stated that proofreading was completely my responsibility. While other publishers still perform this task, it's not always done to an especially high standard. If you have concerns about your ability to produce a polished manuscript, make sure you establish how thorough your publisher will be. It's expensive to hire a professional proofreader, so often corners are cut. There's more on proofreading in Chapter Six.

- **Indexing** — There's often an expectation that authors will compile the index themselves or hire a professional. I was given the choice of paying for it myself or not having an index. But not having an index renders a monograph unusable. Indexing is a complex and time-consuming activity. You'll need to either allow yourself at least a couple of weeks to build your skills and perform the task, or budget the funds to pay someone. I'll explain the costs and practicalities in Chapter Six.

- **Revisions** — as I mentioned in the section on contracts, you're probably required to cover the cost of any revisions after the book has gone to press, i.e., once you've approved the proofs. This is because the publisher often outsources the typesetting and therefore incurs additional fees for any changes. The easiest way to avoid these costs is to ensure you leave yourself enough time to check everything carefully. Also, don't be tempted to make last-minute changes when you're approaching the deadline.

Unless you fear your manuscript requires more attention than your publisher can provide, you're most likely to pay for only the images and the index. Nevertheless, this could represent a significant sum. If money's tight, make sure you understand the costs before committing yourself. Have an explicit conversation with potential publishers about the editorial process. Some publishers helpfully provide this information on their website.[12] In Chapter Six, I'll give you some tips on how you can edit and proofread your own work. Also, I'll explain a lot more about the indexing process, including how to do it yourself or work with a professional indexer.

Unless you're publishing through a gold Open Access platform, it's unusual for a publisher to demand a flat fee, rather than for you to cover specific costs. This should get alarm bells clanging. While writing this book, a friend popped up to tell me she'd received a favourable response from a publisher, but they wanted £3,000 towards the production costs. Now, this would be a lot of money under any circumstances. However, the publisher also expected the author to do the editing, proofing, and indexing themselves. This model strays into the murky world of vanity publishing. It presents all sorts of problems, quite apart from affordability. What happens if the

---

12 For example: www.openbookpublishers.com/section/86/1

peer reviewers condemn your manuscript? Do you still have to pay? Or will the publisher waive that requirement or ignore their advice to guarantee getting your cash? There might be legitimate edge cases, but proceed with caution.

Choosing Between Publishing and Self-Publishing

Perhaps your book idea doesn't fit any of the models outlined in Chapter One. Or maybe you want more control over the whole process. As a control freak myself, I hear you. Fortunately, there are lots of self-publishing options available. By pursuing this route, you can decide on the scope, the cover, the price — and all the other variables.

Self-publishing can also help reach a wider audience. If the price is lower, more people are likely to buy and read your book. Even established academic presses struggle to get books into bookshops. As a self-publisher, though, you'd find it easier to strike deals with individual bookshops and to sell copies of your book through conferences and events. I spoke to an independent researcher who'd sold 3,000 copies of her self-published book through this route. It's difficult to get self-published books into libraries, though. Librarians are understandably keen to ensure they're buying only the best research. While traditional publishers aren't perfect, they act as gatekeepers and build relationships with universities.

Self-publishing vs Vanity Publishing

Self-publishing used to suffer a bad reputation and was often lumped in with vanity publishing. Vanity publishers exist to publish your book, regardless of quality, in return for a fixed fee. They might include services such as editing and proofreading, but they won't give you an honest assessment — that's not in their business interests. Even if nobody buys your book, they've still trousered a fat fee from you. If you're tempted by one of these outfits, be clear on what's included within that fee. Also, take a look at some of their books to get a sense of the production values. Ask around. If you can't get a testimonial from within your network, you should probably steer clear.

Is Self-Publishing Right for You?

Think carefully about the advantages and disadvantages below. What's right for you, right now? Maybe you just go with a traditional publisher for your first book. That way, you can focus completely on writing. If you're looking to pursue a longer-term writing career and turn it into a business, seriously consider self-publishing at least some of your work.

I'm pleased to have had my work published by a few different presses. It provides some validation and has also given me valuable experience which I can now share with you. However, it's unlikely I'd pursue this route again. Mind you, I'd think again if Penguin Random House offered me a seven-figure deal for my memoirs. In the meantime, I prefer the freedom of self-publishing.

With great freedom, though, comes great responsibility: you'll have to do everything yourself. Or find the money to outsource those tasks. If your primary aim is to get a publication and you don't want the faff of doing everything yourself, it's better to find a publisher. Be mindful, though, of how much control you're relinquishing over your own work.

When might it be a good idea to self-publish?

- Your project doesn't fit within traditional publishing lists, e.g., it's wildly interdisciplinary.
- It's challenging in form, e.g., you've written a series of haikus on the economic impact of Brexit.
- You don't want to be part of academic publishing.
- You want to publish your book quickly, either because you have other stuff going on or you fear your research will go out-of-date.
- You want to do something with multimedia.
- You want to have complete control over your own IP.
- You want to keep more of the proceeds from book sales.

When is it a bad idea to self-publish?

- You have no idea what's involved and lack the time to find out.
- You don't have the money to hire professionals to help you with tasks such as editing, typesetting, and cover design.
- You need external deadlines and someone else to hold you to account.
- You want to apply for academic jobs.

- You want the prestige of having been published.
- You need the credibility of peer review.

For monographs, this lack of peer review is a major obstacle. It's not insurmountable, though, as you could hire independent peer reviewers. Unlike in traditional publishing, though, they can't be anonymous. You'll have to identify and liaise with your own reviewers, which might compromise their impartiality. There are potential costs, too. While you might be able to call in some favours, I think it's best to pay people, if you can afford it. This keeps the arrangement professional. If someone is volunteering their scarce time, it's hard to chase and hold them to a deadline.

With self-publishing, you'll need to be the project manager. This means hiring a team of professionals to work with you on the book. They could include editors, proofreaders, and indexers. Marketplaces such as Reedsy (www.reedsy.com) allow you to find publishing professionals, read testimonials, and get quotes. There's also lots of helpful information about self-publishing routes and platforms. In Chapter Six, I also explain the practicalities of working with professional editors, proofreaders, and indexers.

Even if you decide to self-publish, the rest of this book will help you plan, write, and promote your book. Although you won't need to write a book proposal, going through those exercises in the next chapter will give a structure for thinking about your readers and creating a detailed outline for the book.

Applying for an Embargo

When publishing your PhD through any route, there's now a big complicating factor: the embargo. With very few exceptions, doctoral theses are archived and made publicly accessible through the awarding institution's digital repository. This means anybody can read your thesis for free. Understandably, publishers aren't too keen on competing with a free version — why would someone pay £90 for a book when they can just download a PDF? This has two main implications:

1. Your monograph has to be substantially different from the thesis (we'll come on to this in the next chapter).
2. You'll probably need to apply for an embargo.

The embargo states your thesis becomes available to download only after a specified period, usually 1-3 years. Until then, eager readers can see only the abstract and metadata. This gives you an opportunity to finish your book and for those early adopters to buy it.

Unfortunately, there are many snags with embargoes. If you're a funded student, it's likely your maximum embargo period is only one year. That's not enough time to write and publish the monograph. If you're self-funded, you might get up to three years. Even that can be ambitious. The standard is often two years, and you need to provide a copy of the publisher's contract to get it extended.

Publishers are aware of the difficulties. It's inevitable in most cases that your book will emerge from embargo *before* publication day. However, they'll want you to at least obtain the maximum embargo period for which you're eligible. Make sure you establish the procedures for your university and that you have completed all the necessary forms.

You might be asking, can't I stop the university from making my thesis publicly available? After all, it's *my* work. Alas, no. This is frustrating, especially if you're a self-funded student. The rules changed as I was finishing my PhD and I was furious to discover I didn't have complete control over my intellectual property. It's important to clarify, though, that you still own your copyright, not the university. You grant them a non-exclusive license to archive and distribute your thesis. This license doesn't prohibit you from modifying your work or granting copyright to another party, such as a publisher. It's still annoying, though.

If you finished your thesis a while ago and didn't apply for an embargo, you can't do so retrospectively. Your thesis is probably already available and you can't ask for it to be taken down. There's a convincing argument that this free version actually helps sales of your book. It gives prospective buyers a chance to assess your ideas before paying for a more convenient format.

Summary

In many ways, it's never been harder to get a book published. There's a lot of competition, and some academic publishers are chasing dwindling markets. Although this represents a huge challenge to authors, you shouldn't be too despondent. People are still writing, publishing, buying, and reading monographs. By understanding the realities of 21st-century publishing, you'll increase your chances of winning the game. Crucially, you need to also decide on whether you want to be in that game. Does it fit with your career strategy?

There are also benefits to some of these recent changes, especially the technological innovations. It's now much easier to distribute books in different formats and at a lower cost, which means presses such as Open Book Publishers can operate in ways that would've been impossible twenty years ago. And there are now far more options for self-publishing and retaining complete control over your own work.

Everything is still moving fast; indeed, it's accelerating. We won't reach a point where publishing models are firmly established and everyone can just focus on their writing once more. There will be continuous disruption. Make sure you're up to speed with what's happening *now* and how it affects you. Above all, be clear on rights, responsibilities, and costs.

ACTION POINTS

- Apply for an embargo, if you're eligible.
- Decide whether you want or need to make your book available through Open Access.
- Consider your potential audience — can you reach them through traditional publishing?
- Calculate the likely costs of publishing your book — can you afford it?

- Familiarise yourself with copyright law and the potential implications for your book.

As you'll have seen, publishing is a *business*. When you pitch your monograph, you're asking that press to invest their limited time and money in your project. Your next task, then, is to write an irresistible book proposal.

....
TROUBLESHOOTING
....

I want to make my book Open Access but can't afford the Book Processing Charges

I'm not surprised you don't have a spare £10,000. OA is a fast-moving area, so do remain alert to new publishers whose BPCs are more reasonable. If you're in an academic post and require an OA monograph for the REF, see whether your institution would be prepared to help you with the costs. They might even run their own press or be part of a consortium, which means the costs are often waived.

If you're not a career academic, you could consider self-publishing. Although this involves a lot of extra work, you'll retain complete control. What's more important: the prestige of being published or the ability to make your research widely available?

I'm worried about the costs of publishing

That's understandable! This topic isn't often discussed, and it's easy to get caught out. You can limit the potential costs by not licensing images and doing the index yourself. For other possible costs, such as editing and proofreading, speak to potential publishers to establish your likely responsibilities. Anyone who refuses to be explicit is best avoided. If you are responsible for editing and proofreading, I'll share some techniques in Chapter Six to help you do this yourself. I'll also recommend a couple of inexpensive tools.

I don't want to give away my rights (especially when I won't earn much money)

Unfortunately, it's almost impossible to get your book published without signing over your rights. To put it bluntly, publishers are exploiting your IP to make a profit (or to cover their running costs). They won't invest time and money in the production process unless you give them control. You need to decide whether it's important for you to be published. If this is part of your career strategy, it's possibly unavoidable. In that case, look upon this book as a vehicle for getting started. Even if you're not aiming at academia, a publishing contract might bring other financial benefits in terms of salary or job opportunities. Once you're a published author, it'll be easier to explore other options for future publications.

Chapter 4: Creating Your Proposal

> "A person who publishes a book wilfully appears before the populace with his pants down. If it is a good book nothing can hurt him. If it is a bad book nothing can help him." Edna St. Vincent Millay

When you're in the final stages of your PhD, you need to get inside the head of your examiners. You're anticipating what will make them happy and what will make them grumpy. Now it's time to inhabit the mind of a *publisher*. Although their expectations are similar — they want to see evidence of high-quality research — they're also interested in something very different: saleability.

Accepting a book proposal is purely a *business decision*. Even if a press operates as a not-for-profit, they still need to sell books. Nobody publishes a book without believing it'll at least cover its costs. Publishers will have different thresholds, but they're *all* interested in sales. Even if they personally love your topic (which I'm sure they will), they won't accept the proposal unless they can see a *market* for it.

That's harsh if your career strategy relies on getting your monograph published. We have to set aside the unfairness of this system and instead consider how best to work within it. There's no way scholarly presses can publish everything that emerges from graduate schools. Therefore, they have to be ruthless about selecting only the best and most marketable books. We need to make sure, then, that your book proposal is irresistible.

As I mentioned earlier, you need to stop thinking of your project as a thesis. It's now a *book*. Also, you'll have to be far more objective about it. You're trying to persuade someone else to invest a considerable amount of time and money in your project. It's important to see it from their point of view. By doing so, you'll make it much harder for them to say no.

In this chapter, we'll consider who's a suitable publisher and how you should approach them. By doing some background research, you'll greatly improve your chances of them saying yes. We'll also think about how much work you need to have done before contacting a potential editor.

Then we'll get deeper into your book. Writing a strong proposal involves seeing your project from a completely different perspective. Although this is a huge amount of work, the planning you did in the Chapter Two will help enormously. I'll guide you through the common elements of a proposal and explain what happens after you submit it. Even if you decide to self-publish, this exercise will help you understand your market.

We'll begin, though, with the easier task of identifying a suitable publisher.

Identifying a Suitable Publisher

Spending a bit of time identifying a suitable publisher increases your chances of success. As one editor memorably put it, *don't spray and pray*. You're just wasting everybody's time, including your own. Demonstrate that you've done your research to establish you're a good fit.

It also needs to be the right publisher for your career or publishing strategy. If your goal is to get an academic job with a prestigious university, you'll need to aim for an equally prestigious publisher. In the UK, Oxford University Press and Cambridge University Press are the gold standard. And if you're aiming high, you'll need to be patient, too. These presses have incredibly high production and editorial standards, so it can take anything up to seven years for your book to appear in print. If you want that plum job, you'll need to play a long game. As we saw earlier, you also have to give serious consideration to Open Access models to conform to the requirements of the REF.

Maybe you need to move more quickly. If you simply want a wide readership for your book and would like to get it in front of readers ASAP, you'll want a nimbler press. Small presses aren't always nimble, though, as they have small teams and can inevitably take on far fewer books. Maybe you're relaxed and just happy to enjoy the journey. In which case, you'll have more options. If you haven't done so already, go through the exercises in the When's the Right Time, Career Strategy, and Publishing Strategy sections.

By following the process below, you'll probably end up with only a handful of potential publishers. However, they are the presses who are most likely to publish your book. And you're more likely to be happy with the results.

How to Find Publishers

First, take a look at the best books in your field and make a note of who published them. Either browse through your shelves or revisit the bibliography in your thesis. Also consider your literary mascots from earlier. You'll notice the same names popping up repeatedly. If you're lucky, you'll spot a series and identify a gap within it, a gap that you could fill. The Association of University Presses[13] has published a very useful subject area grid so you can see which publishers are active in your area.

Under normal circumstances, conferences are a good place to meet publishers. They'll only bother to attend events that are directly relevant to their subject area. Editors love talking about books and this provides an excellent opportunity to have an informal chat to see whether a full proposal would be welcome. You might discover they're already considering several proposals on your topic, in which case you'll know to focus your efforts elsewhere. Avoid pitching or selling, though — it's not Dragon's Den. Don't trap them in the corner for an hour and tell them about your idea of Foucault for Cats. Especially if you're the tenth person who's approached them.

If physical events aren't yet possible when you're reading this book, social media can also be helpful. Follow relevant publishers on Twitter to get an idea of their interests. You

---
13 https://aupresses.org/resources/aupresses-subject-area-grid/

might also be able to track down individual editors and engage them in conversation. Of course, they're not going to offer you a book contract in a tweet, but you can start forming a relationship and establish yourself in the arena. As I'll explain in the next section, publishers also like authors with a social media presence.

Twitter is also really good for finding out about other people's publishing experiences. Academics might not want to criticise a press publicly, but they'll possibly share the scoop in a Direct Message. I don't want to get sued, so I'm not naming any names here. I've heard many people complain of sloppy editorial standards with certain publishers — even to the extent of misspelling the author name or book title on the cover. This is frustrating when you've put a lot of effort into producing the manuscript. Sometimes, we seek the path of least resistance and then are disappointed with the destination. Like any relationship, it'll be a lot happier if you've got the right partner.

Assessing Publishers

Once you find a publisher you fancy, you need to make sure they're still publishing in your area and that you're a good fit. Publishers work around lists or topics and are unlikely to deviate from them. Once you have a shortlist of potential publishers, look on their website:

- Are they currently accepting submissions?
- Do they still publish books in your area?
- What are their requirements? e.g., do they publish monographs based on theses.

If you haven't done so already, take a look at some of their books. If you can't access physical copies, try the Directory of Open Access Books (www.doabooks.org). If you really don't like the way the book is presented, you might end up disappointed with your own publication. Publishers are unlikely to change their font or print quality for individual authors.

And what's the price range for their publications? Do you want your research to be widely read? If so, don't opt for a publisher who charges £100 for a hardback. Some don't make ebooks available (or the ebooks are even more expensive), so you're relying on readers travelling to large libraries.

Avoiding Scams

As if getting published wasn't difficult enough, there are lots of scammers in operation. If you have a university email address, you'll probably receive emails from companies saying you've been 'specially selected' for publication. While this feels flattering and convenient, don't be tempted. Always do background checks on potential publishers. You don't want to hand over your copyright to someone who'll exploit it purely for their own gain. Although the scammers will at least make your book available, it comes with absolutely no credibility or control. There's lots of helpful information on the Think Check Submit website (www.thinkchecksubmit.org).

Here are some of the basic checks you should make:

- Does the publisher have a proper website with contact details and profiles of editors?

- If any of the team members are academics, check out their university profiles.

- Does the publisher charge fees to authors? (Expecting authors to cover specific costs is different from charging a fee. We looked at some of those costs in the previous chapter.)

- Is there any information on their publishing processes?

- Have you or your friends heard of this publisher? Have you seen any of their publications? Even if you can't afford to buy a copy, you should be able to use the Search Inside feature on Amazon or the Preview on Google Books. If the publisher hasn't enabled either of the features, it's already suspicious.

- Check on Library Hub Discover (https://discover.libraryhub.jisc.ac.uk/) — do academic libraries hold their titles?

Devising Your Strategy

You've probably heard of the Project Management Triangle, a model that illustrates the compromises involved in making a decision. There are three points on the triangle: good, fast, and cheap. Your project can be any two of these, but never all three.

Consider your mission. Can you afford to maintain principles? You can't achieve reputation, affordability, prestige, quality, speed, and all those other criteria. Which are most important to you? For instance, is it worth sacrificing prestige for speediness?

Once you've worked out your priorities, list your publishers and start with the one at the top. Then work your way down. You should only approach one publisher at a time. This is frustrating, especially when you often have to wait many months to receive a response. However, smaller presses will take umbrage if you've also sent your proposal to a bigger press. Given the choice, you'll almost certainly go with the larger press, so they're wasting their time with you. I'll talk more about the timelines later in the chapter.

Approaching a Publisher

Sadly, the vast majority of book proposals are rejected. Often, this isn't a reflection of the idea itself, rather that the proposal was unconvincing or simply not right for that publisher. It's important, therefore, that your proposal is as engaging and well-written as the book itself. A poorly constructed proposal makes it easy for a publisher to say no; a good one will make it hard for them not to say yes — or at least hard for them to not give it serious consideration.

Once you've identified some suitable publishers, check their websites carefully for submission guidelines. If they happen to be deluged with proposals (as is often the case) they might display a polite notice explaining that they're not currently accepting submissions. If so, don't contact them, as they'll be annoyed, and it might compromise any further possibility of working with them. For those publishers who are considering new proposals, make sure you understand their submission process. If it isn't clear from the website (some of them are shockingly bad), then email them.

The requirements of publishing houses vary. Some will expect a full manuscript, others just an outline and a couple of sample chapters. Make sure you give them what they want. No-one is going to sign you up on the basis of a vaguely articulated idea. If you are unable to write a sample chapter or a detailed outline, the publisher will have no confidence in your ability to deliver an entire manuscript. For some publishers, the proposal is part of a package. They'll also want to see a CV and other supporting information.

Making an Informal Approach

You can save yourself some time by making an informal approach in the first instance. This is a good idea if you're not feeling confident about your proposal or suspect it's not something you want to pursue vigorously. Many publisher websites include named editors for the various subject areas, along with their email addresses. Outline your project *briefly* and ask whether they'd be interested in seeing a full proposal. Hopefully, they'll say yes. However, you might get some useful intelligence, such as they already have a similar title under contract, or it's not a good fit for the press. Then you're free to approach the next publisher on your list. First check if there's any prohibition against informal approaches. Large publishers might have more rigid systems.

When I adopted an informal approach for my monograph, the first publisher responded within five minutes to say no! He was very friendly, but also firm — this was not suitable for their market. He suggested a couple of other publishers. If you receive a more favourable response that me, it's still no guarantee they'll publish your book. You're guaranteed a warmer reception, though, which reduces some of the uncertainty and potentially saves you some time.

Keep this email short, e.g. "I've just completed a draft manuscript on X topic/I'm working on a proposal on X topic. Would you be interested in seeing it?" Don't send them your CV, references, and swimming certificates. The shorter the email, the more likely someone will read it. Nobody is secretly craving longer emails. Don't send a manuscript or sample chapters at this stage. And under no circumstances attach your thesis. Naturally, this email should be professional and polite. More on emails in a moment.

Before we get stuck into the proposal itself, I'll address a common question.

How much of your book should you have written?

This perhaps the question I'm asked most often and the one that's most difficult to answer. There are two elements here:

- How much of your book does the publisher need to see? (this should be clear from their guidelines)
- How much of your book is it helpful for *you* to write?

I think it's a good idea to have made substantial progress with the manuscript by the time you approach a publisher. Even if a publisher doesn't request sample chapters, writing at least two gives you a sense of whether this project is viable and how long it's likely to take you. Also writing the introduction forces you to envision the whole book, to consider the overarching themes and the scope. Although the introduction will undoubtedly need revision to reflect the finished book, it does provide focus at this stage.

If you're starting from scratch once your proposal is accepted, it'll take you a long time to complete the manuscript. Give yourself a head start. However, be prepared to listen to feedback from your editor on potential changes — they don't want you to think of the book as *finished*. As the publisher, they'll want to have some input, too. Although changing something you've already written feels like unnecessary extra work, it really is quicker than creating a whole new chapter.

Some people advocate having a full manuscript before you approach a publisher. If you have only a couple of chapters ready, there's a risk that writing the rest of the book will take much longer than anticipated and also that it won't reflect your proposal. The two can diverge. This strategy is unlikely to be appropriate, though, if you want an academic job and need to secure a publishing contract ASAP.

The answer, I think, lies somewhere in the middle. Write at least two chapters, have a go at the introduction, and map out the remaining chapters in detail. Also, create yourself a robust and realistic project plan for completing the manuscript. Use the sprint methodology from Chapter Two to account for all the stages. This conceptual stage is essential. Writing a book isn't just about your subject knowledge. As I explained in Chapter Two, you need both a concept and a point of view, too.

If you go for the bare minimum of a few sample chapters, make sure you have some time available to work on this intensively if the publisher wants to see a full manuscript quickly. If you're years away from finishing the manuscript, there's a risk the publisher will lose interest. Publishers vary, but there is a palpable trend towards tighter deadlines. Increasingly, they require a full manuscript within a year, sometimes just six months.

Writing a Book Proposal

Publishing a book is a business decision, driven by the economic realities of the industry. Consequently, you need to ensure your proposal is a pitch and not a research document. As academics, we're used to talking about our research in purely terms of its significance and originality. While those criteria remain important with a monograph, the *market* is of equal importance.

Also, whereas research proposals are typically written for other specialists, book proposals should be written for a general audience. Most publishing professionals will hold a degree, but not necessarily in your field. As they're the gatekeepers, you'll need to ensure your ideas make sense to them. Only then can your proposal proceed to peer reviewers. This isn't about dumbing down your research, it's about communicating *clearly*. Don't be tempted to copy and paste abstracts or chunks from research plans. You're no longer working on your thesis — this is a whole new book. And don't refer to your thesis in the proposal, either.

Most publishers have a proposal form or template available on their website. If this is the case, you *must* use it. Don't be tempted to adapt it or reuse another publisher's template.

Each press requires different information, and the template structure ensures you provide it. While the questions might seem arbitrary, they cover all the elements of a successful book. It's easy for publishers to say no if you haven't observed their requirements at the outset. Remember, you need to see the book from their perspective. Although they vary, templates typically include:

- Overview
- Proposed title
- Chapter plan
- Physical characteristics
- Audience or market
- Marketing plan
- Author biography
- Competitive analysis
- Readers or reviewers
- Sample chapters
- References

I think it's a good idea to create an exhaustive and generic book proposal first. This serves three purposes:

- It compels you to consider your book from every angle, thereby ensuring its feasibility. This also helps anticipate any questions the publisher might have.
- It provides you with a bank of information from which you can draw. Although you'll need to do some

extra work to satisfy the proposal requirements of each individual publisher, a lot of it will then simply involve copying, pasting, and tweaking.

- You can refer back to this proposal to keep you on track when writing the manuscript. It'll remind you of your original intentions and why you wanted to write a book. That's easy to forget when you're in the middle of it.

Let's take a look at each of these elements in detail.

Overview

Start with *why* again. Why you and why this book? Why does the world need a book on this subject? Maybe nobody has ever written about it before, or perhaps they did a long time ago and now new evidence has emerged. You'll have a hard time making your pitch if it covers well-charted territory. It's not good enough that you want to write the book — somebody must want to read it, too.

Your book needs to stand out in at least one of these areas:

- **Originality** — you're at the cutting edge, e.g. the first person to write about the impact of cryptocurrency on the drug trade. It needs to also be relevant and address a genuine gap. There's a reason why there are no books on Foucault for Cats.
- **Currency** — Many books published only ten years ago will be out of date, especially if they touch upon gender, race, or technology. Of course, that means

- **Comprehensiveness** — are there major gaps in previous studies? Does your book bring together a range of material, thereby saving the reader time?
- **Accessibility** — maybe competing titles are densely theoretical and appeal only to a very narrow market
- **Authority** — does your research lend more weight? If you've conducted an ethnography, for example, you'll have original data.

Most subjects have been covered by previous books, so you need to be clear on what you're adding.

In this overview, you're treading a fine line between emphasising the importance of your research and not overdoing it. Avoid hyperbolic language such as 'astonishing', 'unparalleled', 'groundbreaking'. It's for other people to decide whether this applies to your research. As with a thesis, we can get carried away with the idea of originality. It's hard to say something is completely original, so we're usually aiming to bring a different perspective or insight to existing ideas. Or perhaps using new data with existing methods. There needs to be novelty, but it doesn't have to be earth-shattering.

You must also be clear on why *you* should write the book. What do you offer that nobody else can? Summarise your achievements in the field — if you've authored journal articles or contributed to an edited collection, that'll help your case. Maybe you also have other relevant qualifications. For instance, if you're a Biblical scholar, a first degree in Hebrew or Ancient Greek adds credibility and authority.

And mention here the status of the manuscript. If it isn't yet complete, give a realistic date by which you'd be able to submit it. Use some of the techniques and advice in Chapter Two to map out your project and get a sense of how long it might take.

Here's a sample structure:

- Hook and statement of the book's big idea (don't start with a boring fact, e.g., George Eliot was born in 1819 — that's for Wikipedia).

- More detail on your big idea — give away your conclusion! Publishers don't want to guess your argument and they need to know you have something to say, that you have a point of view.

- Why is this important? What are the implications? What will readers be able to do after reading this book? What's going to change?

- Your methods — you're not justifying them here (this isn't a thesis), you're describing them briefly.

- Who will find this useful? (you need to address this in more detail later on, but summarise it here to get your prospective editor excited).

- Why this press? How does it complement their existing catalogue? This demonstrates you've done your research.

The overview is arguably the toughest part of the proposal. Don't skimp on it, though. You're persuading someone to invest a lot of time and money in your project. If you're struggling to come up with a convincing pitch, this might suggest you need to revisit your scope. Have you tried to keep it too simple? Are you avoiding doing the extra work required to make this a book? The planning and scoping exercises from earlier should help you distil the essence of your project into a compelling overview. You want to pique the publisher's curiosity, not give them a reason to toss it aside. This overview will also form the basis of your blurb, which you'll need to create for marketing purposes.

Proposed title

You shouldn't judge a book by its cover. Especially not in academic publishing, where covers are usually boring. We all, though, judge a book by its *title*. This is how we quickly get a sense of whether it's worth our time (and possibly money). Titles influence our reading decisions and, more importantly, *purchasing* decisions. You need to spend significant time on the title and also be open to your publisher's ideas, if they accept your proposal. The title is quite likely to change during the publication process, as it's subject to input from the editorial and marketing people, too.

Above all, the title needs to communicate the book's contents clearly. You're giving a sense of the focus and scope and not over-promising. If you end up revising the scope of your project, you might also need to rethink the title. As with chapter titles, the book titles should also contain keywords. Most of us rely on search engines to find what we need. Unless our search terms are reflected in the content, we're going to miss potentially useful stuff. Put yourself in the minds of your readers and consider what they might seek. A clear title is also helpful for marketing your book and deciding where it should be shelved. This helps enormously with visibility.

When choosing a title:

- Avoid titles that include quotes. We've all seen those conference presentations where the title is longer than the actual paper. And don't do clever things with punctuation, e.g. (Re)imagining.
- Avoid jargon. Although the intended reader will understand the terminology, the buyer might not. And we need buyers.
- Avoid puns. I'm very fond of a pun myself, but they can cause confusion or bewilderment in international markets.

Many monograph titles are in two parts, separated by a colon. Although this gives you more latitude, the first part still needs to make sense. Some online catalogues won't show the second part (after the colon), so the first part needs to make sense on its own. If your book is called *Much Ado About Nothing: The Government's Response to the Millennium Bug*, it won't make much sense if a potential reader just sees the first part. Also consider the book cover. Most people will see your book online, rather than in shops. They'll get a small image on which probably only the main title will be legible.

Choosing titles is an art form in itself. Ideally, you want an eye-catching main part, followed by a second part that provides more detail. Your publisher will help you, but it's a good idea to come up with a few of your own concepts as a starting point. With trade books aimed at a general and large market, snappy titles are necessary; for monographs, it's more important to be *precise*. Cryptic titles can look poetic, but they're not effective for marketing if people will only understand it *after* they've read the book.

When I published a monograph through my press a while ago, the author wanted to call it: *Lingering on the Borderlands: The Meanings of Home in Elizabeth Gaskell's Fiction*. While this was an attractive title, it presented a few problems:

- I'd have struggled to fit it on the cover and spine, certainly in a font visible to the naked eye.
- 'Lingering on the Borderlands' didn't make any sense without the subtitle. It's a meaningful phrase once you've read the book, but not beforehand.

As this book was aimed squarely at a scholarly audience, we went with *The Meanings of Home in Elizabeth Gaskell's Fiction*. If you need a subtitle to explain your main title, then perhaps that subtitle should be promoted to the starring role.

One of my favourite examples of effective book titles is *City of Beasts: How Animals Shaped Georgian London* by Thomas Almeroth-Williams. Although it's not completely clear from the main part of the title, you get a sense of what it's about. It's also an excellent book. Unless you can come up with something equally elegant, stay literal. And don't allow yourself to become too attached to a title. There's a good chance your title will change at least once, and sometimes close to publication date. Your publisher is trying to anticipate and attract the market for your book and to increase its visibility.

You can also review the titles from your chapter plan to see whether any of them would work as the title for your book. Maybe there were one or two you discarded. It's hard to get any perspective on your own title. And it's important to remember that you won't be buying the book. Test prospective titles on other people and see what they think the book would be about. At the very least, say them aloud. I'm sure many potential buyers were put off *Cooking with Pooh*.

Chapter plan

The chapter plan maps the whole project. List all your chapters, providing a 300-word summary for each. You can break this down into two paragraphs: one identifying the aim of the chapter, the other explaining your approach and materials. If you haven't yet thought through your chapters, then you're not ready to submit your proposal. You are not committing yourself to this exact structure, but a prospective publisher wants to see that you have a plan. If you've already done the planning and scoping exercises, this part should be straightforward. There's no need to outline what's in the introduction or conclusion.

While this might feel like an imposition, it's helpful for you, too. It's easy to create an outline that doesn't really work when you try to write the book. This requirement forces you to confront the full concept and see whether it's feasible and logical. One researcher described this part to me as "annoying but rigorous". You'll also be grateful to your former self when you write your Introduction. Completing this exercise means you'll have some chapter outlines to copy and paste. You'll need to revise them, but it'll make life easier for your future self.

As I mentioned in The Anatomy of a Monograph, make sure your chapter titles accurately reflect their content. Avoid puns, quotes, and double entendres: focus instead on including keywords that will increase your book's visibility in search engine results. Although the publisher will read your proposal in detail, initially they'll scan through to get a sense of it. These titles aren't final. For now, they're working titles to give shape to your project. You might need to revise them later if the focus of your book shifts.

Physical characteristics

The book, rather than you. Publishers are interested in the marketability of the book and also in how much it'll cost to produce. As I mentioned earlier, profit margins are incredibly tight in scholarly publishing, so costs must be kept low.

Length: you need to indicate the length of your finished book. This doesn't have to be exact: a few thousand words either way is an acceptable margin of error. Publishers are increasingly unlikely to publish enormous books, as they incur higher print and distribution costs. Think carefully about the word count, as the publisher might hold you to the upper limit if they accept your proposal.

Often, publisher guidelines state the typical length. If

not, you might get an idea of what's acceptable by looking at some of their existing books. It can vary from 40,000-120,000 words. If your proposal states the book would be 140,000 words, the editor might assume you're incapable of expressing yourself more succinctly, or that this is a largely unrevised thesis. The maximum word count usually includes the footnotes and bibliography, so you'll need to keep it tight.

If you've done the planning exercises from earlier, you should have an idea of your word count. Also, you'll be able to identify areas to cut, in case you need to shorten the manuscript significantly.

Images: you should list any illustrations or images to be included, preferably giving their copyright status. Colour images make a significant impact on cost, so don't include them unless absolutely necessary. Indeed, most publishers won't print in colour, or they'll require you to cover the additional costs. There are usually limits on the number or black and white images, too. Consider what's vital and what's a nice-to-have. If it looks as though your book is expensive to produce, that might deter the publisher.

Audience or market

You and your publisher are likely to have different aims. While you're keen to find a wide readership, they're primarily interested in *buyership*. There's an overlap between the two, though. If you help them understand who'd want to read your book, they can identify the likely market. The audience is the group of people to whom your book appeals; the market is the place where they'll buy it.

Be truthful about the audience. If you're claiming your book is of interest to a wider audience, give examples of similar books that have achieved the same feat. And there's no advantage in claiming it's completely unique. One-offs are difficult to market. Your book needs to be unique yet related to other titles in your field. Yes, it's tricky!

Be specific and thorough. For example, if your book is a critical study of George Eliot's fiction, you could describe the likely size and demographic of its audience, e.g. final year undergraduates, postgraduate taught students, and faculty teaching on Victorian Studies courses. A more niche audience is not necessarily a negative. The publisher might be able to charge a higher price if the book fills an important gap, or if nearly everyone in that field is likely to buy a copy.

Publishers are especially interested in reading lists. Some will ask you to provide evidence that this topic is covered on undergraduate syllabuses and to identify universities who might include it. Naturally, you have no idea whether anyone will buy it or teach it, and the publisher certainly can't hold you to it. However, this information shows you've considered the market and there is at least potential. You could also include details of conferences and events that cover your topic.

Another approach is to broaden your monograph to include better-known subjects. For instance, I was advised to make my book a study of several Victorian women writers and to include some better-known names. Had I been pursuing an academic career, I probably would've begrudgingly done the extra work. Of course, you'd need to consider your commitments and overall strategy to decide whether this is feasible and desirable.

The publisher is interested in your *interpretation* of the market. Although they'll be experts in the broader market, they need a steer from you on this specific topic. They then solicit further advice from expert readers and other advisors. This exercise demonstrates your ability to consider the book from their perspective.

Marketing plan

Some publishers want a marketing plan included within the book proposal; others send a separate questionnaire later in the publishing process. Even if it's not required right away, it's a good idea to give marketing some serious thought now. Building an online presence takes time. Many publishers now ask for details of your blog and your Twitter handle. There's an assumption that you're active on social media and know how to disseminate your research. They want authors who are publicly engaged with their topic and have online followings.

Although social media are influential, conference papers are arguably more important. Giving frequent talks on your topic establishes you as an expert on your topic. Also, you can include links or flyers to promote your book. Overall, publishers want to see that you're *active*. Their own marketing activities are often limited to catalogues, so they'll be expecting you to promote the book. While this might seem as though they're relinquishing their responsibilities, you as the author are best placed to talk about your work. Hearing an author discussing their work is far more effective than seeing an advert.

So, make sure you have an online presence (see Chapter Seven) and also identify events where you can speak. Ideally, you'll want evidence of having conference proposals accepted. You could also include details of any special interest groups in which you participate. These groups often allow book announcements and informal talks. You can lay a lot of the groundwork while you're writing the book, then it's easier to get people to pay attention when it's published.

Author biography

This is where you explain why *you* are uniquely qualified to write this book. Describe your background, including higher education qualifications, professional experience, and any awards. Also include details of any professional associations in which you are active. This indicates promotional possibilities and also that you are a networker. Keep it relevant — they don't want to know about your hobbies or pets — and restrict it to a couple of paragraphs. Don't just include a CV, unless you're asked for one.

Like the Overview section, the author biography is likely to be used in publicity material. This will appear on the book jacket and on the websites of book retailers, such as Amazon. You should write it in the third person, e.g., "Zoe Clarke is a researcher specialising in …" You'll get another opportunity to revise it, but for now you're using this biography to convince a publisher that you're the right person to write this book.

Competitive analysis: It might seem odd to draw attention to rival books. However, competing titles demonstrate interest in this topic. If nothing else has been published in this area, that might suggest oversight, but equally it could mean nobody wants to read about the topic. Publishers need to understand where your book fits — where will it be shelved in libraries, where should it appear in catalogues, and where will it show up on the websites of online book retailers.

Identify 3-4 titles with which your book would be competing, including those not yet published (you'll find forthcoming titles on publishers' websites and authors' social media profiles). For each, write a couple of lines on how your book compares, specifically explaining how yours is different. This is not an opportunity to disparage your competitors, rather it's an exercise in demonstrating why your book is necessary. Maybe the other books are out-of-date, incomplete, or not in the right format. Editors don't want to simply publish more of the same, so tell them why your idea is significant. As I mentioned above, your book needs to be unique, yet related. It can't exist in isolation. While it must make an original contribution, it should also be part of a bigger picture.

Here, you can elaborate on the Overview section of your proposal, emphasising where your book stands out in terms of originality, currency, comprehensiveness, accessibility, or authority. This is helpful for you, too, as it'll give you focus during the writing stage.

Readers or reviewers

Publishers send either your proposal or completed manuscript (sometimes both) to external reviewers. These people are experts in your field — usually current academics — who are in a position to comment on its relevance and quality. Typically, publishers ask you to nominate anything from 3-6 potential reviewers. These can't be people with whom you have a close personal or professional relationship. For instance, don't suggest your supervisor, a collaborator, or your mum, even if she's an expert in your chosen field.

There's no need to approach these people directly. You provide the publisher with their full contact details, along with professional title and institutional affiliation, and they'll do the rest. Even if you find someone who's ideal, they might lack the time or the inclination to act as a reviewer — that's why you need a few names. Although some publishers pay a small fee (around £100), others rely on goodwill and reciprocity: *if I read this manuscript, somebody else might read mine.*

When considering potential reviewers, ask yourself:

- Who's published recently in your field with a similar target audience?
- Who do you think would be fair-minded?
- Who hasn't had any substantial involvement in your thesis or other research projects?

Once they've been appointed, don't contact reviewers. This compromises the peer review process. Your publisher will contact them and make all the necessary arrangements. Don't be tempted to send them extra information or make helpful suggestions. And definitely don't email them to ask what they thought of your book.

The press won't necessarily use your suggested reviewers. They'll have their own pool of people and some of the larger presses include academic advisors on their boards. You might also be asked for a list of reviewers to *exclude*. This isn't an opportunity to protect yourself from intellectual rigour, but to eliminate anyone who has been openly hostile to your work. Although this is rare, it does happen. Of course, a lengthy list of nemeses would be a red flag to a publisher, so use this device sparingly.

Sample chapters

Publishers often request at least two sample chapters at the proposal stage. It should go without saying they must be typo-free. Don't send a rough draft. Imagine those chapters are going straight to press and prepare your work accordingly. This means also taking care with the presentation and formatting. And don't simply send them a couple of chapters from your thesis. Publishers never want to see a thesis. If you're struggling to complete two chapters, it'll be tough for you to write an entire book. These sample chapters don't have to be sequential, but they should make sense on their own.

If you've completed the planning and scoping exercises from Chapter Two, you should already have an outline for your chapters. In Chapter Five, I'll guide you through turning those outlines into a draft. Then in Chapter Six, you'll get it ready for submission by applying editing and proofreading techniques.

References

If you're an independent scholar — i.e., you're not affiliated with an academic institution — it might be worth including a couple of academic references. This isn't essential by any means, but it can help validate your credentials. Some publishers might think someone who's been out of academia for a long time isn't up to date with the latest research, methods, or styles. You'd need to contact any referees in advance to check they're happy to be approached. They'll also appreciate some background details on your project to help them comment on your expertise. It's unlikely they want to read an entire manuscript, but your draft proposal will give them a sense of the book.

Not all publishers require or even welcome references. They're more useful if you're not well established. In some cases, you could include your examiners' reports (if they've agreed you can have a copy). These documents should comment on the strength of your research and whether it's of publishable quality. A reference might not directly impact upon the outcome, but it could help the visibility of your proposal.

Submitting Your Proposal

Most book proposals are sent by email these days, but you should check the publisher's preference. Occasionally, they'll want a printed version, as it's easier to read sample chapters. Whether your submission is electronic or hard copy, your covering letter or email is the first chance to make an impression. Don't just write "please see attached my proposal". Engage with the publisher and make them want to open your attachment. Briefly introduce yourself and your proposal, explaining why you think it would be of interest to them. Mention you're familiar with their catalogue and then outline how your book would fit within it. Include contact details so they can ask any questions and thank them for their time. Wherever possible, identify a named individual through the publisher's website. Often, they'll include a list of editors and their subject specialisms, along with their email address.

Make absolutely sure there are no typos in your covering note. If you are addressing an individual (as you should be), double-check the spelling of their name. Start with "Dear..." rather than "Hello...", as formality will convey a greater sense of professionalism at this stage. Use their full name and avoid titles unless you know what they like to be called. Deciding on whether someone is a Mr/Mrs/Ms/Miss/Dr or Professor is problematic and getting it wrong can cause unintentional offence. Never start with "Dear Sirs" — they'll think you're a dinosaur. My press receives at least two emails each year addressed to "Dear Sirs ...", even though the website provides our names (and indicates we're both women). I gleefully hit the delete key.

Always use a sensible email address for communicating with publishers — sk8trboy88@hotmail.com doesn't look professional. Either use your university address, if you have one (ensuring that it won't expire imminently), or create a suitable address elsewhere. While we're on the subject of your online presence, bear in mind that some publishers are inquisitive souls and might Google you (just as prospective employers routinely do these days). Make sure there isn't any online evidence of your having displayed a cavalier attitude towards deadlines, or been overly critical towards one of their other authors.

Don't simply copy and paste huge chunks of your proposal into the email. This should be more of an elevator pitch, preferably just a one- or two-sentence summary. Above all, keep this email brief — you've already given them a lot to read.

What Happens Next?

The publishing process doesn't move quickly. If you've spent any time in academia, then you'll be well prepared for the barely perceptible rate at which it sometimes progresses. It's rare for a publisher to come straight back with an enthusiastic and unequivocal acceptance. Once you've submitted your proposal, wait at least two months before chasing the recipient. Don't pester them, as they're likely to say *no* just to get some peace and quiet. Even if the publisher expresses interest, don't expect speedy responses. They'll be working on a number of projects at any given time and dealing with a bulging inbox. Give them a gentle prod, e.g. "is my proposal still under consideration?" The average time for reviewing a proposal is three months.

With large publishers, there'll be a strict process for the editor to follow. Even if they love your proposal, they'll have to spend time calculating the likely production costs, assessing the market, and sizing up the competition. They then need to convince their colleagues that your book is viable. Those colleagues will be championing other proposals, too. All publishers — even large ones — receive far more proposals than they could ever hope to publish. They'll also solicit feedback from expert readers. They have to be selective and go through a multi-stage process. Remember, this is a business decision.

If you really want to work with a specific publisher, or your options are limited, you'll need to be patient. If there are other potential publishers, let them know you're going to submit it for consideration elsewhere. Then it's up to them to either accelerate the process or release you. Don't issue idle threats, though — they could call your bluff. Larger publishers will be far less flexible, too. They'll have procedures and committees for overseeing the acquisitions process.

Generally, there are four potential outcomes after you submit your proposal:

- The publisher turns down your proposal outright. Usually either because it's a poor proposal or not right for their list.

- They request more information. Perhaps there's some detail missing from your proposal, or they want additional supporting evidence. They might even ask if you'd be interested in approaching the topic from a different angle or broadening your scope. This could be the case if the idea fits with an existing or forthcoming series.

- They offer you an advance or pre-publication contract. Although this sounds exciting, it's not a guarantee. This only commits the press to *reviewing* your full manuscript. The contract sometimes also stipulates you won't submit the manuscript to anyone else. There's no commitment for the press to publish your book, though. Once they've received the full manuscript, they'll send it out for peer review again and use those reports to decide whether they want to publish it.

- They offer you a full book contract. In this case, the press is committed to publishing the book (although the contract often stipulates that it must be of 'publishable quality'). Often, you'll only receive a full book contract if the completed manuscript has received favourable peer reviews.

Readers' Reports

If the publisher thinks your proposal has potential, they'll send it out for review. This usually involves two or three readers who are familiar with your field (they might be people you suggested on your proposal). They're encouraged to reflect on:

- The suitability of the content for the intended market.
- The need for such a book within that market — is there an identifiable gap?
- Appropriateness of the writing style — how much work will it need? Is it written in the right voice for the intended market?
- Scholarly rigour — is your research thorough and of a high academic standard?

You normally get to see those reviews. In some cases, the editor will urge you to act upon specific comments, or they might leave it to you to decide what feedback to implement. If all the reviews are unfavourable, your proposal is likely to get rejected at this stage. Alternatively, they could contact you with questions or to request more sample chapters. They might even ask you to reframe your entire proposal. If this happens, you shouldn't feel despondent — it means they care enough to invest some time in you. The publisher might like the idea in principle but need it to fit more closely with the rest of their list. It's not unusual for this stage to take anything up to a year, with emails bouncing back and forth. Most publishers aim for three months, though.

This is probably the worst part: waiting for the verdict. Academics are busy people, and it takes a long time to provide thoughtful feedback on a detailed book proposal or manuscript. Some publishers provide commentary on the reports, giving you a steer on what they expect you to do; others will just say, "here you go". If the reviewers have been harsh, the editor might attempt to soften their comments. Academic reviewers occasionally forget there's a human at the other end of that manuscript. It's important to remember that negative reviews won't end your writing career. If the editor is inviting you to respond to the reviews, then you're still in the game. They'll be interested to see how you respond to criticism, too. If you flounce off, they might conclude you're too much of a handful.

Peer reviewers are there to *advise* publishers, they don't make the final decision: they're consultants, not executives.

As such, they make *recommendations*. Often, these recommendations differ or are even completely contradictory. After all, they're just opinions. However, your willingness to engage with these reviews and consider their concerns could make the difference between rejection and a book contract.

Your publisher is likely to also send out your full completed manuscript for peer review. Hopefully, this formative input should ensure you get an easier ride next time. I've included more detailed guidance on implementing feedback from readers' reports in Chapter Seven.

Dealing with Rejection

Unfortunately, the most likely response to your proposal is an outright "no". If you're lucky, the publisher might give you some constructive feedback. Perhaps your book isn't right for their list, or they lack the capacity to take on any more projects right now. You should treat their decision as final. Don't respond by telling them they're wrong or otherwise impugn their judgement. And don't beg. Publishers have long memories, and it will jeopardise any future chance of working with them. Rather than sweeping off in high dudgeon, focus your efforts on the next publisher, bearing in mind any feedback received. Many successful authors have been turned down by multiple publishers. Perseverance is key.

In the early days of my press, I turned down a proposal on the grounds it was far too niche. I took the time to politely explain my reasoning, adding that I'd welcome future approaches from the author. Unfortunately, he responded with several emails, informing me I was wrong. Naturally,

I'd rather not hear from him again. Another author wanted me to publish a scholarly biography of her (completely obscure) ancestor. After I declined it, she kept pestering me at conferences.

Why publishers say no

- The proposal is weak — it's badly written or incomplete.
- The idea isn't new — there are already good books on the subject.
- The author lacks a profile — the publisher is unconvinced as to the author's ability to market their book or for it to attract enough attention.
- The book isn't right for the publisher — it's outside of the publisher's normal subject area.
- The book is a barely disguised thesis — the author has made minimal attempts to adapt it.
- The book won't sell — the potential audience for your book is just too small and the publisher is unlikely to make any money. Perhaps you've been vague or unrealistic about the market.

By researching your market and writing a really strong proposal, you can mitigate against these reasons.

It's important not to take rejection personally. Publishers turn down manuscripts all the time, *good* manuscripts, too. They can only ever accept a tiny percentage of what's offered to them. Their reasons for turning you down are only ever about the book and its place within the publishing marketplace, not because *you* aren't good enough.

Make sure you're not using rejection to reinforce any negative stories you're telling yourself. This prevents us from reflecting and learning. Hopefully, publishers will be kind and provide constructive feedback. There's very little that can't be fixed if you're willing to put in the time and effort, e.g., improving the quality of your writing, finding a different angle, or trying a more appropriate publisher.

A while ago, I coached a newly minted PhD on his book proposal. Unfortunately, the first publisher he approached responded in a patronising and unhelpful manner. Although he was bewildered and despondent after their response, he regrouped and approached the next publisher on his list. He's now a superstar in his field and has an impressive list of publications that would put much older academics to shame.

Rejection is part of academia and, indeed, life. Think of all the times you've said no to people: admirers, chuggers, door-to-door salespeople. They were all desperate for you to make their day by saying yes. But you didn't. Not because you're a bastard, but because the offer wasn't right for you. It would be expensive (and exhausting) if we all went around saying 'yes' to everything.

It's OK to silently fume for a couple of days, but then get yourself going again. See what you can learn from that rejection to make your next offer irresistible. If the rejection is purely because they've already published a similar title, then this is absolutely no reflection on you. This is why an initial informal approach can be worthwhile.

Publishers are happy to see proposals for different books, unless their reason for rejection was the quality of your writing. If quality was a problem, explain how you've worked to improve it. Otherwise, they'll judge each approach on its own merits. The fact that they've turned down one proposal from you has no bearing on the outcome of future submissions. Keep going.

Working with a Publisher

Assuming the publisher says yes, it'll be the beginning of your working relationship. Whereas writing a thesis is usually a solitary endeavour, writing a book means being part of a team. And those team members are stakeholders in your project, too, as they're investing their time and money. Having a team on your side is good in terms of support and accountability, but you also lose some control. With a PhD, there's often quite a lot of flexibility in how you manage your schedule. Now, though, there are other people who need you to fit with *their* schedules.

Publishers vary, but it's helpful to get an overview of how they operate.

What do Publishers Do?

Regardless of their size, all publishers cover similar activities, divided into these areas:

- **Editorial** handle the initial stages of acquisitions and contracts. You normally approach an editor in the first instance, and they'll be your main contact. They'll also liaise with you as you write your book and organise peer review at the appropriate points. At the end, they'll oversee editing, proofreading, and indexing. As we'll see later, although they're *overseeing* these activities, you might be performing them yourself.

- **Production** turn your manuscript into a book. This includes typesetting, cover design, and ebook formatting.

- **Marketing** promote and publicise your book, for example by circulating catalogues and contacting libraries.

- **Sales** get the right books to the right people in the right places. This can include shipping, warehousing, and working with intermediaries such as distributors.

For huge publishers, there will be teams of people looking after each stage. With small publishers, there might be just a couple of people doing everything. Some publishers — especially the larger ones — outsource some (in a few cases, all) of these activities to companies called book packagers. This means you might find yourself dealing with a wide range of people, all with their own pressures and deadlines.

If you decide to self-publish your book, this overview gives you a sense of all the work you'll have to do.

Typical Timeline

The timelines will vary, too. Some publishers will make this information available on their website or you'll receive an author's handbook when signing the contract. Here's a typical timeline, though:

- You submit your proposal, usually along with at least two sample chapters.
- Your proposal is assessed by the acquisitions editor.
- If they think it's a good fit, the acquisitions editor pitches your proposal to their colleagues. This first stage takes around 3 months.
- If their colleagues agree, your proposal is sent out for peer review. This often takes 3-6 months, sometimes longer.
- You then revise and resubmit your proposal in response to reviewers' comments.
- If the editor still thinks this is a viable project, the contract and terms are agreed at an editorial board meeting.
- You sign the contract and agree a deadline. Commonly, this is 12 months.
- Then you write the book, in accordance with guidelines provided by editor, e.g., on formatting and style.
- You submit your full manuscript.
- The editor checks everything and (typically) sends it out for review again.
- You make any final edits, and these are checked by a clearance reader.
- The manuscript is copyedited and proofread, either by you or the publisher. Sometimes the index is compiled

at this stage, too.
- Your book is then typeset, and the cover is produced.
- You check the proofs, and any final tweaks are made.
- Your book goes to press and is distribute.
- You celebrate, then get on with promoting it.

You can familiarise yourself with typical processes and approaches, but stay flexible. Every publisher will operate differently, and you'll need to adapt to their way of working. Timescales will be elastic, too, and you'll be expected to provide most of the elasticity. Some presses are better these days at turning around a book more quickly, but some will move at a languid pace. If speed is important to you, check the information available on their website and also talk to other people who've been published recently.

Summary

Publishers are seeking the right concept, by the right author, at the right time. Even though you're an expert, that's no good to editors if there are already several decent books on this topic, or nobody's actually interested in this area at the moment. That's why you need to consider your book from the publisher's point of view. It can't be all about you, as you won't be buying the book.

Getting a book proposal accepted might make writing your thesis seem easy. It's worth the effort, though, so please persevere. Writing a really good proposal will give you an immediate advantage, both improving your chances of getting published and improving your chances of finishing the manuscript. By crafting a solid proposal, you'll develop the concept of your book and get a strong sense of where it's going. If you lack the time to write a proper proposal, you don't have time to write the book.

You'll probably need to keep adapting that proposal, too, for different publishers and for the various stages of the acquisitions process. Even if an editor expresses interest in your idea, you still need to win the approval of committees and external readers. If you're aiming for an academic career, you'll almost certainly need to brace yourself and accept the process. Each publisher will have their own requirements, both for the proposal and the book itself. You'll need to be patient and persistent.

ACTION POINTS

- Identify and assess potential publishers.
- Find out who you should contact and by what method (i.e. do they favour an informal approach in the first instance, or are they expecting a full proposal?)
- Create a generic book proposal that you can adapt for each publisher (carefully following their requirements).
- Establish how much of your book you want to write in advance. Even if you go for the minimum, make sure you've *scoped* and *planned* the entire book (see Chapter Two).

- If your proposal is accepted, familiarise yourself with the timeline and requirements.

Ultimately, a good proposal helps you produce a better book, and faster. It's finally time to start writing.

TROUBLESHOOTING

I'm struggling to write a book proposal — this is harder than writing a book!

I agree with you! It might be helpful to think of the proposal as part of writing the book. Although this document is perceived as being for the benefit of the publisher, it's important stage in developing the concept of your book. It forces you to contemplate the project from the perspective of your reader. By understanding more about them, you'll be more focused and motivated. Producing that generic proposal will also highlight any flaws, such as sketchy chapters or an unwieldy scope. Although this is unwelcome intelligence, it's much better to discover these problems before you get deep into writing.

My book proposal keeps getting turned down

Firstly, it's perfectly normal to experience rejection. Publishers can only accept a tiny percentage of the proposal submitted to them. Before you resubmit it elsewhere, ask yourself:

- Is this the best book proposal you could possibly write? Did you ensure this was a *business* document, rather than a research outline? Remember, publishers are interested in *buyer*ship, not just readership.

- Are you approaching the right sort of publisher? Is your book a good fit for their list? And do they have a gap that you're filling?
- Have you thought through the concept? Are you offering something original, or a thinly disguised thesis?

Assuming you've already covered these points, decide how long you want to spend on persevering. How important is this to you? If you're seeking an academic career, it's worth talking through your proposal and strategy with a friend on trusted colleague. That'll help you see your idea through someone else's eyes. If you're not aiming at academia, you could explore self-publishing instead.

A publisher is interested in my proposal, but I'm worried it'll take too long for them to publish the book

If you're aiming at one of the prestigious university presses, you can expect the publishing process to take several years. Unfortunately, there aren't any shortcuts. Consider what's the priority for you in relation to your career or publishing strategy. For academic job applications, it might be enough to have your book under contract with the likes of OUP or CUP. If you need to actually have a book *published*, it's worth staying open-minded. There are smaller university presses that move faster. Do your research and ask around. Maybe you need to move quickly this time, but you can aim higher with your next book.

Chapter 5: Writing Your Manuscript

> "Getting the first draft finished is like pushing a peanut with your nose across a very dirty floor."
> Joyce Carol Oates

It might feel as though we've covered a lot so far, and you possibly haven't even done any writing yet. That preparation was vital, though. Now you'll have a clearer sense of what you need to do. If you haven't yet done the planning and scoping exercises from Chapter Two, please hop back there now. Don't be tempted to skip those exercises, though, as it'll make it much harder to write your book.

Everyone always wants to know how long it takes to write a monograph. Unsurprisingly, it takes longer than you think. Often, everything makes perfect sense in our heads. Then when we transfer it to the screen, it looks like a plate of spaghetti. Also, you probably haven't written a book before. Although you have experience of a big writing project, the monograph presents other challenges. You'll almost certainly make mistakes and not go about it in the most efficient or elegant way. You're learning and writing at the same time.

Mindset is crucial. You're no longer thinking like a PhD

student. Apart from the fact this is a book, not a thesis (have I mentioned that before?), you'll need to find different ways of working. The strategy you used for finishing your PhD is unlikely to be effective now. You'll need to develop new skills and ways of working.

In this chapter, I'll help you become a professional writer. We'll build effective routines and templates for boosting productivity, overcoming procrastination, and staying on track. I'll also introduce you to the idea of building a writing fortress — creating the right conditions to ensure you maintain a consistent output. Of course, there are many obstacles in your way. I'll explain how to avoid perfectionism, deal with competition, and recognise when you've done enough. Once you have that baggy first draft, it's time to get someone else's perspective. I'll offer guidance on soliciting and implementing effective feedback. Although you want to keep your draft in a folder marked Top Secret, sharing it with early readers is the best way to turn it into a great book.

So far, you've been thinking like a project manager, working *on* your book. Now you'll be working *in* the book and creating that elusive first draft. First, let's think like a writer.

Thinking Like a Writer

If you're not doing so already, you need to think of yourself as a professional writer. After all, you're writing a book. Although there are some badly behaved authors, the successful ones these days are highly disciplined. That's not to say they find writing easy, rather that they've found ways of motivating themselves. Maya Angelou famously locked herself in a hotel room every morning with a bottle of sherry and a copy of the Bible. She understood that writing can't happen unless you create the right conditions. As you'll see from her example, we all need to find the conditions that are right for us. Mind you, I'm not convinced a breakfast sherry is good for productivity.

When I was writing my MA dissertation, I received an astonishingly unhelpful piece of writing advice. One of my advisors told me I shouldn't even *start* writing until all the ideas were fully formed in my head. Only once everything made complete sense should I open that Word document. Then, apparently, it would all appear on the screen in a continuous stream. As you'll have guessed, this didn't happen.

I kept telling myself I wasn't ready to write *yet*. Consequently, I had to apply for an extension and ended up writing the dissertation on my honeymoon. My topic was nineteenth-century bigamy, and I had a book called *The Road to Divorce* on my bedside table when I was supposed to be celebrating my nuptials. Remarkably, I'm still married.

I believe some people find writing easier than others — they can write fairly fluently and confidently. I refuse to believe, though, that anyone sits down and writes a complete draft of a paper or chapter. These myths, perhaps unconsciously, are designed to reinforce imposter syndrome. When a senior academic tells us we shouldn't be struggling, that makes us think we don't belong.

This (mythical) approach also gives us an illusion of control, something we desperately crave right now. We don't want to acknowledge the chaos, the resistance, the feelings of helplessness. How we establish that control, though, is by creating and refining processes that work for us. Often when I'm coaching researchers on writing, they'll explain their process to me and ask, "is that OK?" They're seeking approval. But there's no 'right' way of writing, only a way that's effective for *you*. And by 'effective', I don't mean one that consistently produces thousands of perfect words each day. I mean a process that helps you achieve realistic goals within a realistic timeframe. It's much better to consistently produce 500 words a day than to strive unsuccessfully to write 2,000 words every so often.

At the other extreme there's the suggestion that writing is torturous. I don't buy that, either. As is often the case, the truth lies somewhere in the middle: writing takes effort. And it's iterative. As Ernest Hemingway famously said, "The only kind of writing is rewriting." He also enjoyed a cocktail of champagne and absinthe while writing, which might have affected the quality of his first draft. Good writing is hard. But it's incredibly satisfying and worthwhile. Get out of the PhD mindset and all the accompanying bad habits and self-flagellation. You're now a professional writer with your own way of doing things.

Not Thinking Like a PhD Student

Not only do you need to start thinking like a writer, you should also *stop* thinking like a PhD student. If you're still in PhD-mode, those thesis tics will creep into your manuscript. In Chapter Two, we looked at the main differences between a thesis and a monograph. Now we'll take a closer look at style.

One of the main differences between the two forms is that a book is less defensive. In a thesis, we're obliged to footnote almost everything, providing evidence for our claims, and relying on third-party support. We're also expected to include an extensive literature review to situate our claim to originality and significance. Once you've got your doctoral gong, though, it's more acceptable for you to make (carefully reasoned) pronouncements. Nor do you need to provide a blow-by-blow account of your methodology. As a fully qualified academic researcher, it's assumed you know what you're doing.

Recently, I spoke to a researcher who was told by peer reviewers that her monograph still read like a thesis. She was labouring her original contribution too much instead of "just getting on with it". There are all sorts of apparatus required in a thesis, because it's part of an examination. As in any examination, the emphasis in a PhD is demonstrating what you know. You need to be more courageous with a book and aim instead to share what's important.

> **In a thesis, you demonstrate what you know; in a book, you share what's important.**

Your book needs to be more focused, better written, and to appeal to a wider audience. Although you've been encouraged to write a thesis and get it published, no publisher (or reader) wants a thesis. You can get away with some truly horrible writing in your thesis, provided your argument is clear and original. It won't be tolerated in a book, though.

If you're aiming for a wide readership, publishers expect

you to write in an engaging way, using clear examples and lively case studies. It will be obvious to them if you've just done your best to cobble together the more presentable bits of your thesis. There's a good chance you might need to rewrite your thesis line by line. In a thesis, we're showing off that we know this stuff — "Look at me, I can use the word 'ontological'!" But in a book with broader appeal, is that going to deter readers? Of course, there's a place for technical language, but only when it enhances rather than hinders meaning.

Many books on academic writing focus on word choice or writing in an academic style. Although this is an area that causes a lot of anxiety for researchers, it's often a distraction from the more important matter of *structure*. Sometimes, an overly academic style is used to hide a shaky argument. Fancy words and convoluted sentences treat the symptom rather than the cause. Consequently, I'm not going to talk much about style here. In any case, that'll vary enormously according to your discipline and field. It's much easier and quicker to sort out your style if you have a sound underlying structure. I think the best way to improve your style is to learn from others.

Reading Like a Writer

In his memoir *On Writing*, Stephen King insists: "If you want to be a writer, you must do two things above all others: read a lot and write a lot." King spends equal amounts of time reading and writing because he wants to learn from what other people are doing. Yes, even wildly successful authors are still learning. That's how professionals hone their craft.

It's the same with any craft you want to improve. If you're learning to play guitar, then it's a good idea to watch some incredibly accomplished musicians, like Sister Rosetta Tharpe. If you search on YouTube, you'll find some amazing videos of her. She was one of the great pioneers of the electric guitar and many famous musicians have learnt from her. If you're an artist, you can look at works by the great masters. By zooming in on those paintings and analysing the brushwork, you can work out exactly how the artist has achieved that effect.

I want you to read like a writer. Once you've extracted the meaning from a journal article or book, go back and observe the writing style. How is the information conveyed? Was it a struggle to understand it? If it's Judith Butler, then yes. Is it engaging? Did you enjoy yourself? Or was it a bit of a slog? And how is it structured? How has the author built up the arguments? And are there any particular words or phrases or expressions that are useful? Obviously, you can't steal the ideas, but there's no reason why you can't use a good verb or a nicely turned phrase. You can collect those as you're reading them and using them in your own writing. Look at your literary mascots to get a sense of style. What do you want to incorporate? And what should you avoid? In *Stylish Academic Writing*, Helen Sword explains:

> By imitating the successful and making their skills our own, we can collectively evolve the common type of academic writing into something truly worth reading.

There's an unhelpful myth that it's not really academic writing unless it sends the reader into a coma. So much of it is written in a deliberately clunky style that makes people feel excluded. That's not what most of us want to do. Should we be producing work that creates barriers? Or do we want the widest possible readership for our ideas? If possible, think about how far you can go with your own writing. In the Bibliography, I've included some suggested further reading on writing in different disciplines. In short, imitate the style of writing *you* enjoy reading. Don't become part of the problem.

Boosting Your Productivity

Although successful authors differ in their working methods and preferred tipple, most of them share a core habit: they create blocks of time for *deep work*. If you've not seen it already, I recommend watching Cal Newport's TED Talk on deep work. Newport, a prolific writer and professor, argues we need blocks of time during which we completely immerse ourselves in a task. We often *think* we're focused, but we're only engaging in *shallow* work, as we're constantly distracted by emails, notifications, and other people.

And it's not just the distraction itself that causes a problem. In his book *Deep Work*, Newport explains the concept of *attention residue*. When you switch from one task to another, your attention doesn't immediately follow. Some of your brain cells are still working on that original task, such as mentally composing a response to an infuriating tweet you've just seen. Although you're now looking at your book again, it doesn't have your full attention. You're still smarting.

These distractions are undemanding and provide immediate gratification. With deep work, the payoff is much bigger, but you have to wait a long time. It's human nature to seek an easy win, that dopamine hit of social approval or the satisfaction of having responded to an email. We sacrifice our longer-term goals in the pursuit of instant gratification.

This state of semi-distraction is seriously affecting our ability to pursue demanding activities such as writing. How can you examine a complex question from all angles if your brain is also composing replies and seething from online interactions? Two hours of deep work is worth a whole day of multitasking. We often tell ourselves we need a vast and clear schedule to get any writing done. What we actually need is frequent and relatively short sessions of deep work.

Creating Blocks of Deep Work

If you're going to finish your book, you need to decide exactly *when* you're going to write it. With large projects, it's easy to imagine we're making progress just by *thinking* (or worrying) about it. Thinking is certainly encouraged, but we also need to take consistent action. It's those small, consistent actions that add up to the outcome of a finished manuscript. As Stephen Pressfield writes in *Nobody Wants to Read Your Sh*t*, "[W]hen we think in blocks of time, we acquire patience. We break down that overwhelming transcontinental trek into doable daily or weekly transits."

For a tight schedule of 6-12 months, it's vital to get into a routine. I know routines sound dull — we want to write when our head is bursting with ideas. Unfortunately, that tends to happen at inconvenient moments. Routines can be dull, but they're also *predictable*. Once we've established a predictable writing process, we get a much better sense of how long everything takes. If we know we can reliably crank out 1,000 words each week, it's easier to plan those 12-week sprints (see Chapter Two). And consistently hitting those targets provides evidence of progress. There's nothing more motivating than knowing we're finally getting somewhere.

Once you've planned that 12-week sprint and worked out your goals for each week, you can start fitting everything into your schedule. Start by blocking out any completely immovable objects, e.g., work commitments, medical appointments, and important social engagements. Now see if you can find at least a couple of blocks for deep work. Don't be too ambitious at first. It's much better to start small and gradually build up than to be defeated by an unrealistic goal. That just leads to despondency.

Schedule those blocks of deep work in your usual calendar app or diary. This is a commitment just like any other. Of course, there's always the risk you'll delete it, but this does at least introduce a little bit of friction. If other people have access to your calendar, be vague or enigmatic — just record yourself as unavailable. Otherwise, they might think your writing time is negotiable.

If you have enough flexibility in your schedule, you should also consider the best time of day for writing. If you're a morning person and trying to work on your book in the evening, you could be making life unnecessarily difficult for yourself. Could you swap your tasks around to make better use of your energy? Are you doing something in the mornings that doesn't require much brainpower? Likewise, if you're an owl, could you keep some evenings free?

I write best in the morning while my brain is alert and fully caffeinated. Also, I'm less likely to have become distracted by emails and other intrusions. I can often return to my writing in the afternoon, but only after I've already made a strong start. My absolute peak is 8.00-10.00, so I try to avoid scheduling routine stuff during those hours. By protecting this time most days, I make consistent progress on my books. For those of you with full-time jobs, you'll have a lot less flexibility. Then it's a case of setting some limits on your job and being very careful how you allocate your free time.

Using Smaller Blocks of Time

If you have a lot of responsibilities, you probably can't accommodate more than a couple of deep work sessions each week. You can still use those smaller blocks of time, though. It's a matter of suiting the action to the time slot. In *Getting Things Done*, David Allen explains four criteria for choosing actions:

- **Context** — e.g., location, equipment available.
- **Time available** — if it's just 5 minutes, this limits what you can do.
- **Energy available** — how mentally taxing is the proposed task?
- **Priority** — what results in the biggest payoff?

Context

If you need to take a one-hour train journey, is there anything you could achieve in this time? Is it possible to take a laptop? If not, could you hand-edit a printed draft? When I worked at a university, I had a 12-minute train commute. You wouldn't think that's enough time to achieve anything meaningful. Nevertheless, I'd often use it to write the opening sentences of a chapter. They're always the hardest and most time-consuming. If I tried to do this at home, I'd keep re-reading what I'd already written. For these micro sessions, I'd take nothing but that first paragraph and focus on just one sentence.

Time available

You can't get much writing done in five minutes, but it's certainly long enough to check a few references. That type of systematic task is suited to short bursts, especially given it's quite dull. Unlike writing, there's no need to build up momentum or hold lots of information in your head. Conversely, if you find yourself with an unexpectedly empty afternoon, could that be a good opportunity for sustained work on a problematic chapter?

Energy available

It's essential to identify our best hours for writing and make sure they're not occupied by lower priorities. Equally, we want to avoid pushing ourselves too hard at times that aren't right for us. If you're a morning person but have a couple of free evenings, find some less demanding activities to do then. Finishing your book isn't all about big ideas. Much of it involves organising material, which is something you can do when you're low-powered.

Priority

When you have competing priorities and it's not clear which you should confront first, consider which you *most* want to finish. That euphoria of having completed an unattractive task is motivating and also clears your mind. Maybe there's also a task you can complete now that'll save you time in future, for example, requesting scans from an archive, ordering books through inter-library loan, or organising your research material.

ACTIVITY

Once you've got a sense of your project, see if you can organise the tasks by time and energy. For example:

- 5-minute jobs, e.g., checking references.
- 1-hour jobs, e.g., outlining a chapter section.
- 2-hour jobs, e.g., reading a journal article.
- One-day jobs, e.g., drafting a chapter section.
- Entire weekend jobs, e.g., planning and scoping a chapter.

Now you identify the types of job involved in each week of your sprint and add them to your weekly schedule.

Embracing Darwin Days

On 1st October 1861, Charles Darwin wrote to a friend, "But I am very poorly today and very stupid and hate everybody and everything." Ever had a Darwin Day? Me too. For Darwin Days, we need Darwin Jobs. That's a list of tasks that aren't mentally demanding, yet nudge us closer to the finish line. They might include those 5-minute activities, such as checking references, or more sustained but easy tasks like formatting a document.

In some cases, though, these feelings are a sign that you need a Duvet Day instead.

Using the Pomodoro Technique

Another way to manage smaller blocks of time is to measure them in *tomatoes* with the Pomodoro Technique. *Pomodoro* is Italian for tomato, and it refers to those novelty tomato-shaped kitchen timers. The technique was devised by Francesco Cirillo back in the 1980s. Here's what you do:

1. Choose a task or activity, e.g., write paragraph.
2. Set your timer for 25 minutes (it doesn't have to resemble a tomato).
3. Work on your task without any interruptions — so, don't check email, make a cup of tea, or talk to the cat. If anything unrelated pops into your head (which it will), quickly make a note of it and return to your task.
4. When the buzzer or bell sounds, take a 5-minute break and record your progress.

5. Repeat, taking a longer break for every 4 tomatoes completed.

The science behind it shows that most of us can focus for only 25 minutes before our mind wanders. That's when we start faffing and seeking distractions. A 5-minute break allows our brain to relax, but it's not long enough for us to lose momentum or forget what we were working on.

The Pomodoro Technique is highly effective for most of us because it enforces short bursts of focused activity and encourages us to break our work down into more manageable tasks. It might take you a little while to get used to it, but soon you'll start thinking of tomatoes as a unit of labour, "Hmm, that looks like a three-tomato task."

You'll be surprised by what you can achieve in 25 minutes, too. It depends on the type of writing (e.g., descriptive, analytical, contextual), but 500 words are feasible if you know what you're going to write. Complete a tomato each day and guess how much you'll have accumulated by the end of the month? 10,000 words. That could be a draft book chapter.

Everyone is different, so you'll need to experiment to establish an approach that suits you. Some find 25 minutes too long, or require 10-minute breaks between tomatoes; others need a giant 60-minute tomato to make any progress. You might not even find it helpful at all. Some types of work suit this format better than others.

If you're struggling to fit everything in your schedule at the moment, just make a commitment to yourself to complete one tomato a day. Once you've squashed a tomato for five days in a row, see whether you can squeeze in two per day. The key is to not overstretch yourself by setting an unrealistic target. It's much easier to take a short walk every day than it is to run a marathon once a week. Think small and consistent, not big and sporadic.

For me, the real strength of the Pomodoro Technique is in getting started when resistance is high — "I'll just do one tomato today." Then I miraculously find myself capable of completing another tomato. Sometimes we need to doggedly pursue one tomato at a time; other days, one tomato is enough to find that motivation.

Building Your Writing Fortress

Even if you've successfully found time to write, you have defend that time *and* use it productively. You must create the right conditions for writing to happen. In other words, you need a *writing fortress*. This usually means either hiding yourself away, or communicating your needs clearly and repeatedly. Tell somebody you want to work uninterrupted for 30 minutes, and it'll be a matter of moments before they insist on asking whether you fed the cats. Or they'll feel able to destroy your concentration so long as unnecessary questions are prefixed with, "I know you're busy, but ...".

It's hard getting colleagues and family members to respect those boundaries. One solution is to ensure those blocks of deep work are scheduled and upheld. If you plan a writing session, then do something else, it signals to everyone else that this isn't really a priority. If you stick to the schedule, though, everyone gets used to this routine (including you), even if they don't necessarily like it. Agree times when you'll be fully engaged with shared activities and clearly communicate when it's time for your writing. This might involve firmly reminding household members of those agreements. As with any fortress, you have to repeatedly repel attackers.

We also need to be aware of the enemy within: ourselves. When other people are constantly disrupting us, we have the perfect excuse for not having done any writing. If we are on our own, there's no-one else to blame. This is really annoying. That's why we need a routine to get started.

Devising a Start-up Routine

It took me a long time to realise I couldn't simply sit at my desk and expect to launch straight into academic writing. I'd sit frowning at the screen and wonder why nothing was happening. After 10 frustrating minutes, I'd decide to check my email or browse Twitter, as if that was going to help me focus.

Just as we wouldn't expect to compete in the 110m hurdles without warming up, we can't write cold. We need to ease ourselves into it gradually. This way, we can almost sneak up on ourselves and start writing academically before our brains have realised what's happening. We can do this by creating a start-up routine or algorithm — a series of steps leading to an intended outcome.

The advantage of effectively programming ourselves is that it doesn't leave any room for judgement. Ask yourself, "Should I do some writing this morning?" and your brain will frantically come up with at least a dozen reasons why it can't possibly happen now. Instead, follow a clear set of instructions that have already been established.

The steps of your start-up routine will depend very much on your personal preferences, but here's what it might include:

- **Make a cup of tea or coffee** — some people like to use a special writing mug. This mug is only used when writing, so it signals to the brain that they're moving into this mode. Maybe you favour special writing pants instead, or even a hat.

- **Get comfortable** — if you're not sitting comfortably, you're likely to develop aches and pains. Once this happens, you associate writing with physical pain, and your body (as well as your mind) will recoil from it. Spend a few moments adjusting your workspace. Perhaps you can optimise your chair, raise your monitor, or get a cushion.

- **Switch off the internet** — the internet is a giant conspiracy to prevent you from getting any work done. Make sure you've downloaded everything you need in advance, so you don't disappear down any rabbit holes.

- **Do 5 minutes' freewriting** — freewriting is whatever's in your head, rather than structured thoughts. This gets you warmed up, clears your head, and helps get those synapses firing. You're writing without putting any pressure on yourself to produce anything sensible. Alternatively, you could type out a quote from a journal article.

- **Tackle an 'easy' tomato** — when I say 'easy', it could also be 'exciting' or a least marginally more attractive than all the other tomatoes. The aim is to give yourself a quick win that gets you motivated.

Be prepared to experiment with your start-up routine and reflect on the outcomes. Maybe you'll need some extra steps.

Adding a Shutdown Routine

You might think writing *too much* is a nice problem to have. Over time, though, it can cause problems. Without an exit strategy, we're tempted to keep writing until exhaustion sets in. Or our mind is buzzing with distracting thoughts when we're trying to switch off. A shutdown routine helps you ease out of writing mode and also prepares for your next session. Again, the exact steps depend on your personal preference, but here's what it might include:

- **Use bullet points to quickly jot down any ideas** — this gets them out of your head and removes the fear of forgetting them. You'll also have a clear outline for the next session.

- **Make a quick note of what you want to do tomorrow** — e.g. I want to finish the introduction to Chapter 2, then check the references. Again, you won't need to spend time tomorrow trying to remember what you'd intended to do.

- **Do 5 minutes' freewriting** — this helps you reflect on your session and come out of academic mode. You might create some prompts, such as "What went well today?" or "Is there anything I could try tomorrow to make my writing session more productive?"

- **Update your progress chart** — this gives you visible evidence of progress, and it's very satisfying. I'll share an example in a moment.

- **Tidy your workspace** — clearing the clutter might make your desk seem more inviting tomorrow. If your desk also happens to be a dining table or in your bedroom, it also means you're not distracted by the sight of your writing materials when you want to relax.

With these routines, you're aiming to remove the friction caused by having to make decisions, e.g. "What should I do today?". Also, they help us form habits. It takes a while for good habits to become established, so you'll need to pursue those routines for at least a month before the resistance dissipates. Bad habits (such as rewarding yourself with cake) become hardwired within a couple of days.

ACTIVITY

Create your own start-up and shutdown routines and place them somewhere visible.

Creating Accountability

Although I'm organised and self-motivated, I can seldom be trusted to write on my own. Even if I set aside some time for writing, there's often a very good reason why it can't possibly happen today: a complicated email to write, a query to answer, an errand to run. I'll definitely write *tomorrow*, but today (sadly) it's not possible. My solution to this problem is to create *accountability*. I'm much better at upholding commitments to other people than to myself.

Working in a Panopticon

As I write this, a Russian PhD student called Natasha is watching me. Well, I think she's getting on with her own work, but I certainly feel as though I'm being watched. Every time I decide I'm tired or feel the urge to check Twitter, I remember my commitment to Natasha: she's going to finish making notes on a paper, while I complete a draft of this chapter.

We're connecting through Focusmate (www.focusmate.com). This online tool matches you with a stranger so you can watch each other write. Yes, it does sound a bit creepy, but it's incredibly effective. You choose a 50-minute slot through the online calendar, then click on the link to connect with your partner. You have a brief chat at the beginning to introduce yourself and explain what you're going to work on. Then you get writing. At the end, you have another brief chat to share what you've achieved. Over time, you'll see familiar faces and build relationships. I've mentioned some of my regular Focusmate partners in the Acknowledgements.

While random pairings might not be your cup of tea, perhaps you could make informal arrangements with another writer? One of the advantages of this dreadful pandemic is that we've found new ways to connect. Although video conferencing has been around for years, few people would have thought to either facilitate or even attend a virtual writing retreat. If you're still part of a university, some of your colleagues might organise online writing events. Or you could create your own with Zoom.

Apart from the accountability, these events also create solidarity. When we're stuck at home, wrestling with a slippery draft, we assume everyone else is out having fun. That's infuriating. When we can see other people struggling, we realise we're not alone and also that writing is difficult. It's not that we're rubbish at writing, it's because we're trying to do something that's officially difficult.

Now you're in the chair and being supervised, we can start writing ...

Breaking it Down

I've coached thousands of academic writers over the last six years. By far the biggest problem is the expectation of producing perfect writing, instantly. Unless they know *exactly* what to say, they can't commit it to the screen. They spend hours in the futile pursuit of constructing the world's most perfect sentence. The solution is simple (although not necessarily easy): give yourself permission to write rubbish, then gradually improve it through stages of revision. In the words of Harvard Professor William J. Perry, "First you make a mess, then you clean it up."

I find most people need at least five stages to produce a finished piece of writing. I've experimented on myself and others, and this is broadly the approach that tends to work.

The Writing and Editing Cycle

- **Zero Draft** – a loose and sketchy collection of ideas, just for you! You absolutely don't share this with anybody else. Pick out the good ideas and develop them in the ...

- **First Draft** – here there's some attempt at structure, but the main aim is to develop your ideas without worrying about how everything fits together. Then you're ready for the ...

- **Second Draft** – now you're refining those ideas, thinking about and strengthening your argument, dropping anything that doesn't fit. You're starting to consider your reader and perhaps sharing it with a trusted colleague or friend. With their input, you move on to the ...

- **Third Draft** – this is where you're clarifying, improving consistency, signposting and implementing any feedback. Once this is done, you proceed to the ...

- **Final Draft** – only now do you address the tiny details, such as whether that should be a semi-colon or a dash. Proofreading is unbelievably tedious, so you don't want to spend time perfecting drafts that are still changing.

You might need fewer or more steps. If you're a social scientist, you might be writing in a more structured way from the outset, as there are usually strong conventions that need to be followed. For those of you writing in a more exploratory way, you'll probably find it easier to apply structure retrospectively. This way, you're not inhibiting yourself. Whatever your approach, you need to break it down into stages. There's no such thing as writing efficiently. And multiple drafts relieve some of the pressure. As Stephen Pressfield writes, "If we know we're going to do fifteen drafts before we're done, we don't panic when Draft #6 is still a mess."[14]

I've found most people work in a way that seems profoundly inefficient: scribbling in different places, transcribing, highlighting, consolidating, and sifting. It feels chaotic, but it's the only way they can get to the final draft. This is a very physical approach, and that's fine. Often people ask me "What writing approach should I se?" My answer, much to their annoyance, is "The one that's right for you."

The fundamental point is that you shouldn't be trying to write and edit at the same time — they should be different stages of the cycle. Here's why ...

Writing on the Right Side of the Brain

You've probably heard the idea that the two sides of our brain govern different activities. While it's not scientifically accurate, it's a useful model for improving writing productivity. The left side of the brain is concerned with anything analytical, logical, or linear; the right side, meanwhile, is cre-

---

14 *Nobody Wants to Read Your Sh*t*

ative — making imaginative leaps, using intuition, and spotting connections. If we're seeking to create something new, we need to deploy the *right side* of the brain. It's impossible to move logically through something that doesn't yet exist.

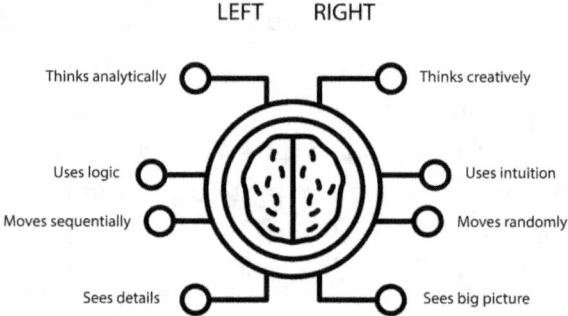

However, the two sides of our brain are often in conflict. The right side spends five minutes cranking out a dozen words, then the left side devotes the next hour to deciding whether they're the *correct* dozen words. You're switching between writing and editing, getting tired in the process, and not making much progress. The trick is to keep writing and editing separate. Our desire to leapfrog straight to the third draft is often about impatience. Instead, think about the craft and the process.

Find an approach that works for you. But, whatever you do, break it down. Writing then editing. This is tough to do. It takes practice. You won't ever lose the urge to edit, but you can learn to *resist* it. If you've ever tried meditation, you'll know how hard it is to let go of thoughts about mundane matters when you're supposed to be focusing on your breath. With practice, though, you'll let go much quicker.

Here are some tips to make it easier:

- **Switch off your spellchecker** — those wiggly red lines are insistent and distracting.
- **Write longhand** — on the computer, it's too easy to delete and rewrite endlessly. As you type up your handwritten draft, you'll be editing it simultaneously.
- **Schedule separate sessions for writing and editing** — start treating them as completely separate activities. Sitting in different locations might help, too, if that's possible.

You also need to avoid the tyranny of the blank page by starting with a plan.

Planning a Piece of Writing

In Chapter Two, I got you to map out your book, then outline the individual chapters. Now you're going to focus on the writing itself. You can't just sit down and write a chapter — that happens only in our imagination. Instead, as ever, you need to break it down. You can apply these techniques either to a whole chapter, or to a main section within a chapter. Whichever you choose, make sure you know how many words you've allocated from your word budget.

Thinking About Your Reader

First, consider your reader. You've already done this for your book proposal, but now you're getting more specific. What does your reader need from *this* chapter or section? Ask yourself?

- **Who is the audience?** — what's their background, e.g., undergraduate, postgraduate, faculty?
- **What do I want them to know?** — what do I want the reader to take away from this chapter or section?
- **What do they want to know?** — what questions might they have in their heads? Are they seeking particular evidence for claims you've made in the main introduction?
- **What do they already know?** — what assumptions can you make about their knowledge? You then don't need to waste your word count on unnecessary information. Do they already believe in the importance of your topic?
- **What don't they know?** — what are they unlikely to know that you'll need to explain, e.g., context on obscure concepts?

This exercise primes your brain to focus on what's important and to eliminate everything else. Of course, you can't know exactly who will read your book. And you can't cater for everyone. You'll need to make some judgements based on the largest potential audience. For example, explaining concepts could be boring for expert readers, but essential for undergraduates or taught postgraduates. Keep basic explanations as short as possible, so readers can easily skip over them.

Creating a Storyboard

All writing, regardless of discipline, needs a story. There should be a beginning, middle, and end, with a narrative arc that propels the reader. Earlier, you planned the overall story for your book. Now you'll do the same for the chapter or section. It's time to get out the sticky notes again.

- Find a BIG piece of paper or an empty wall
- Write your start and end points on sticky notes and place them at either end of the space. Your starting point might be: asking a question, challenging a popular misconception, or identifying a knowledge gap. The end point is your resolution or conclusion. As I explained in Chapter Two, a chapter should come full circle and answer any questions it poses at the beginning.
- Use the sticky notes to work out the steps you'll need to guide your reader from beginning to end. Don't worry about the sequence just yet — get all the ideas out of your head and on to notes.
- Review your notes critically. Which belong to the story? Are any merely confusing sub-plots? You don't want more than half a dozen.
- Spend some time experimenting with different sequences on your storyboard. You can take photos to easily compare variations.
- Once you're happy with a sequence, make a note of the word allocation for each sticky note.

This approach also helps you break down your chapter or section into smaller blocks. You can then choose one of the sticky notes and start writing around it. You're only ever focusing on one note or block at a time. You'll find it much easier to plan your time around small blocks, rather than around entire chapters.

Building a Wireframe

A storyboard might be enough to get you going, but some writers need more detail. A wireframe is a model that's used for planning the structure of a page. It provides you with an outline around which you then write. This is also another opportunity to apply my Rule of Three.

- Decide on the three main points you want to address in this chapter or section.
- Then break down each of those main points into three sub-points.
- Next, map out your introduction and conclusion with bullet points (see Anatomy of a Monograph section for the elements you need to include).
- Review the outline to ensure it's following a logical sequence.
- Allocate word counts for each of points.

Here's an example based on a 6,000-word chapter:

Introduction (a total of 900 words)
- Why is this important? (250 words)
- Setting context, e.g., historical background (325 words)
- Methodology or approach (325 words)

Main Point 1 (a total of 1,500 words)
- Sub-point 1 (500 words)
- Sub-point 2 (500 words)
- Sub-point 3 (500 words)

Main Point 2 (a total of 1,500 words)
- Sub-point 1 (500 words)
- Sub-point 2 (500 words)
- Sub-point 3 (500 words)

Main Point 3 (a total of 1,500 words)
- Sub-point 1 (500 words)
- Sub-point 2 (500 words)
- Sub-point 3 (500 words)

Conclusion (600 words)
- Summary (200 words)
- Implications for the field (300 words)
- Call to action (100 words)

Please note, this example isn't prescriptive, it's just to give you an idea of how to break down your chapter or section. You'll need to consider what's appropriate for your field and topic by consulting your literary mascots.

These approaches can be effective because they separate structure from content. It's difficult to create a structure *and* content simultaneously, but that's exactly what we attempt when we dive straight into writing. Inevitably, your writing will deviate from that initial plan, but in Chapter Six I'll demonstrate some editing techniques to help you reimpose order. Give yourself a loose structure to start writing, then tighten it up later with editing. Don't try to do everything at once.

With an outline of your writing, you're ready to get going. You can either start writing around those points, or transplanting existing chunks from your thesis. If you completed the auditing exercise from Chapter Two, you might've identified some content you can reuse. Once you start fitting it into this new structure, you'll have a clearer sense of the gaps. Then you'll use the bullet points as prompts for creating additional material to fill them. Don't be tempted to simply reuse the structure from your thesis. This is a completely different project.

Staying on Track

It's hard to get an objective sense of our progress. And emotions are a terrible judge of what's really going on. What we need, then, is evidence. A writing audit is a good way of engaging the neocortex and bypassing that unhelpful limbic system (see Chapter One). This template helps you move through the different drafts and sections of your thesis and also shows you exactly where you are. You might notice that the stages in this example correspond to the Writing and Revision Cycle. At a glance, you can see what you've done and what's left to do.

Section	Word target	% Complete	STAGE				
			Zero draft	1st draft	2nd draft	3rd draft	Final draft
Introduction			☐	☐	☐	☐	☐
Literature Review			☐	☐	☐	☐	☐
Chapter 1			☐	☐	☐	☐	☐
Chapter 2			☐	☐	☐	☐	☐
Chapter 3			☐	☐	☐	☐	☐
Chapter 4			☐	☐	☐	☐	☐
Chapter 5			☐	☐	☐	☐	☐
Chapter 6			☐	☐	☐	☐	☐
Conclusion			☐	☐	☐	☐	☐

Make your own, or download a copy from www.howtopublishyourphd.com. Create a more detailed version of the audit that includes all the sections of your monograph. It's a Word document, so you can quickly adapt it to suit your own monograph structure and stages. Add the corresponding numbers from your word budget, too. Try to break it down into small chunks that correspond to either notes your storyboard or bullet points on your wireframe, so you're able to tick off at least one of them each session. You need that sense of achievement.

Tracking your word count makes sense when you're in the intensive writing phase. It's immensely satisfying to see yourself edging towards the target. At later stages of the Writing and Revision Cycle, it's no longer meaningful. Indeed, you might be deleting words. You'll need a better measure. Perhaps you're now aiming to reduce the word count? Track this instead. Note where you are now and what you're aiming for. We'll be looking at editing techniques in the next chapter. Once you have a strategy that works for you, you can build it into this audit template.

The trick is to keep moving.

Avoiding Perfectionism

Often, we grind to a halt because we're trying to get something perfect: "I need to get Chapter 1 absolutely right before I can progress to Chapter 2." Six months later, you're still wrestling with Chapter 1, and you have three weeks left to finish the rest of your monograph.

The Pareto Principle describes the idea of uneven distribution, that roughly 80% of the effects come from only 20% of causes. It was developed by Italian polymath Vilfred Pareto, who discovered that around 20% of the pea pods in his garden contained 80% of the peas. Then he calculated that 80% of the land in Italy was owned by 20% of the population, and it spiralled from there. Although this isn't an exact formula, you might find that the bulk of your writing emerges from 20% of your time. That remaining 80% is spent trying to get everything exactly right — making endless revisions and worrying whether it's good enough. Rather than maintaining a strong momentum, we slow right down, and progress becomes imperceptible. Then despondency descends.

We can also use this 80/20 rule to set some limits. Aim to get your chapter 80% polished, then move to the next one. Ideally, you should also get some feedback at this stage. With the benefit of perspective — either through taking time away from your writing or getting someone else's feedback — it'll be much easier to fix that final 20%. For now, you're focusing on executing your plan, ensuring you've created blocks of writing to cover all the areas of your map or outline.

If you think of a chapter as *finished*, you'll be less prepared to make necessary changes during the editing phase. You need to retain some flexibility in your manuscript. It's like building an IKEA bookcase: if you tighten all the bolts too soon, it'll be much harder to manoeuvre (and some of the bits are almost certainly the wrong way round). With a full draft, you can get a sense of your whole project, strengthen your argument, and work out what needs to be added or deleted. Writing a book is an iterative process. Pursue *progress*, not perfection. Or use my mantra: "lower your standards and keep going".

Sometimes we're unwittingly committing acts of self-sabotage. Although we might fantasise about finishing our manuscript, part of us doesn't want to stop. Finishing means submitting ourselves to judgement and relinquishing control of this book. Big projects like PhDs and books are also good excuses for getting out of all sorts of unpleasant social engagements. Other people accept these excuses quickly and without argument because they're terrified we'll tell them about our research. To avoid judgement, we either set impossible standards for ourselves or allow the scope to widen.

We're seized with the possibility that this book could be even greater, if only we pushed for a bit longer.

Although unleashing your Theory of Everything on the world is a tantalising prospect, it's completely unrealistic. Get this book finished, then develop your ideas further in the next one. You're not attempting to have the last word on this subject. Hopefully, you'll write further books and contribute to debates in other ways. Produce the book you're capable of writing *at the moment*, and don't be tempted to drastically change your scope — even if you discover someone else is writing on the same topic.

Dealing with Competition

It's almost certain that other people will publish on your topic, maybe even while you're writing your book. I can tell you've just broken out into a cold sweat. You'll no doubt remember this advanced state of paranoia from your PhD. Every time you saw a journal article on your topic, you shrieked, "That's exactly what I'm researching! Everything I've done is now obsolete." Then you calmed down, read it slowly, and realised the author was taking an entirely different approach.

When you encounter a competing book, assess it carefully. Ask yourself, "is this the exact book I would have written, with absolutely no changes? Would I be happy to put my name to this?" If not, you have a different book to write. In any case, there's room for multiple perspectives. Scholars, especially PhD students, will want to read more than one book on a topic. Reading multiple perspectives helps us understand our own position. Nobody writes the definitive book on any topic, regardless of what their Twitter bio might suggest.

The concept of *multiple discovery* (sometimes referred to as *simultaneous invention*) describes how two people, working completely independently, can come up with the same idea at the same time. Even if the *concept* is similar, though, the *point of view* will differ. You have a unique perspective. While you shouldn't radically change your book in response to someone else's publication, it might help you strengthen or refine your argument. You can emphasise what's unique about your approach, experience, or data. Use competition to stimulate your ideas, rather than as an excuse to stop.

Overcoming Procrastination

Sometimes, we just get stuck. Our brain refuses to cooperate, then we start panicking. In *The War of Art*, author and screenwriter Stephen Pressfield describes our daily battle to overcome resistance. Even though we know we should be writing, there's a powerful pull away from the desk. We feed resistance with our fear, that fear of getting started. As Pressfield writes, "Master that fear and we conquer Resistance."

If you're experiencing that overwhelming feeling of resistance, spend some time considering why. Once you've identified the problem, you can find a solution. Are you finding it ...

- **Dull?** Pick a bit that interests or excites you and start there. There's no need to start at the beginning and slog through. Indeed, it's often easier to write the introduction once you've got everything else in place. Choose the most attractive sticky note or bullet point from your plan.

- **Frustrating?** What's missing? Perhaps you don't have the right piece of data or an appropriate quote. This doesn't happen often, but occasionally we're trying to write too soon.

- **Hard?** Are you giving yourself a mammoth task? Does your to-do list say, "Draft Chapter 3"? If so, break it down into more manageable chunks and just focus on one at a time. Keeping breaking it down until it feels manageable, even if that's just writing a sentence.

- **Chaotic?** It's time to return to the planning stage. A few years ago, I was writing a chapter for an edited collection. Nothing seemed to fit together, and I was stuck in an endless loop. Eventually (after a lot of catastrophising), I took a step back and created a storyboard. I realised that I was actually writing two different chapters. They were in conflict with each other and pulling me in different directions.

- **Futile?** Start with why. Remember those reasons for writing a monograph in Chapter One? Take a look at them again.

Freewriting can help you here, too. The idea is that you write continuously — no stopping to edit or think — and access those reasons lurking at the back of you mind. You could give yourself specific prompts, such as:

- Why am I finding this difficult?
- One of the challenges I'm facing is ...
- Another approach I could take is ...

You can also use freewriting to recover your mojo. Try prompts such as:

- What excites me about this piece of writing?
- How will I feel when it's finished?
- Why is this book important to me?

Not only will you feel inspired, you'll also have started writing. Removing the need to sound 'academic' can help you write more freely.

If you're still struggling, just commit yourself to one tomato. You only need to do 25 minutes' writing. Maybe that's enough to get you going, then you're ready for another tomato. Even if this doesn't work, at least you'll have done a little bit of writing. Perhaps it's a Darwin Day and you can just perform some light duties. Or you need some time away from your desk.

Reviewing Progress

If entire weeks are passing with no evidence of progress, it's a sign you need to sit back and review the situation. It's impossible to create a plan that works magically in all circumstances — our current self is trying to imagine how our future self will perform and what will be happening around us. Reality is always much more complicated (and tiring). Schedule some time each week to consider how it's going, ideally by asking yourself questions. For example:

- How much did I achieve this week?
- Was it in line with what I hoped?
- If yes, what made it a productive week?
- Could I recreate these conditions?
- If no, what went wrong?
- Were there problems I could've anticipated and prevented?
- What could I do differently next week? New location? Different time of day?

And look at where you are on your overall plan. Roughly on target? Sailing ahead? Or languishing behind? If you're struggling, you can consider:

- What's slowing me down?
- Am I striving for perfection?
- Or trying to do too much?
- Is my timescale simply not realistic?
- Is there anything else I can stop doing to make more time for my book? At least temporarily?

Do some calculations, too. How many useful words can you write in a typical session? How many do you need? Of course, this is a rough calculation, but it gives you an idea. Once you know your personal best is 500 words a day, it's hopeless to routinely aim for 1,000. This helps you come up with a more *realistic* plan.

If you haven't done so already, introduce some accountability. It's hard to uphold commitments to ourselves, so make arrangements to send your draft to somebody else by an agreed date. This doesn't have to be an entire chapter, you could just email them 500 words after the weekend. And they don't even need to read it — your accountability partner is simply verifying that you've completed your assignment. It's better, though, if this person can also give you some constructive feedback.

Getting Feedback on Your Writing

During your PhD, your supervisor (hopefully) gave you feedback at different stages of your draft. This is unlikely to happen with your monograph. You might get a hands-on editor who's willing to provide some formative feedback, but most will be interested only in the full manuscript. Of course, you'll get extensive feedback from your peer reviewers, either on sample chapters or your entire book. It's a good idea, though, to solicit constructive feedback at an *earlier* stage.

Although receiving feedback is uncomfortable, it forces us to see our own work from a different perspective. Potentially, your book will be read by thousands of readers during its lifetime. The best way to make those people happy is to expose your ideas to readers as you're producing them. You'll need to recruit some beta readers. I think the most effective reviewers are those from different fields or even disciplines. This is because:

- You can't presume familiarity with the concepts you're using, so it forces you to be clear.

- Someone outside your field is unlikely to start tearing apart your methodology or suggesting bright ideas on how you could make this into a completely different book. That's not what you need at this stage.

- You get the benefit of a different perspective on your work. Someone looking in from the outside will spot things nobody else will see.

You don't want someone who's too different, though. It might be hard for a theoretical physicist and an Elizabethan poetry expert to give reciprocal feedback, unless both have an informal background in their respective topic. And someone whose brain goes into a spasm when they see a table of numbers isn't a good choice for your quantitative analysis.

Make reciprocal arrangements with *other writers*. This ensures good dynamics: it's a collaboration, rather than you asking a favour from somebody else. Also, we give much more constructive feedback when we know that other person will also be critiquing *our* work. It doesn't have to be the entire manuscript, either. I often get writers to swap a 2,000-word writing sample. Their partner can then flag sentences that are unclear or paragraphs that lack an obvious point. Once we've had our attention drawn to these problems, we find it much easier to notice them in other areas of the manuscript. You might be able to find potential partners on Twitter or through other academic networks.

What Feedback Do You Need?

In the early stages, you're seeking high-level input on the structure and arguments — the absolute fundamentals of your book. It's not helpful for someone to point out all the small grammatical errors on something that's likely to be reworked multiple times. Equally, when you reach that elusive final draft, you won't be too pleased if someone suggests an entirely different structure or new ideas.

First, then, consider what stage you're at and what input you need:

- Structure?
- Arguments?
- Flow?
- Style?
- Grammar and spelling?

Direct your beta readers accordingly so they can focus their efforts. If possible, provide them with a list of questions to answer. For example:

- Is the topic of this chapter or section clear from the introductory paragraphs?
- Does the argument progress clearly across the paragraphs? If not, where does it break down?
- Is the argument supported with evidence? Please indicate any areas where the evidence is weak or missing.
- Does the conclusion resolve the questions posed in the introduction?

- Is the language clear? If not, please flag any confusing jargon or word choices. Were there any sentences or paragraphs you needed to reread?

Above all, you don't want people's opinions, e.g. "I like this". Instead, you want them to point out where they didn't understand something, or it was confusing. They're not telling you how to rewrite it, rather they're providing a commentary on their experience as a reader. As Neil Gaiman explains:

> When people tell you something's wrong or doesn't work for them, they are almost always right. When they tell you exactly what they think is wrong and how to fix it, they are almost always wrong.

Feedback isn't about getting gold stars, it's about improving our writing. While writing is usually a solitary activity, publishing is a profoundly social act. All writing ultimately needs an audience, otherwise it's just a secret diary. The more you engage with that audience while you're writing, the more engaging your book will be. And you'll received more helpful feedback by sharing a less polished version. Your reviewers will be feel uncomfortable with pointing out problems if they think you're about to submit your manuscript.

For guidance on implementing more substantial feedback, see the section on Readers' Reports in Chapter Seven.

Summary

Our brains are remarkably clever at achieving sophisticated feats of self-sabotage. Either we seize on competing priorities as an excuse for wriggling out of writing, or we allow other people to repeatedly hijack our physical and mental space. By thinking of yourself as a professional writer and taking your craft seriously, you can create the right conditions for that book to emerge. Unfortunately, you can't just use someone else's writing process — it's a matter of building routines that are effective for *you*. Although this requires a lot of trial and error, you'll become far more productive than you ever thought possible.

Rather than hurling yourself straight into the writing, think about how it'll fit into your week. Then use some of the planning techniques to ensure you've given yourself enough structure to get going. When working on a book, you'll probably spend more time on planning than on writing. A good plan helps you keep moving. You'll know exactly where you're going and whether you're on track. If you do grind to a halt, spend some time considering *why*. Are you pursuing perfectionism? Do everything you can to *keep moving*. And don't be tempted to start writing a completely different book. It might *seem* less painful, but that's just because you haven't yet discovered the problems in that more attractive project.

If you're struggling to keep yourself in the chair, introduce accountability by making commitments with other writers. Combining accountability with a routine can result in remarkable progress. And progress is wonderfully motivating. Make sure, too, that you're involving other people in your Writing and Revision Cycle. By soliciting constructive feedback from trusted partners, you'll improve the quality of your book and also get some much-needed encouragement. Involve your readers at every stage.

ACTION POINTS

- Identify some blocks of deep work (~2 hours) in your weekly schedule.
- Make a list of activities you could complete in smaller blocks of time, e.g., 1 hour, 30 minutes, 10 minutes. Include some Darwin Jobs for days when your brain refuses to cooperate.
- Create start-up and shutdown routines for your deep work sessions.
- Decide how you'll create accountability, either by using a site like Focusmate, or making arrangements with friends.
- Use the storyboard and/or wireframe techniques to plan your next piece of writing.
- Download and adapt the Writing Audit template (or create your own).
- Schedule some time with yourself each week to review progress.
- Identify a trusted friend or colleague to give you feedback on your writing.

Once you have a full baggy draft of your book, it's much easier to get a sense of the central argument and narrative. We'd much prefer to have this in place before we start — that would be much easier, wouldn't it? But life's seldom like that. Once you have something that looks a bit like a book, you can identify and strengthen that Golden Thread. Identifying this elusive thread can involve making some big changes. You might need to move, delete, or redraft entire chapters. While this feels scary and time-consuming, it results in a much better book. And it'll be easier to finish. That's what we'll be doing in the next chapter.

TROUBLESHOOTING

I'm finding it impossible to write — there's no time!
One of the most useful (but infuriating) coaching questions is, "What are you *avoiding* doing?" Often, we *know* what needs to happen, but we immediately discount it. In this case, it might be *what are you doing so you can avoid your book?* We tell ourselves we can't possibly stop doing something, but it's precisely that activity that's getting in the way. For me, it's usually experimenting with new software or binge-watching *Call My Agent*.

Is there something you need to stop doing temporarily so you can finish your book? Although it's painful, you can limit the pain by sticking to your plan. Is it better to have three months of spending all your weekends on the book, or three years of feeling guilty that you're not making any progress?

Look again at your weekly schedule and see if you can identify some blocks of time for deep work, even if it means jettisoning something else. Could you get up earlier and do a couple of tomatoes before work?

I'm in the grip of perfectionism — I can't stop editing while I'm writing

This is a common and stubborn problem. Set yourself some stricter (yet realistic) limits or targets, e.g., 200 words per hour. You want a target that's a slight stretch, but not in the realms of fantasy. That way, you won't have time to fiddle with it endlessly. Make sure you set an alarm and can see the word count.

Now think of yourself as being in creator mode. Your task here is simply to create 200 words on a specific topic. The editing is somebody else's responsibility — that somebody else is your future self, of course, but that's for another day. By creating clearly defined roles for yourself, it's easier to separate these activities.

I'm making time to write, but not seeing any progress

If this keeps happening, review your practices. What's getting in the way? Distractions? Perfectionism? Lack of planning? Are you giving yourself too much structure? Not enough? Have you used the Rule of Three to provide clear goals for your sessions? Maybe those goals are too big and you need to break them down into more manageable chunks. Make them as specific as possible, e.g., *write a paragraph to explain con-*

cept of X. Start by giving yourself one small goal per session. Once you can achieve that goal consistently and comfortably, you're ready to stretch yourself.

Chapter 6: Getting Ready for Submission

"The first draft of anything is shit." Ernest Hemingway

The best academic writers are those who can put themselves in the mind of their reader. What does the reader want to know? Rather than, what do *I* want to tell them? Your main objective as an academic writer is to guide the reader from A to B along the most direct route. There should be no confusing detours, digressions, or cul-de-sacs. In our heads, those ideas exist in three dimensions, and we understand how they link together. Your reader, however, is approaching these ideas for the first time and they need to understand them in a linear format.

Hang on! Didn't we spend a lot of time earlier creating a plan? Surely that means our manuscript follows a logical structure? Not necessarily. Although your manuscript should have some shape, it's almost certainly bulging in odd places. This is because our writing often takes us in unexpected directions. Dr Pam Lock, a Victorianist and writing retreat facilitator, described it to me perfectly. Some writers are watercolourists, while others are sculptors. The watercolourists sketch their concept and gradually build up the layers of detail. They start with a strong image of how they want it to appear, and it steadily emerges on the canvas. Sculptors, on the other hand, start with a big lump of an idea, then whittle away until it assumes a recognisable form. This method can be scary. And it involves quite a lot of swearing. You can probably guess which I am. If you're a fellow sculptor, the first part of this chapter is for you, as we'll confront that big lump.

Although a publishing contract means some highly trained eyes will be peering at your manuscript, don't use this as an excuse for not checking your own work. With the exception of the biggest presses, most publishers won't check your work line by line. Often, they're mainly checking areas such as consistency and then relying on peer reviewers to point out glaring errors. Otherwise, they're expecting you to produce the best possible quality manuscript.

In this chapter, I'll guide you through a five-step editing process:

1. Structure — getting the main elements in the right place.
2. Flow — arranging your paragraphs in a logical order.
3. Signposting — providing a roadmap for your reader.
4. Clarity — ensuring consistency and eliminating ambiguity.
5. Details — making tiny tweaks through proofreading.

This process is certainly time-consuming, but adopting a systematic approach helps you move faster. You need to get the structure and flow right before you tinker with the details. There's no point in perfecting a paragraph if you're going to delete it tomorrow because it doesn't fit. We'll start with the biggest tasks, and work through to the tiniest elements, such as spelling and punctuation. Of course, that's probably the last thing you feel like doing. In which case, you need to either put aside some funds to hire a professional proofreader, or be really nice to your friends. I'll outline the practicalities and costs of working with proofreaders and also recommend software that'll save you time and money.

First, we need to tackle the structure.

Strengthening Your Structure

To get a sense of the structure, you need to step away from the laptop. MS Word is a word processor (and not an especially good one), so it won't help you with structuring a long document. It's mostly good at crashing when you've forgotten to save, then triumphantly recovering a version from three weeks ago. Map out your book instead. You're revisiting the planning exercise from Chapter Two. This is an opportunity to reimpose order and to consider whether there's a *better* structure.

As before, you'll need:

- An empty wall or other blank space.
- Some oblong sticky notes.

- Lots of square sticky notes.
- Marker pen (or preferably a lovely big set of Sharpies).

Write each of your chapter titles, not the numbers (and they might be working titles at this stage) on the oblong sticky notes and position them in a horizontal line at the top of your space. Now use the smaller sticky notes for jotting down the elements of each chapter – this might be subsections or key ideas – and arrange them vertically under each chapter heading. Eventually, you'll have a map of your book that you can see all at once. Now you can scan through and see what's happening. Here's what to look out for:

- Are the chapters proceeding in a logical sequence? If you need to reorder them, write the new numbers on some extra sticky notes and position them above the chapter titles.
- Do any of the chapter elements belong elsewhere? Flag them on the note.
- Can you spot any duplications across chapters? Make a note to delete the duplicated content and add a signpost or link (e.g. "As I discuss in chapter 2...").
- Have you spotted any gaps that need to be filled, such as some context to link two sections?
- Is there anything that doesn't fit? Are there diversions or digressions that might confuse the reader? Mark those with a red X.

Scan horizontally and vertically to check the book makes sense from all directions — remember, your reader won't necessarily progress from start to finish. Keep your book proposal in front of you, too. Have you followed the structure of your chapter outlines? If not, did you make a conscious decision to do it differently? Or has there been some scope creep? Don't be tempted to address any of the smaller details at this stage — that comes later. For now, you're getting the structure right, establishing the foundations of your book.

I appreciate it's tough to delete chunks that represent hours of work down the research mines, but a tighter narrative helps make your argument clearer. Those deletions aren't lost, either. You can turn them into journal articles, blog posts, or add them to a future book. You might want to carry out this activity over a couple of days. If you have the space, it's a good idea to leave the map at least overnight. Then you have a bit more perspective when you return to take another look. If you want to experiment with different versions, you can take photos or recreate them with a digital tool, like Trello or Jamboard. It's also a good idea to show your map to someone else. Talk them through the structure and ask whether it makes sense.

Once you're happy with the map, you can begin moving those chapters and sections around in the manuscript. Before you get stuck in, make a copy of your unedited manuscript. Once you've started hacking away at your work, you won't remember what it looked like originally. Add comments for yourself on the original version to flag where you've made changes, e.g. "I've moved this section to the beginning of chapter two." This helps you keep track of what you've done and it's vital if you need to unravel any of your changes. If you're juggling too many files on the screen, you could use a printed copy for documenting changes.

Improving Flow

If you imagine your book as a house, the previous step was all about getting the foundations right. Now we're going to think about the bricks or building blocks. You probably have a lot of these building blocks, but they're not necessarily in the right order. We'll achieve a logical flow by rearranging them. Importantly, though, we're still ignoring the smaller details for now. You don't order the cushions until you've built your walls (unless you're one of those smug couples on interior design programmes).

In writing, your building blocks are *paragraphs*. Like the book (or the house) itself, they need to be well structured and substantial. Consequently, a paragraph normally shouldn't be shorter than three lines. In novels, there might be a very short paragraph for dramatic effect, but there's not really a good argument for doing that in a piece of academic writing. A paragraph should contain one key concept: no more, no less. Otherwise, you're either slowing down your reader with unnecessary words or overwhelming them with too much information. Each paragraph break allows your reader to take a short pause before they move onto the next concept. And each paragraph should be connected to the previous paragraph. There's a clear sequence for the reader over which your argument builds.

In our heads, this is how we write all the time. We are rational beasts who build logical arguments. In reality, though, our writing gets out of control. Even if we start with a fairly tight plan, our thoughts go off in other directions and we're tempted to squeeze in *just one more idea*. Sometimes, this works to our advantage. As we're writing, our thoughts and arguments are developing — we're adding layers of meaning. While it's important to allow ourselves this freedom, we then need to reimpose order with a reverse outline.

Reverse Outlining

While every writer is different, nearly everyone benefits from the technique of reverse outlining. I think it's the best way to improve the flow of your argument and produce a coherent manuscript. There are many different approaches to this technique and there's no right way of doing it. I'll share my approach with you, which you can then adapt.

Step One

- Print a draft of your completed chapter.
- Number the paragraphs in the margin.
- For each paragraph, write a concise bullet point summary (it should fit on one line and describe the purpose of that paragraph, e.g. providing historical context on XXXXX, explaining theory of XXXXX, outlining the chapter).

You now have a compact list, which is much easier to work with than scrolling back and forth through a monster Word document. It'll take you 2-3 hours to reverse-outline a 10,000-

word draft, but it's time well spent. As you've probably noticed, this is a more granular version of the book mapping exercise we did earlier.

Step Two

Next, scan through your bullet list and remain alert for the following:

- Are your paragraphs following a logical sequence? Or are you hopping around?
- Are there any duplications? We all have a tendency to say the same thing in slightly different ways.
- Can you see gaps where you need to add a segue? Or maybe a subheading to indicate a change of topic?
- Are there giant leaps that require additional context? Are you taking your reader with you, or leaving them behind?
- Can you spot digressions that might confuse the reader? Have you got excited about a related topic?
- Are there any paragraphs that are doing too much work and should be divided? If your bullet point is long and complicated, this suggests a paragraph that needs simplifying.
- Or are there some paragraphs that are lacking a specific point and can be ditched? Did you struggle to find a point to the paragraph? These chunks often represent our thoughts. Although they were necessary in working out our overall argument, they're not required in a final version.

Step Three

Edit the bullet point list by getting everything in the right order. Also, flag any necessary insertions, deletions, or consolidations. You can then use the revised list as a model for your draft. As before, make a copy or a backup first, just in case you regret some of the changes. Also, ensure you *cut-and-paste* paragraphs when you're moving them, rather than copying – otherwise you can end up with duplicates. You can add comments to record what you've done, too.

Optional Step Four

It's common for us to rely too much on secondary sources and using quotations from more established academics to make an argument, especially when we're making the transition from PhD student to academic author. Consequently, our own voice gets lost, and the monograph becomes a synthesis. To ensure your voice is evident, you need to remove some of that scaffolding.

Using your reverse outline bullet point list, devise a colour-coded scheme to flag the different types of writing in your draft. For example:

- RED = secondary sources
- AMBER = context
- GREEN = original argument/findings/conclusions, etc.

You could simply circle each bullet point with the corresponding colour or use a highlighter pen on the text itself. Either way, you'll quickly get a sense of the balance in your chapter. Is it a sea of red? There's no right balance between secondary sources, context, and originality, so spend some time thinking what might be appropriate for your book. Perhaps you could prune a secondary source from a six-line block quote down to a one-sentence inline quote. Then you've got more room to add your own insight.

Reverse outlining is beautifully simple, but it's also time-consuming. If you need to get a sense of how long it'll take for your book, try it out on a small sample of your writing, say 2,000 words. If you've read a piece of academic writing that was easy to follow, I'm willing to bet the author spent some time on reverse outlining.

Remember:

- Each paragraph should propel your reader from the introduction to the conclusion.
- Be prepared to delete anything that doesn't fit the narrative.
- A logical flow helps your reader understand the argument.
- Your argument must be evident throughout.
- Don't worry about smaller details at this stage – you're purely getting your paragraphs in the right order.

Adding Signposts

Once you've got your structure in place and those paragraphs in the right order, you can start adding some signposts. Signposts help your reader navigate around this very long piece of writing — they need a sense of where they've been, where they are, and where they're going next. Signposts might include descriptive headings, cross-references, or emphasis of argument. They're not very exciting to write, but they can make a big difference to the reader's experience.

Some people argue that signposts are just for theses. This tiresome apparatus should be quietly ditched when making the transition to a monograph. I agree signposts can be inelegant and occasionally disruptive, but we need to consider our reader and how they *use* our book. I'm employing the verb *use* rather than *read* for good reason. They're probably reading your book alongside a dozen journal articles, a few book chapters, and maybe a racy novel. It's unlikely they'll have time to read your work in long sessions and might therefore be dipping in and out over a few weeks or even a couple of months.

Although we like to think they're carefully reading our book from cover to cover, they might only be interested in one specific chapter. As you'll know from your own experience, researchers need to be selective. Consequently, they need reminders about what you've already covered and clear summaries of your arguments. Once they reach chapter 4, they won't remember (or even have read) something you mentioned in chapter 1. Effective signposting can also encourage them to read the rest of the book — look what's coming up if you stay tuned! They're constantly making decisions about whether this book is a good investment of their time.

Here are some examples of signposts:

Chapter or section outlines

At the beginning of every chapter or section, you should explain how it's structured. This isn't spoiling the fun, it's helping your reader understand what's coming. They can then focus on the arguments. Yes, they're dull to read (and even less exciting to write), but they're immensely helpful when you need to remind yourself of what a chapter covers. Few of us have time to reread entire books, so these summaries help refresh our memories. Especially if we've been sloppy with note-taking.

Mini-conclusions

This means summarising your arguments as you go. Although you'll have explained your claim in some detail, following it up with a succinct summary helps the reader follow your overall argument by adding emphasis. You can think of this as a sub-total. Remember, your reader shouldn't be struggling to fathom your argument or its significance. Don't make them do all the heavy lifting.

Some academic writers insist it shouldn't be necessary to repeat your argument. If it was strong enough in the first place, your reader will have understood it. Realistically, though, most of us have the attention span of a gnat. Our minds are constantly distracted by competing priorities, phone notifications, and trying to survive a pandemic. Mini-conclusions also make us feel confident that we have indeed grasped the argument.

Emphasis of argument

Similarly, you might want to remind your reader of related

arguments. For example, "As I argued in Chapter Two, this text ….". This way, you're creating connections and allowing them to form a conceptual map in their mind.

Cross-references

If you've explained a theory or concept earlier on, for example, in your introduction, you don't want to repeat it in a later chapter. However, you still need your reader to know that you've talked about it. In this case, you can say something like, "Here I apply the theory of X, which I discuss more fully on p3." "In this section, I draw on the theory of X, which I explain in my introduction." You don't want your reader thinking, "Why hasn't this author explained her use of this theory?" You have! It's just elsewhere.

Be careful of referring to specific page numbers, though. While it's possible to create these references in Word, they'll almost certainly get lost at the typesetting stage. Instead, point to specific sections. This is easier to do if you've broken down your chapters.

Headings and sub-headings

Headings and sub-headings break up the text, giving the reader natural pauses. They also allow you to provide accurate signposts to specific pieces of information. Those headings provide an essential roadmap for navigating the book. As I mentioned earlier, these headings should be *descriptive*, giving a clear sense of what's to come. If your headings just say 1.1, 1.2, it'll be easy for readers to get lost. Numbering might be the convention for your discipline or publisher, though, so check what's required.

A sub-heading is also a useful expedient for masking a gear change. Perhaps your reverse outline has exposed a big leap between paragraphs and you're not sure how to add a segue. If so, adding a sub-heading signals the change of topic to the reader. This device should be used sparingly. A chapter can't be a loose collection of ideas.

Think about what you appreciate as a reader. We tend to revisit books that are well organised, with strong signposts and indexes. Take another look at your literary mascots and find examples of signposts. How do those authors introduce chapters, emphasise arguments, and link between sections?

Ensuring Clarity

You've got the structure, flow, and signposting in place. Now it's time to achieve clarity in your sentences. I hope you resisted fiddling with them during the earlier stages, as it's much easier to start with the big stuff and work down. For the moment, we're specifically interested in the *structure* of the sentences, rather than spelling and punctuation. That comes at the *next* stage.

Sometimes bad things happen to good sentences. We know what we mean; it all sounded good in our head, but then an absolute monster emerges on the page. I mentioned earlier the importance of introducing pauses between paragraphs for your reader. You also need pauses within sentences. If you think of a musical score, the composer adds pauses or rests through notation and also varies the tempo. It would be quite dull if the whole piece moved at a consistent pace.

It's the same with writing. We need to give the reader a rest and not make the tempo too predictable.

One of the easiest ways to make our writing clearer is to write shorter sentences. It's always tempting to squeeze as many ideas as possible into one triumphant sentence — "There's this, and there's that, and oh yes, here's another thing!" This is exhausting for your reader, as they'll probably have to re-read it several times. Even if you like writing jumbo sentences, I'm willing to bet you don't enjoy reading them.

Unless unavoidable, sentences shouldn't be longer than three lines. Any longer and the human brain struggles to process all that information. When you spot a long sentence in your writing, read it aloud. If you turn blue halfway through, it's definitely too long. If you can't say it, you shouldn't write it either. If there's a good reason for exceeding three lines, then follow it up with a shorter sentence. This allows your reader to come up for air.

Academic writing doesn't need to be complicated. While the ideas themselves are complex, that's all the more reason to keep the writing simple. Convoluted writing is often hiding a lack of meaning or substance. Don't produce writing that you wouldn't want to consume. I talk to many researchers who are made to feel stupid by badly written books and articles. They assume the problem lies with them, rather than with the author who didn't consider the reader. While these researchers persevere and eventually grasp the arguments, the convoluted writing has caused unnecessary stress and wasted their time. We can all help each other by pursuing clarity over fanciness.

Wrangling with Words

Writing style is a huge area and one that varies enormously according to the discipline. I've included some suggestions for further reading in the Bibliography. Here, though, are six techniques[15] that'll tighten your prose:

1. Use power verbs

Routinely, we resort to relatively weak verbs, like have, make, do, and show. If we replace those with more specific verbs, it makes our writing stronger, more precise, and easier to follow. For example, *establish* is much stronger than *show*. This first example is fine, but it's vague and weak:

> "In what is known as the Golden Age of detective fiction, the majority of writers were women."

If we use instead the verb 'dominated', this sentence is suddenly much stronger:

> "Women writers *dominated* the Golden Age of detective fiction."

It's also a lot more concise. You can see there are far fewer words in the second sentence, but it says exactly the same as the first sentence.

Before getting carried away with power verbs, make sure you understand the conventions in your discipline. In some areas, you're expected to be more tentative and use verbs like

---

[15] Some of these techniques are adapted from Helen Sword's excellent book *Stylish Academic Writing*. If you were kind enough to read my previous book *How to Finish Your PhD*, you'll already be familiar with these techniques.

suggest rather than *demonstrate*. Take a look at your literary mascots to get a sense of the appropriate vocabulary.

2. Avoid Zombie Nouns

Zombie Nouns are nominalisations, or nouns that have been formed from verbs, adjectives, or other nouns. They often end with -ism, -ity, -ness, or -ation. Indeed, *nominalisation* is itself a zombie noun and we have Helen Sword to thank for the more memorable name.[16] Like zombies, these words suck the life force from our writing. In her excellent piece for the *New York Times*, Sword offers this example:

> The proliferation of nominalisations in a discursive formation may be an indication of a tendency toward pomposity and abstraction.[17]

I'm sure you can understand it perfectly well, but it's not much fun to read, is it?

When we read, our brains are scanning for words we recognise to help us derive meaning. While we *understand* zombie nouns, it takes us much longer to parse them. Using vivid nouns keeps your reader alert and engaged.

Consider this example:

> The development of the category of middlebrow fiction during the interwar period intended to effect the containment and delineation of the type of mass-market literary fiction which had aspirations

---

16 For an entertaining explanation, watch Helen Sword's TED-Ed Talk – https://youtu.be/dNlkHtMgcPQ.

17 https://opinionator.blogs.nytimes.com/2012/07/23/zombie-nouns/

> to the status of high culture. Middlebrow literature had strong associations with the middle class and its increased power and with innovations in the mechanisms of literary circulation, such as libraries and book clubs. Factors which made a significant contribution to the definition of middlebrow fiction, in accordance with the assertions of the critics of the interwar period, included its tendency to lack seriousness and authenticity; its use of content and form which was taken as evidence of failure to challenge the reader; its tendency towards soothingness and palliation, and, most significantly, the class position of its readership and authorship.

You can see there are lots of words such as *containment*, *delineation*, and *contribution*. And then some wholly invented terms like *soothingness*. This is all jarring for the brain. There aren't that many concrete terms that we can understand and hold on to. Anyone who's skim-reading will struggle to get a sense of your argument. Here's the same paragraph again, with many of those nominalisations removed:

> During the interwar period, the category of middle-brow fiction was developed to contain and delineate the type of mass-market literary fiction that aspired to the status of high culture. It was strongly associated with the increasingly powerful middle class, and the new mechanisms of literary circulation such as libraries and book clubs. Factors which made a significant contribution to the definition of middlebrow fiction, according to the critics of the interwar period, included its failure to be serious or authentic; its use of content and form which failed to challenge the reader; and its palliative tendency. The most significant defining factor was the class position of its readership and authorship.

You can see here the language is much more vivid and concrete. It's easier to read and, again, it's much shorter, too. If you find a zombie noun in your own writing, consider whether there's a simpler alternative. Could you turn a noun into a verb? For example, "the defendants were all in violation of the statutes," becomes "the defendants *violated* the statutes". While the style of the first example is more common in academic writing, it's completely unnecessary.

3. *Clarify ambiguous words*

We know what we mean when we write *this* and *it*. But our readers probably won't, especially if the *this* or *it* has become separated from the subject to which it refers. In the example below, you can see that *this* could either refer to the idea of work becoming bound up or it might relate to the idea of the emphasis. The reader could go back and reread the previous sentence to work out what is meant by *this*. But that's extra work and you're slowing them down.

> For middle-class young women, work had now become bound up with notions of patriotic duty and self-improvement, even though there was still considerable emphasis placed on the central importance of women's domestic role. ***This*** had changed social attitudes to the idea of women's paid work outside the home.

You could say 'This emphasis' rather than just 'this'. Yes, that's repetitive, but that's better than being ambiguous.

4. *Eliminate unnecessary words*

If you bury your arguments under lots of extra words, it's much harder for you reader to follow them. Examples abound in academic writing, such as "on a regular basis" rather than just "regularly", or "an increased appetite was manifested by all the rats," instead of simply "all the rats ate more". There's no extra information conveyed in the wordier version. Look out for these habits in your own writing. Often, we're up against the word limit anyway, so going through and eliminating these unnecessary words can help.

5. Keep related words together

When you have a related noun and verb, make sure there's not a huge clause in between them. Otherwise, your reader is likely to forget the noun was at the beginning of the sentence. They have to go back and reread it. In this example, the noun is *writers* and the verb is *set*. There shouldn't be more than about ten words in between. Or perhaps you could use parentheses if you do have to include an extra piece of information in between.

> Many novice **writers** at the beginning of their academic careers, hopeful of the production of elegant and impactful academic prose and delusional about the amount of work achievable in any given amount of time, *set* themselves excessively ambitious targets.

6. *Use words consistently*

As you're reading through, make a note of the terms you're using. Have you applied them consistently? For example, do you in some places refer to Great Britain, and the United Kingdom in others? Also, check your tenses. Are you veering between past and present? There's no right answer to what tense you should deploy, but it might relate to the stage of your thesis. For example, in the Introduction, "I will argue that..."; in the main body "I argue that..."; in the conclusion, "I have argued that...". It's up to you, but be consistent.

Try these techniques on a small section of your book, around 2,000 words. This'll give you a sense of how much work you'll need to do and how long it'll take:

- Use power verbs
- Avoid zombie nouns
- Clarify ambiguous words
- Eliminate unnecessary words
- Keep related words together
- Use words consistently

There are a couple of tools to help you, too. On Helen Sword's The Writer's Diet (www.writersdiet.com) website, you can paste a 100-word sample of your writing for analysis. You'll get feedback on areas such as zombie nouns and ambiguous words. There's also a Word plugin available, along with lots of other resources. The Hemingway Editor (www.hemingwayapp.com) gives you a readability score and also flags use of the passive voice. As Sword explains, "[s]tylish academic writers spend time and energy on their sentences so their readers won't have to".[18]

Checking the Details by Proofreading

Proofreading is perhaps the one task I dislike even more

---
18 *Stylish Academic Writing*, p. 62.

than housework. And that's not a statement I make lightly. Although we often make terrible proofreaders of our own work, the responsibility usually lies with us. While some publishers still do some proofreading, it's not always performed to an especially high standard. In any case, you want to send the manuscript to your editor in the best possible shape. Then they can focus on the big stuff, rather than getting distracted by typos.

This is the *final* stage of the Writing and Revision Cycle. You don't want to spend time proofreading work that's still under development. This activity can be compromised if you overshoot earlier parts of the project. Make sure you've allowed some time and also added some contingency. It's not something that can be rushed. Indeed, proofreading needs to be painfully slow. Most people would expect a top speed of 2,000 words per hour. That's where the manuscript is relatively clean, and you're not slowed down by lots of errors. Are you now frantically calculating how long it'll take for your manuscript? Probably somewhere from 30-60 hours. You don't want to be proofreading full time for a week — that would be miserable — so you'll need to allocate enough time over a longer period and develop a strategy to use it effectively.

In this section, I'll give you some tips on making proofreading easier for yourself. Then we'll look at the costs and implications of hiring a professional to help you. Finally, I'll introduce some software that'll make proofreading less tedious. Software doesn't necessarily save you time, but it helps you become much more systematic and accurate.

How to Make Proofreading Less Painful

Before you start proofreading, consider what would make it easier for you. Here are some ideas:

- **Print your manuscript:** if you're working on the screen, it's far too tempting to get carried away and make sweeping changes. Moving paragraphs around will almost certainly wreck your flow and create additional problems. Working on paper is less tiring, too. A different font might help you get some perspective on it, too — it then looks less like your writing. I try to make my manuscript look like the final publication, with proper formatting. Then I can think of it as a book, rather than a random collection of documents.

- **Do it in short bursts:** your eyes will get tired, and also it's unbelievably boring. If you're yawning and staring at the same page, you've become ineffective. I recommend using the Pomodoro Technique to keep your eyes and brain sharp.

- **Read sloooowly:** if you're a fast reader like me, this is excruciating. But there's no point in proofreading quickly — you'll just miss half the mistakes and have to start all over again. Boo. Aim for no more than 2,000 words per hour (or 800 per tomato). I follow each line with a ruler. This prevents me from skipping ahead, and I can also use it to hit myself when I keep spotting the same daft mistake.

- **Use a screen reader:** software that reads your text to you. This functionality is built into Word and Scrivener, and can be added to Google Docs. *Hearing* your writing makes missing words more conspicuous. When we read silently, our brain often fills in the gaps.
- **Crowdsource some help:** not many people will love you enough to read your entire manuscript, but perhaps you can bribe them to check a section for you. Even better, organise a reciprocal arrangement with another author. Most of us suffer from persistent writing tics or repeated misspellings. If someone points those out in a small sample, we then know what to address in the rest of the manuscript.

It's hard to detect inconsistencies in our own writing, especially at the end of a long project. If you can afford it, a professional proofreader will bring fresh eyes and perspective.

Hiring a Professional Proofreader

If you have the money, it makes sense to outsource the proofreading. Perhaps you're dyslexic, you've struggled to write in English, or you don't want to look at the wretched thing any more than is absolutely necessary. In this case, make sure you hire a professional. In the UK, I recommend approaching the Chartered Institute for Editing and Proofreading (www.ciep.uk). Their members are fully qualified, and some have extensive experience with academic writing. You can also find someone with a background in your subject area. This isn't necessary, mind you, as they're just checking for tiny details at this stage.

Although professionals will save you time and worry, they're also expensive. Proofreading is a laborious process and you're paying by the hour. The cost for an 80,000-word manuscript is likely to be at least £800. If you plump for someone charging a significantly lower fee, they're likely to be reading less carefully. You've probably seen adverts for proofreading services at very reasonable rates. These companies invariably outsource the work to distributed freelancers who are badly paid and not necessarily native English speakers. They're just relying on the spellchecker in Word. You could do this yourself and spend the money on treats instead. Bear in mind, though, that even great proofreaders won't catch everything. No-one has a success rate of 100% on a complex document like a monograph, but they're likely to do a better job than you.

Great proofreaders are also in demand. You'll need to negotiate a start date with them and make sure they have the final manuscript ready to start work. They'll have lots of other projects booked in with little flexibility in the schedule. As you might have guessed, working with a proofreader is likely to mean completing your book even earlier. This is another part of your project to manage. Although you're saving yourself some time, you lose some control and flexibility.

What do Proofreaders Do?

There's often confusion over the roles of editor and proofreader. To complicate matters further, there are also different types of editor. Here are descriptions of the various roles, along with the typical rates you can expect to pay.[19]

Developmental Editors ...

- Provide detailed feedback on how to improve the structure, focus, and overall style of your book.
- Suggest other ways to organise it.
- Make substantial changes to sentences to improve clarity.

A developmental editor won't give you feedback on the subject matter itself, although they might point out logical flaws in the argument. Also, they won't tackle smaller details like spelling and grammar. This is an expensive and time-consuming job. Developmental editors need to spend a lot of time understanding your book so they can pull it apart. Consequently, you can expect to pay at least £5,000 for this service. You could buy a lot of sticky notes with that money.

Line Editors ...

- Refine style.
- Boost clarity.
- Check grammar and use of language.
- Ensure consistency of formatting.
- Apply a style sheet you provide.

Line editing can be especially helpful if you're writing in a second language and worry that your syntax is erratic or

---

[19] Based on an 80,000-word manuscript and the rates quoted by the Chartered Institute of Editing and Proofreading.

inconsistent. If money's tight, you could hire a line editor to work on just one chapter. They'll normally use track changes in Word, so it'll be easy for you to see what they've corrected. You can then find those errors in your other chapters.

You might expect to pay £2,800 for a monograph.

Copy-editors ...

Generally leave the style alone and make only small changes to your sentences. They're much more focused on the tiny details and often combine this work with proofreading. This is known as a proof-edit.

This usually costs in the region of £2,400 for an 80,000-word manuscript.

Proofreaders

Unlike editors, proofreaders won't change the sense of your text. They don't routinely point out that you've used the wrong word or that you've made a factual error. Their role is to spot spelling mistakes, grammatical errors, and typos. This is why they don't need to be an expert in your subject. If there are peculiarities in your field that might confuse them, provide a short briefing document.

Some proofreaders will also help with formatting, ensuring that headings, figures, and citations are consistent. They'll need a copy of the guidelines for your publisher. Naturally, this takes extra time, so it'll be factored into the cost. Academic proofreaders offer to check references, too. Again, this needs to be explicitly agreed in advance and it'll cost you more. They're not going to check whether you've quoted the correct page number, though, they'll just be scanning for inconsistencies in formatting. It's much easier to use Zotero!

Remember: they almost certainly won't catch everything. With proofreading, a 95% accuracy rate is considered decent. For a manuscript comprising 80,000 words, this could leave you with 4,000 errors, which doesn't sound decent at all! Although most proofreaders will exceed this threshold, you'll still need to go through everything yourself. The best solution is to check it thoroughly *before* sending to your proofreader.

Proofreading generally costs around £2,000 for a book of this type.

Proofreaders and editors normally state an hourly rate, which makes it hard for you to calculate the likely costs. They're reluctant to specify a rate per 1,000 words, though, as the quality can vary so much. Those 1,000 words might contain 3 errors, or 300. They'll probably want to see a sample so they can give you an accurate quote. This sample gives them an idea of how long it'll take and the types of problem they'll be dealing with. Also, they can decide whether they can really help you. Authors sometimes think they need a light edit, but they're actually asking for a substantial rejigging. To keep the costs down, do everything you can to make the manuscript as clean as possible before sending it to them.

Before you hire a proofreader or editor:

- Be clear on what your publisher is doing — will your manuscript be professionally edited and proofread?
- Obtain a style guide from your publisher. This should

explain spelling conventions and other details.

- Make sure you're getting a professional — search the database of the Chartered Institute for Editing and Proofreading.
- Clarify what they're going to do — e.g., copy-editing, proofreading, formatting.
- Prepare a briefing document to explain anything that might be confusing.
- Decide how you'd like them to work — e.g., tracked changes in Word.
- Consider deadlines — by what date will you need to get the final draft to them?

If you want to hire a professional but have limited funds, work out what's most important to you. Or what stage is most difficult or unattractive? If you follow the exercises at the beginning of the chapter, you'll be able to get your manuscript in much better shape. Maybe you just wheel someone in at the end to check all the tiny details. Alternatively, you can do it yourself with the help of some software.

Using Software

While Word's built-in spellchecker is much better these days, it's worth investing in a dedicated tool, especially if neither you nor your publisher is employing a professional proofreader. There are dozens of tools out there, but here are the three I've used: Grammarly, ProWritingAid, and PerfectIt.

Grammarly

Available as a web-based tool and a Word plugin, Grammarly (www.grammarly.com) checks your spelling and grammar. The free version offers only a limited number of checks, but the premium product is highly sophisticated. You can specify the style of writing, e.g. academic, and Grammarly gives you detailed feedback. It currently costs $30 per month, or $144 per year.

I used Grammarly for checking the final draft of my monograph. It took almost two days for me to work through all the suggestions. Although the majority of suggestions were irrelevant, every so often Grammarly would flag an embarrassing error. Admittedly, those two days were really quite boring, but it was quicker than checking everything manually. Also, it did it all systematically. Left to my own devices, I'd have got bored and started switching between tasks.

However, I found some of the grammar suggestions pedantic and archaic, such as screaming about all my split infinitives and occasional use of the passive voice. Overall, I thought Grammarly was dogmatic and possibly too detailed. It was taking me a long time to work through (what were to me) irrelevant suggestions. I now use ProWritingAid instead.

ProWritingAid

ProWritingAid (www.prowritingaid.com) is, I think, much better suited to book authors. Unlike with Grammarly, you can upload your entire manuscript and check it in one (very long) session. It also works in Word, Google Docs, or Scrivener. Alternatively, you can download their desktop app.

It's not compatible with mobile devices, though, so it's not a good choice if you work on an iPad.

Although it's slower than Grammarly, ProWritingAid gives you much more feedback on your writing style. While Grammarly is proficient at flagging all the errors, it won't necessarily help you become a better writer. ProWritingAid provides valuable feedback on areas such as:

- Repetition, cliches, or overuse of words.
- Length of sentences.
- Readability.
- Consistency, including missing closing quotation marks.
- Plagiarism — the Premium Plus version includes 50 plagiarism reports that compare your writing with webpages and published works (it's similar to TurnItIn).

Currently, ProWritingAid costs £20 per month or £79 per year. If you're feeling flush, you can buy a lifetime license for £399.

PerfectIt

Another option is PerfectIt (www.intelligentediting.com), which works differently from Grammarly and ProWritingAid. While those other two get stuck into the writing itself, PerfectIt is much more focused on consistency and applying a house style. For instance, it'll pick up if you're using different spellings of the same word, such as co-operation and cooperation, and find missing brackets or quotation marks. PerfectIt also flags placeholders (e.g., XXX) and abbreviations that haven't been spelled out in the first instance. It works much more like a proofreader than an editor.

You can either customise the built-in style sheets or create your own. Ideally, you should obtain a style sheet from your publisher to ensure you're following their requirements. Once you've defined your preferences, PerfectIt hunts down deviations and potential errors.

This definitely isn't a passive option. You'll need to spend time telling PerfectIt what to find, otherwise it can't possibly be effective. The longer you spend defining your style, the better job it'll do. This could be a good choice if you feel confident in your writing style or have already worked with a line editor.

You could achieve the same result with Word macros and wildcard searches, but it would take you a lot longer. PerfectIt asks what you want, then applies it systematically. If you hire a professional editor or proofreader, they'll almost certainly have PerfectIt in their toolkit. The cost is around £50 per year and there's a free 14-day trial available.

Tips for Using Software

Although software will help you to be systematic, it does have limits. For instance, it'll only catch *rule-based* errors, e.g., *if there's a full stop, the next letter should be capitalised*. ProWritingAid or Grammarly won't notice that you've referred to three case studies in the introduction, but there are only two in the chapter. These are errors that only the human eye can catch.

Whatever tool you use:

- Make sure you understand how the tool works so you can get the best out of it.
- Allow enough time — it's not necessarily any quicker than manual proofreading.
- Tackle one stage at a time, e.g., grammar, spelling, style.

Tools are only as good as the artisan who uses them. It's part of your professional development as a writer to learn both the tools and the craft.

Applying Formatting

Your publisher will almost certainly have a house style, which you'll enforce consistently during the proofreading stage. They'll probably have formatting requirements, too. These requirements often govern elements such as layout, pagination, headers, fonts, and margins. They'll want your manuscripts to be presented in a certain way to make it easier for the typesetters. It's also important to keep everything as clean as possible. A messy manuscript slows down the production process and also increases the chances of errors appearing in print.

Word documents can easily end up in a complete pickle, especially if you're copying and pasting from different documents. Here are some potential areas to address:

- Create and apply styles consistently across the entire manuscript. e.g., making sure all block quotes look the same or that all captions are italicised.

- Use headings logically and hierarchically, e.g., Heading 1 for a chapter title, Heading 2 for a section, and Heading 3 for a sub-section. This'll make it much easier to generate a table of contents.
- Insert proper footnotes (don't just put them in brackets after the text).
- Never use spaces instead of a paragraph indent (this is a heinous crime).
- Only use one space after a full stop (the convention for two spaces comes from the days of typewriters, and I bet you're not using one of those).

One area you'll need to check carefully is the citation format. This is where I must make a confession. Although I checked these requirements before starting my monograph, I disregarded them. I thought to myself, "they can't possibly want an inline format like Chicago, I'll just use MHRA as usual". Big mistake. Inline styles like this (Oliphant 1867b, 258) are certainly unusual in my field, but that's what the publisher wanted. What's more, they used a particular flavour of this style, too, which meant I had to change quite a lot of my citations manually. I think it looks clunky and disrupts the reading experience. But it's not my publishing house, so I'm not queen. Lesson learned. It took me an entire weekend to (very grumpily) go through nearly 1,000 citations.

How Much Time Do You Need for Editing?

One of the questions I'm asked most often is, "how long does editing take?". I offer two equally exasperating answers:

1) As long as you need.

2) As much time as you have available.

You might end up against the deadline with no wriggle room. In which case, you'll have to go like the wind (see below). Otherwise, it depends on several factors: length, complexity, your speed, and how much other stuff you've got on. Ideally, you should dedicate a 12-week sprint to editing. Go back to your weekly planner and add in some deep work sessions for editing.

Think about how much energy you need for the different editing tasks. Applying consistent formatting is much less demanding than getting a clunky paragraph to make sense. The session length and time of day will depend on the stage you're at:

- **Structure** — it's much better to approach this in long stretches so you can hold the entire book (or at least large chunks of it) in your head. If you're working on your manuscript alongside lots of other responsibilities, block out a series of weekends for this activity and lock yourself in a room with lots of snacks.

- **Flow** — you'll need at least an afternoon to reverse outline a book chapter. It's not too mentally demanding, though, as you're just trying to get everything in the right order rather than creating anything new. This is also a satisfying activity.

- **Signposting** — although this is a relatively straightforward task, again you need to remember what you've said earlier in the book. It's best done in longer sessions, although it won't require a lot of energy.

- **Clarity and Details** — wrangling with those sentences and words is both fiddly and challenging. However, it can be achieved in shorter sessions that fit around your other tasks. If you have lots of non-writing responsibilities, could you squeeze in a tomato before breakfast or after dinner? Oddly, I find these activities easier when I'm tired. I'm better at simply plodding through the stages and not coming up with any bright ideas (you don't want ideas at this stage).

- **Proofreading** — this is another activity that can (and indeed should) be done in short bursts. You absolutely don't want to spend an entire day proofreading. On the other hand, it's not much fun if the proofreading drags on for months. Find the sweet spot for you. You should be able to establish your typical proofreading speed on a sample, which means you can then make a fairly accurate plan.

For many writers, this is the worst part of the project. Revising your own work can feel soul-destroying. You're no longer coming up with new ideas, making insights, or identifying connections — it's just the seemingly endless drudgery of getting everything in the right place. The best way to get through it is to be systematic. Devise a realistic plan and work through it methodically. There are no magic tricks or wormholes that'll get you there any quicker.

Having said that, what do you do if you run out of time? What if you've only just finished writing and there's only a couple of weeks before you're due to submit your manuscript? Here are some suggestions, in order of preference:

1. Negotiate an extension with your publisher. They might be reluctant, especially if the project has already been delayed. Ask for the minimum extra time you'll realistically need and make sure you stick to it. Contact them as soon as you realise you're in danger of missing the deadline.

2. If you're doing paid work and it's possible, take some annual leave or reduce your hours for the next few weeks. Cancel or postpone any other commitments, if you can. Clear your schedule and throw yourself into editing.

3. Accelerate and cut corners! Focus on reverse outlining to improve the flow of your argument. Then make sure you use a tool like ProWritingAid to catch most of the smaller errors. Cutting corners at this stage means you'll have to spend more time once the manuscript comes back from the publisher's editor or peer reviewers. You're not saving yourself any time overall, but it gets you out of an immediate hole.

Checklist

After weeks or months of feverish editing, you've probably lost any grip on reality. Work through this checklist to make sure you've covered everything.

Have you ...

- Identified your core argument?
- Stated your argument clearly in the introduction and conclusion?
- Provided evidence to support your argument?
- Explained the significance or implications of your argument? i.e., answered the *why* question.
- Addressed any research questions posed at the beginning?
- Added enough context to explain your argument?
- Arranged the material in a logical sequence?
- Inserted signposts to guide the reader?
- Included all relevant citations in the right format?
- Solicited and incorporated feedback?
- Checked and implemented the style guidelines?
- Proofread everything?

Then you're ready to go!

Don't aim for perfection, else you'll still be beavering away in 10 years' time. You've got other stuff to do. Write the best book you can within the timeframe, then submit.

Summary

Editing a manuscript is often a Sisyphean task. We correct one problem, then immediately notice a dozen more. There's no way of avoiding it, though — you have to go *through* the task, not around it. The answer is to be systematic and work through the stages we covered in this chapter:

1. Structure — getting the main elements in the right place.
2. Flow — arranging your paragraphs in a logical order.
3. Signposting — providing a roadmap for your examiner.
4. Clarity — ensuring consistency and eliminating ambiguity.
5. Details — making tiny tweaks through proofreading.

Although it doesn't necessarily feel like it, this staged approach is much more efficient than embarking upon an editing frenzy. It'll be more satisfying, too. As with writing, make sure you keep moving and don't get stuck on one stage. Inevitably, there will be slippage, but you don't want it to become a landslide. You can download and adapt an Editing Audit from www.howtopublishyourphd.com.

The techniques I've outlined are by no means prescriptive. You'll undoubtedly find better ways of working to suit both you and your project. They're certainly a good starting point, though. Reflect on the techniques afterwards (you can use freewriting prompts) to discover how you might adapt them. By focusing on your craft in this way, you'll develop some valuable skills for future writing projects. Everyone needs their own writing and editing process that works for them.

ACTION POINTS

- Be absolutely clear on how much editorial support is provided by your publisher.
- Budget enough time for editing and proofreading.
- Work through the tasks systematically.
- Track your progress and adjust your course, if necessary.
- Use software to help you (although accept its limitations).
- Think about your reader. Always.

Once that's done, you're almost ready for final submission. Although there are a few more tasks to complete, you can enjoy a much-deserved break while your manuscript goes through the review process. In the next chapter, I'll explain those final stages, including dealing with readers' reports, checking proofs, and indexing your book. We'll also consider ways of promoting your work. For now, though, you've earned a cup of tea and a rest.

TROUBLESHOOTING

I'm running out of time and haven't yet started editing

Stop writing ASAP! You need to set yourself some limits, potentially by reducing the scope or lowering your standards. As I mentioned earlier, you're not aiming for perfection during the writing stage. You just want a baggy full draft to work on. Then you'll need to plan your editing time very carefully. Cancel any non-essential commitments and establish a clear schedule for working through the editing stages.

If you think the structure is fairly sound, focus your efforts on reverse outlining. Then use ProWritingAid to sort out consistency, spelling, and grammar. There's absolutely no wriggle room now, so don't be tempted to add new material or make big changes at this stage.

It's all rubbish!

It's difficult to get any perspective on our own work. If possible, leave a gap between writing and editing. I find two weeks is enough for me to not be consumed with self-loathing. Any sooner, and I can instantly zoom in on all the flaws and ignore the parts that make sense. Above all, telling yourself it's rubbish just slows you down — it's another form of procrastination: *This is all rubbish, so I should just stop trying.* Keep going.

Although a monograph needs to be more polished than

a thesis, it still doesn't have to be perfect. With infinite time and a trust fund, we could perhaps produce something close to perfection. But people want to hear about your ideas now. With monographs, we're seeking original and relevant insights, not the most perfect sentences ever constructed. Indeed, there's a high tolerance for clunky writing in academia. If you've expressed yourself clearly and thought about your reader, you'll automatically put yourself among the best writers.

I really need some help with proofreading, but I can't afford it

First, be clear on what your publisher is offering. They might already employ a professional proofreader. If you have an academic affiliation, check whether your institution would cover at least part of the cost. There are a few grants available through scholarly associations, too, although competition is stiff.

Otherwise, use both PerfectIt and ProWritingAid to catch as much as possible. There are free trials available for both tools, so you could avoid paying anything at all if you can complete these tasks in a fortnight. You'll need to spend some time learning how these tools work and configuring them correctly. Once you've used them both, read the manuscript yourself, slowly and carefully.

Be wary of anyone offering cheap proofreading services. It takes around two weeks to do a thorough proofread of a monograph. If someone says they'll do this for £200, they'll be going too fast or just using tools you could access yourself.

Chapter 7: Publishing and Promoting Your Book

> "The key to everything is patience. You get the chicken by hatching the egg, not by smashing it."
> Arnold H. Glasgow

You'll probably remember from your PhD that the submission date was only the end of *one phase*. Although that date was the huge goal you'd been aiming for, it wasn't actually the end. There was the small matter of the viva, making corrections, and submitting the final version. It's the same with a monograph. You've already done a lot of work in planning, producing, and polishing your manuscript, but there are still a few more big tasks to complete before it becomes a book.

Because we get so focused on the writing, we forget about those other tasks. They sneak up and catch us unawares, and we don't have enough time to deal with them effectively. Also, it's hard to get a realistic idea of exactly what's involved and where our responsibilities lie. Unfortunately, publishing schedules tend to be tight and it's usually the author who's expected to be flexible. If you're a first-time author, how do you best prepare for this uncertainty?

In this chapter, I'll clarify these final stages and what

you'll need to do. First, we'll look at readers' reports. While it's overwhelming to receive a long list of requested changes, implementing a structured approach makes this task more bearable. As I'll explain, you're not required to accept every recommendation. We'll develop a process for deciding what's right for your book and create a plan you can execute.

Then we'll look at getting the final version of your manuscript together so your publisher can typeset it and produce the book cover. At this point, you'll be expected to check proofs and verify details, such as copyright permissions. This is your last chance to get everything right. As we'll see, additional errors often creep in during the production process, which means it's important to remain vigilant during these final stages.

Increasingly, authors are required to either compile their own index or to cover the cost of hiring a professional indexer. Either way, this affects your timescale and possibly your bank balance, too. I'll explain what's involved in indexing your own book and how much time this is likely to take you. If you have the money, it's worth paying an indexer. I'll outline the likely costs and the implications for your schedule.

Your book also needs an audience. In the final part, we'll look at the many ways in which you can promote both yourself and your work. While traditional methods, such as conference and book reviews, are still valid, they need to be complemented by new approaches, including blog posts, podcasts, and online academic networks. I'll help you create a marketing plan that's right for you and also give you an idea as to when you should start promoting your book.

The order in which the information in this chapter applies depends on your own publishing timeline. For instance, your book might've already been peer reviewed. If you're nervously awaiting your readers' reports, you can be working on your marketing plan in the meantime. First, let's prepare ourselves for those reports.

Dealing with Readers' Reports

You might've already received readers' reports on sample chapters, in which case you'll be familiar with the format. Many publishers also request a review of the full manuscript. Depending on your contract, they might be relying on favourable reports before going ahead with publication. This stage, then, can be pivotal. And stressful. I waited over a year for my reports. It's fair to say I wasn't in a receptive mood when they finally arrived.

It's tempting to react quickly to readers' reports. Allow time for an emotional response first, though. That initial response might be anger, frustration, resentment — all of the above. You've already done a lot of hard work on this book and now you're potentially being asked to do a lot more. Typically, we fixate on the negative comments and allow those to churn endlessly in our heads like a full load of laundry. Go back and read all the comments more slowly. If possible, get someone else to read them. They're more likely to provide a balanced view.

Above all, don't take any comments personally. The reviewers are acting on behalf of the publisher to ensure this is a viable book. Everyone's priority is to maintain standards.

Nevertheless, some reviewers get carried away with imagining the book *they* would write, rather than focusing on what's in front of them. Although the review process is uncomfortable, it'll make your book better. One of my reviewers must've spent ages going through my manuscript, as they made hundreds of suggestions on how it could be made clearer. This was invaluable. Although I was obviously delighted with the other reviewer who thought my book was great, this wasn't especially constructive feedback.

Implementing Feedback from Readers' Reports

Make sure you read the reports thoroughly (I read them quickly and spent the next couple of days sulking). Then print them out and go through with coloured pens to flag the different areas:

- **Green** = the reviewers' positive comments (hopefully there'll be some). It's so easy to lose sight of the good bits and end up in a pit of despair. Highlighting these bits ensures a positive and receptive mindset.
- **Amber** = comments you want to implement.
- **Red** = suggestions you want to reject.

Keep the **green** comments in a file you can refer to during moments of despond.

Triage the **amber** parts into small, medium, and large. And group together by type, for example:

- Style
- Clarity
- Flow
- Structure
- Evidence / citations

By grouping them together, you'll get a better sense of how much work needs to be done. It'll also help you move much faster. Although it's impossible to be precise, you can set aside more realistic blocks of time for each activity. For instance, improving the style of a specific paragraph is a small job; removing all instances of the passive voice could be a much bigger undertaking. A typical comment from reviewers is that the book still sounds like a thesis. This would involve going through your manuscript systematically and considering your use of language.

For the **red** areas, think through your reasoning. For instance, you might need to explain the consequences of major changes. One of my reviewers wanted me to significantly extend the scope of the book. Quite apart from being unqualified to write the book they craved, it would've taken me at least another couple of years. For a different publication, a reviewer wanted me to read and cite a document that was only available in a Scottish archive. It would've cost me several hundred pounds and a couple of days for a peripheral footnote. Seemingly minor requests can sometimes involve a disproportionate amount of effort. Where possible, suggest a compromise. In the first example, in my conclusion, I acknowledged the existence of other potential paths for extending the scope of the research; in the second, I signposted the resource, without doing an 800-mile round trip to read it.

Responding to Readers' Reports

Your publisher might have a template or guidelines on how to respond to reviewers' reports. If not, explain what you're going to implement and provide a timeline. Although you can be strategic in exactly what you implement, it's unwise to dismiss everything wholesale. If there are major criticisms with which you disagree, explain why you don't think they're valid for your book. Acknowledge the point and then explain. Remember: these responses are for the editor, not the reviewers — you're not communicating directly with these anonymous people. You don't want to be either combative or submissive. Instead, you're seeking a dialogue and making a case for your book. You're convincing the publisher this is still a viable project.

Typically, you should explain:

- What you're going to implement, including how and when. For anything major, this should be a full paragraph, e.g., how you're going to make it sound less like a thesis.

- What you're not going to implement, along with reasoning. For example, "While this is a valid point, I think it's beyond the scope of this project."

- How long it'll take you to implement the feedback. You should choose a deadline that's realistic for you, but don't make them wait too long. Hopefully, the triaging exercise above will help you get a reasonable idea of timeframes. In Chapter Six, I provided you with editing techniques to make this easier. All these tools should allow you to devise a schedule.

You don't have to respond to every point individually. For example, if the reviewers have picked up a lot of typos, just explain that you're going to proofread everything thoroughly before resubmission.

Once you've resubmitted your revised manuscript, your publisher might send it to a *clearance reader*. This reader checks through everything again, especially whether you've implemented your agreed changes. They're also making sure you haven't got carried away and completely revised the scope of your book. If you had to make corrections to your PhD, your internal examiner would have performed this role for your thesis.

Then you're ready for the final submission.

Including Your Acknowledgements

If dealing with readers' reports made you crotchety, I now have a more pleasurable task for you: writing the Acknowledgements page. Some writers, I suspect, spend longer crafting the Acknowledgements page than writing the actual book. You're not Gwyneth Paltrow at the Oscars, so don't go overboard. It's easy, though, to cause offence by missing someone important. Start a list and add to it as people pop into your head. If it's a long list, group them by category, e.g., colleagues, friends, librarians, pets.

Of course, you need to thank everyone at the publishing company and any freelancers who've assisted you, such as proofreaders, editors, and indexers. It's also good practice to acknowledge your peer reviewers, even if they were a bit fierce. They still took the time to read your manuscript in detail and provide feedback.

I've seen a few authors include something like, "Thank you to all my friends who provided unfailing support. You know who you are." This is *clever*. There's no chance of omitting anyone and the author's friends will assume it includes them, even if they were mostly a disruptive influence.

As you'll have noticed from other books, it's customary to insist that any errors remain your responsibility, regardless of whether someone else completely misled you. Hopefully your restraint will be rewarded in a future life.

There might also be space to include a dedication. Either one that appears on its own page, or in a prominent position at the front. This is usually just a few words long.

Getting Ready for Final Submission

Once you've implemented feedback from your reviewers, you have a final manuscript that's ready for the production process. Before submitting it to your editor, make sure you've followed all the requirements. These requirements will vary between publishers, but here are some typical points to check.

Have you …

- Obtained copyright clearance for any third-party materials and completed the necessary forms?
- Provided images in the correct format?
- Followed the publisher's formatting specifications, e.g. creating a table of contents, including a list of figures, or using endnotes rather than footnotes.
- Compiled and checked your index, if it's required at this stage?
- Included any additional content, such as Acknowledgements?

Before you press *send*, check everything carefully. Don't think, "Ah, well, I've got plenty of opportunities to revise it later." One author drove me to the edge of reason by requesting dozens of changes on the proofs. He hadn't checked his references properly in the first place, thinking 'it would be easier' to do so once he had the PDF. He then requested dozens more changes once the book was in print. Don't do this to your publisher.

Assuming you've followed all the publisher's requirements, your book then goes into *production*. Typesetters lay out the text and images, designers produce a front cover, and marketing people start creating awareness of your forthcoming book. You'll soon see your name pop up on booksellers' websites and maybe on social media, too. This will be either motivating or terrifying, depending on how you're feeling at this stage.

The production process usually moves at a faster pace. There are whole teams of people involved — some of them outsourced — and they're used to working on dozens of titles simultaneously. Publishers now become much more focused on deadlines. Once your book is listed as forthcoming, they'll want to ensure it actually manifests, especially if there are pre-orders or scheduled publicity campaigns. Consequently, you won't get much time for checking your proofs.

Checking the Proofs

You might imagine there's no need to check the proofs at this late stage. After all, you've checked the manuscript thoroughly and repeatedly, and so have several other people. However, errors creep in at different stages of the production process. I've heard stories ranging from a few dozen random (and wrongly placed) commas, through to 10,000 typos introduced at the typesetting stage. And, no, that's not a typo in itself — 10,000 errors. I'm not entirely sure why this happens, but it's fun to speculate.

My best guess is that publishers are increasingly outsourcing the production work to third parties. They have their own processes and software, which aren't necessarily compatible with the publisher's (or yours). Given these third parties are usually based overseas, it could be cheaper for them to re-key entire books than to invest in industry-standard software. Also, distributed teams are working on the book at different times and in different locations. It's easy for someone to be working on the wrong version and then overwrite somebody else's changes. Whatever the reason, this all means you need to remain alert.

Larger publishers will have online proofing systems which you *must* use. Here you mark up any required changes and add comments. Sometimes, this system will also show you any changes that have already been made to your manuscript. In the absence of a proper user guide, spend fifteen minutes poking around to get a sense of the functionality. You'll probably find at least one feature that'll save you time. This task is fiddly and tiring, so do it in short bursts to ensure you remain effective. This stage is purely for spotting typesetting errors or typos. Your publisher might charge you the cost of implementing any more significant changes.

Make sure you check the book cover carefully, too. It's not unheard of for author's names to be misspelled, especially if they're unusual. And go through the blurb. Sometimes this content is rekeyed, rather than copied and pasted, and errors are introduced.

The manuscript (now sometimes referred to as the *typescript* by this point) will keep reappearing in your inbox at different stages. Check it each time, even if you've already done so earlier. Of course, you don't want to have to proofread the entire manuscript more than once. Perform a couple of spot-checks, though. If you see an error that wasn't there before, contact your editor to verify you have the correct version. You shouldn't have to do all this stuff, but the realities of 21st-century publishing are that many corners are cut. You might've seen the press coverage on Susie Dent, the lexicographer. Her book, ironically named *Word Perfect*, was littered with errors, after the publisher accidentally printed an earlier draft.

Indexing Your Book

Just when you thought you'd finished, there's yet another task. And it's a big one. Although the index appears both at the end of the book and at the end of the project, its importance can't be overstated. An index boosts the usability and value of a monograph and increases the likelihood of librarians buying a copy. We like to think that everyone will read our book from cover to cover. In reality, though, they'll be jumping to the specific bits they're interested in. No doubt you've made extensive use of indexes as a researcher, but you might not have given much thought to compiling one yourself. While your publisher might arrange the index for you, increasingly, they're asking academic authors to take responsibility instead. In this case, you have the option of hiring a professional indexer, or trying to do this work yourself.

There's a popular myth that you can just use software to create an index. Although indexers these days certainly use software rather than little cards, the *art* of indexing must still be performed by a human. Indexers create a *map of the book*, including multiple access points for readers, who are all seeking different information. You can't just use Ctrl or Cmd + F to find what you want, because you need to know the exact terms used by the author. For instance, if you wanted to look up childbirth in a book, you'd have to search for related terms, such as midwifery or obstetrics. An indexer does the work of gathering together those related terms. They're also making important decisions around whether something is worth including, or it's just a passing mention. They'll also pick up *implicit* mentions, where the author talks about a topic without referring to it explicitly. These are impossible to locate without reading the book carefully.

Some publishers just ask you to submit a list of keywords. They then go through later and add in the page numbers. Although this is a relatively quick exercise and won't cost you any money, the index won't be very good. Indexing is a skilled job and very time-consuming for amateurs. Authors *can* make good indexers, but it can be hard to step back from your own work sufficiently to do a good job, especially if this is your first attempt at an index. Publishers often say on their websites that authors make the best indexers of their books, as they understand it better than anyone. However, I think this is a weaselly excuse for not covering the cost of the work.

I have the good fortune to be married to a professional indexer, which means I don't have to pay. I probably made a vague promise about taking her out for a slap-up dinner, but have been saved by lockdown. If there weren't an indexer in the next room, I'd definitely be paying someone else to perform this task. If you can afford it, hire a professional; otherwise, allow yourself enough time to create an index that boosts the value of your book. We'll look at both approaches now.

Working with a Professional Indexer

You might be concerned that the indexer won't understand your book; to reassure yourself, pick an indexer with a strong background in your subject area. Remember that indexers are expert readers of complex texts and they will read your book very carefully. You can find a professional indexer via the Society of Indexers Directory.[20] Also ask for recommendations from colleagues or your publisher. And you could take a look at your literary mascots. If you think those indexes are done well, see whether the author has named the indexer in the acknowledgements (this is a good way of making an indexer happy, by the way).

Once you've identified a suitable indexer, contact them early in the publication process, as they often get booked up with work. They will be used to managing slippery schedules, but keep them informed of any changes as they come up. If you approach more than one indexer for a quote, let the unlucky candidates know that you've gone elsewhere.

The cost depends on the length and complexity of your book. Typically, it'll range from £500-£1,200. You might pay more if you require a specialist indexer, for instance, in areas such as medicine and law. In some cases, you can ask for the cost to be deducted from your royalties. Publishers will only agree to this, though, if they feel confident you'll actually earn some money. If you're in an academic research post, it might be worth enquiring to see whether your department would at least make a *contribution* towards the cost of indexing. This is more likely if they have their eye on the Research Excellence Framework (REF).

Indexing Your Own Book

If you decide to index your book yourself, don't be tempted by some of the automated indexing tools out there. Automated indexes generated from document searches are not really

---

20 www.indexers.org.uk/find-an-indexer/directory/

indexes at all. They don't include the vital component of human analysis that decides whether a topic should be in the index, and how to represent it.

There are two different approaches to indexing currently used by publishers. Firstly, indexes can be compiled at the end of the publishing process, from page proofs (usually a PDF). Copy-editing and typesetting are all completed, any figures or images will be in place and the page numbers will be fixed. A fast turnaround is often required, with proofreading and indexing to be completed within a month or less.

Secondly, indexes can be *embedded* into a Word manuscript. This might be done at the final draft stage: some publishers expect the draft you submit to them to have an embedded index already prepared. Or it might be done later in the process but before the book is typeset. Embedded indexing can save time in the publishing process and means books can be published more easily in various formats. The index automatically updates to reflect the changed pagination and includes hyperlinks in e-book editions. Embedded indexing in Word is fiddly and complex. Professional indexers use expensive specialist software to make this easier.

Before embarking upon your index, you should thoroughly familiarise yourself with your publisher's requirements — they're likely to have strict rules on both the format and length. Once you're clear, you can get going with the art of indexing. The most accessible guide to the process is Nancy C. Mulvaney's *Indexing Books*.

If your publisher has specified a maximum length for the index, then don't exceed it; they'll just ask you to cut it down, creating a lot of additional work for you. And whatever you do, follow their instructions on the maximum number of page references following an entry – normally between six and eight. A long string of page numbers is of no use to your readers.

It's better and easier to start at the beginning and work your way through the book, rather than making a list of keywords and searching for them. The latter approach can seem quicker, but you may miss implicit discussion of key topics and be tempted to add passing mentions. You need to think *conceptually* rather than literally. Give yourself plenty of time: indexing is intense intellectual work, and even professional indexers can only manage a maximum of four hours a day. Authors usually spend 2-4 weeks on indexing their own books.

Checking Your Index

Whether you write your own index or work with a professional, you'll need to review it. When you do so, consider the following questions:

- Are all the main concepts and topics represented in the index?
- Are the words used for the index entries clear? Will they make sense to your readers?
- Are there long strings of page references, or long page spans, that have not been broken up with appropriate subheadings?

- Do the cross-references make sense? Or are they creating endless loops?
- Are the page numbers accurate? It's worth spot-checking to make sure.

If you've worked with an indexer, or your publisher hired one, refer any queries to them – they'll be best placed to sort out any issues. There are links to more detailed guidance for authors on the Society of Indexers website.[21]

Promoting Your Book

Around 4 million books were published in 2020. How many of those did you notice? How many of those authors *wanted* you to notice? All of them! Unless you're a celebrity who's written a children's book, it's hard getting people to pay attention. In fact, it can be even harder than writing the book itself. In short, nobody wants to read your work any more than you want to read theirs.

It's a misconception that being published means you get a marketing machine behind your book. Although your publisher will do *some* promotion, it's likely to be limited to inclusion in flyers and catalogues. There's now a much greater weight of expectation placed on you as the author to promote your work. While this might sound as though they're shirking their responsibilities, it makes sense. As the author, you understand both the material and the audience. Also, readers want to connect with authors, not with organisations.

....
21 https://www.indexers.org.uk/about-indexing/authors-indexes/

Some publishers will request a marketing plan at the proposal stage. For instance, they'll want to know about your online presence and any speaking engagements. Other publishers will send you a separate marketing questionnaire once you're approaching the submission date. Either way, you need to start promoting your book while you're still writing it. Yes, as if you didn't already have enough to do. You're looking to generate interest and establish your audience. This is often referred to as *publicity*, while promoting the published book is *marketing*.

In this section, I'll guide you through the many ways in which you can promote both yourself and your book. We'll start with traditional methods, such as book reviews, before moving onto more recent innovations, including podcasts and social media. Then I'll help you put together a marketing strategy that's right for you and your book.

Before engaging in any of these promotional activities, you'll need a blurb.

Writing a Blurb

Whatever form of promotion you pursue, your blurb will be crucial. This piece of text appears all over the place: on the back cover, on Amazon, in library catalogues. It's how you entice the reader to buy or borrow your book. One university librarian told me she wouldn't buy titles where the blurb was incomprehensible. She'd assume the book was equally incomprehensible and therefore not useful. Although you probably don't feel like doing any more writing at this stage, you'll need to spend some time on crafting your blurb. Your publisher might provide some input, but you can't wriggle out of this task. In any case, you should be the person who best understands your book.

A blurb isn't the same as an abstract. An abstract just summarises a publication — its purpose is to distil the essence into a paragraph. A blurb, on the other hand, is designed to *sell* a book. Whereas readers will use apparatus such as the table of contents and index to assess the relevance of your book, *buyers* will initially see the blurb, either in a publisher's catalogue or through an online bookstore. A blurb is more emotional than an abstract: you're mainly concerned with answering the *why* question. Abstracts are more concerned with the *what* and the *how*.

You should already have a summary or overview from your original book proposal. You'll want to tart it up a bit, and your argument or scope might have shifted in the meantime. Also, your blurb needs to be much shorter, around 150-200 words. You're not trying to rewrite the book in 200 words, rather you want to give a sense of it to the reader. Why should they spend their time (and possibly money) on this book? What problem is it going to solve for them? What gap does it fill, what misconception does it correct? In what way is it unique?

In the book itself, your writing style needs to be fairly restrained — after all, you're a serious academic author. On the blurb, though, you're *selling*. While you don't want to sound like you're flogging duvet covers at the local market, you do need a more excitable register. You want to inspire people to read your book. And you can inspire them by demonstrating genuine enthusiasm for your subject. As with your chapter titles, the blurb also contains important metadata for search engines. It needs to be intelligible to both humans and machines.

You can use a simplified version of the template we used for your book proposal and also incorporate some of the other elements from your pitch. This time, you'll focus on:

- Statement of your big idea — what's the problem or gap you're addressing?
- Why is this important? What are the implications or consequences of this gap?
- How are you addressing it? What methods or approach are you taking?
- Who is this book for? It's definitely not for everyone. If you're specific, potential readers are more likely to recognise themselves and identify with your book.
- What are the benefits to the reader? What will change after they've read your book? What will they be able to do differently?

Yes, it's difficult to squeeze all that information into 200 words. I'd suggest starting with a long version, then cutting it down. Allow yourself to write around those five points, creating an entire paragraph for each of them. Then go through each paragraph and whittle it down, removing anything that isn't essential. You'll need to revise it several times, so don't expect the final version to emerge immediately. If possible, work on it over a couple of days to get some perspective on it. Read it aloud to ensure everything makes sense, and also get other people to give you feedback.

Here's the blurb from my monograph:

> Once dismissed as a "purveyor of dangerous inflammatory fiction," Florence Marryat has suffered a reputation as a trashy and formulaic novelist, unworthy of critical attention. Critics have consistently overlooked the radicalism of her work, which confronts themes such as marital violence, single motherhood, and female sexuality. By gathering evidence from across the range of her fiction, Catherine Pope establishes Marryat as an important feminist writer – one who challenged prevailing ideas of femininity in both her life and her work.
>
> With a life neatly spanning the Victorian period, Marryat (1833-99) was well placed to experience and to observe the ways in which women's lives were transformed during the nineteenth century. At the time of her birth, a wife's legal identity was entirely subsumed into that of her husband; by her death in 1899, women had benefitted from momentous changes that granted them a separate identity and greater rights over their bodies and personal property. As Pope argues, Marryat contributed to the debates that heralded these changes, partly through her ability to produce sensation novels at a prodigious rate, and also by pursuing a scandalous and thoroughly un-Victorian lifestyle.

You should be able to identify some of the devices from the template. I haven't explicitly addressed the audience, but it should be easy for potential readers to understand whether it's relevant to them. As you'll see, it should be written in the third person.

My example is by no means prescriptive and there's room for improvement. However, it'll give you an idea of how you might construct your own. Look at your literary mascots to see how they've presented the blurbs. Also, browse library catalogues and online bookstores to get more inspiration. Above all, be prepared to spend some time on this activity. You'll be seeing the blurb in lots of places, so you want to be proud of it. And make sure you check everything carefully before submitting it to your publisher. Although they'll almost certainly read it, errors do slip through. It's very hard to change a blurb once it's online.

Journal Articles

Some people suggest you write journal articles to promote your forthcoming book. Well, not necessarily the book itself, rather *yourself* as someone who's an expert on this topic. There are a few problems with this tactic:

- Unless you have very few commitments, you won't have time to write a book *and* journal articles.
- Journal articles aren't that widely read in some fields, anyway.
- Peer review can take years, so the articles might not emerge until after you've finished your book. Although that's still useful publicity, they might not explicitly mention your book.

This isn't to say you shouldn't publish journal articles. Just be clear on how this activity fits with your strategy and time commitments. If you end up with a rogue chapter or section that doesn't fit your book scope, it could enjoy a future life as a journal article.

Otherwise, conferences and talks are probably better. This gives you an opportunity to beta-test some of content. You'll no doubt get some questions that'll help you see the research from a different perspective.

Conferences and Events

In-person events are still one of the most popular methods for book marketing. Consider the popularity of literary festivals, such as Hay and Cheltenham. Readers are desperate to see and hear the authors behind the books. Once they've built that emotional connection with you, they're more likely to buy your book. They might even be queuing up for a signed copy.

If you're giving a conference paper, make sure it's easy for people to buy your book or recommend it to their university librarian. For physical events, your publisher will almost certainly send you some flyers or at least provide a PDF for you to print. Don't be tempted to make one yourself unless you're really good at that sort of thing. A scruffy flyer gives a poor impression of the book.

When speaking at online events, include a link to the book in your speaker biography, slides, and any handouts. If possible, display a copy of the book in the background. Even though it's easier and cheaper to attend virtual conferences now, don't go overboard. Be selective, as it still requires time and effort to put together a good talk. Include the preparation time in your overall plan.

Book Reviews

Book reviews are far less influential than they used to be, but they remain a core part of your promotion strategy. Your publisher will probably have a list of journals to whom they routinely send review copies. Given the cost of production and postage, publishers won't be flinging copies around willy-nilly. They'll expect you to engage in a range of other promotional activities.

If you want a specific journal to review your book, you can ask the publisher to send a copy. They'll usually want to know some details about the publication and when the review is likely to appear. They're wise to academics requesting 'review' copies when they just want a freebie and have no intention of actually reviewing it anywhere. Usually, publishers send the book to the journal editor, who then forwards it to the reviewer. There will be a limit on how many copies they'll distribute, so think carefully about the best journals to review your book. Publishers might be happier to share ebooks — especially PDFs — but reviewers are often less happy to read them on screen. As reviewing is unpaid, getting a free book is a large part of the incentive.

You could also approach bloggers in your field and ask them for a review. You'd need to make it worth their while, though. It's a lot of work to read, digest, and review a monograph. At the very least, you should offer them a free copy.[22] Either use one of your author copies, or invoke your discount to make it more affordable. Otherwise, you could offer to contribute a guest blog post, either about the book itself, or reflecting on the process of writing it. One distinct advantage of blog posts is that they usually appear much faster. It can take several years for a review to appear in a journal. While you're waiting, look out for preprints[23] you can promote on social media. On H-Net, scholars in the Humanities and Social Sciences can submit their book for review[24] and also make an announcement. As this site boasts 100,000 members, it might be a good place to start.

Let your publisher know if you spot a review out in the wild. They can then promote it on social media and include pull-out quotes on other publicity material. One academic author told me she was asked to provide some 'puffs' for her book. She was obliged to approach people and send them her manuscript before publication. The timeline was tight, so it was unlikely they'd have the opportunity to read it properly. That didn't matter, though — the publisher just wanted a quote.

If you're unfamiliar with puffs, they're the literary equivalent of soundbites. They appear on the front cover and usually say something like, "A groundbreaking study," "an extraordinary achievement," or "jaw-dropping" (quite a useful

---

22 I've received emails from a few academics, asking me to buy and review their book. This is cheeky!
23 This is the version submitted by the author, before it's been through the peer review and editorial process. Some journals allow authors to share this version in advance.
24 https://networks.h-net.org/reviews

non-committal one, in case you're ever asked to write a puff). Unfortunately, this is standard practice in trade publishing; I'd not heard of it before in scholarly publishing, though. I really hope it doesn't catch on.

Awards and Prizes

Some of the big scholarly organisations offer prizes for monographs, especially for first-time authors. One snag is that you often need to submit between 3 and 6 copies to the judging panel. Your publisher won't necessarily cover the cost, so you need to consider carefully whether you've really got a chance of appearing on the podium. It's debatable, anyway, how much difference an award makes, unless it's a very famous one. However, getting this form of recognition can certainly boost your esteem, if not necessarily your sales. Identify any prizes for which your book might be eligible. Note the deadlines and work out what you need to do.

Mass Media

Unless your book is topical, it's unlikely you'll get interest from the main TV channels. That normally only happens with trade authors, as their publishers will have all the right connections. One of my authors was featured on a prime-time BBC programme, but the original interview was slashed to about 30 seconds. It made no difference to book sales, either.

There's a better chance of being featured on radio or in online articles, assuming your research topic is currently trending. The website Help a Reporter Out (HARO),[25] connects journalists with experts and can be a good way of getting featured on different channels. It's not guaranteed, though. Even if a journalist quotes you as a source, your contribution might be edited out of the final version. Sometimes the article is never published at all, or it appears a long time after the interview.

In any case, the main media channels are far less dominant these days. Most of us tend to follow a mix of YouTube channels, podcasts, and blogs, rather than a couple of big broadcasters or publications.

Podcasts

Podcasts have exploded over the last few years. Unlike radio stations, they can serve niche audiences and are available in a convenient format. Although academia has been slow to grasp the potential of podcasting, the situation is improving. Websites such as H-Podcast[26] and Pod Academy[27] offer lists of podcasts, along with reflections on the medium. And the New Books Network (www.newbooksnetwork.com) is a consortium of scholarly author-interview podcast channels.

Don't be tempted to dive straight into starting your own podcast, though. It's technically difficult and can also take years to build an audience. Maybe that's part of your longer-term strategy, but first become a guest on someone else's

---

25 https://www.helpareporter.com/
26 https://networks.h-net.org/node/84048/pages/114315/academic-podcast-roundup
27 www.podacademy.org

podcast. Established podcasters are always looking for guests, and they can connect you with different audiences. Do your research before committing yourself. Make sure it's an established podcast, and listen to a few episodes to check you're happy with the quality of both the content and the audio.

Blogging

Around ten years ago, nearly everyone had a blog. Then they realised how much work was involved and quietly abandoned them. However, the limits of social media and questions of ownership and control have led to a resurgence in academic blogging.

You can use a blog to:

- Share articles, like your own personal repository.
- Talk to other researchers and get feedback on your work in progress.
- Improve public engagement by making your research more widely available.

Blogging can be a highly effective way of promoting your book. Blog posts are indexed faster by Google and show up in search results much sooner and more prominently than traditional (or static) webpages. Also, it's easy to configure your blog to broadcast new posts through your social media channels and to subscribers.

Before you start blogging, consider what you're trying to achieve:

- Build an audience?
- Increase book sales?
- Attract a publisher?
- Earn money? (unlikely, but some bloggers achieve this through ads or affiliate links)
- Get a job?
- Or is it purely for your own edification?

And how does this fit with your career strategy?

There are a few reasons why you *shouldn't* blog:

- You're researching a controversial topic and don't want to deal with the hassle. Unfortunately, anyone blogging on topics such as gender, sexuality, or climate change will attract tiresome trolls. Although you can make your blog anonymous, obviously that means you can't use it to promote your book.
- You haven't got time.
- Or it's a displacement activity to avoid getting on with your book.

Creating Your Own Blog

If you decide to go ahead with your own blog, take a look at some other academic blogs. What do you like and dislike about them? There's no right way to blog, so you're completely free to come up with your own format.

In terms of blogging platforms, WordPress is still the

world leader. Although it's not perfect, WordPress offers several advantages:

- It's widely used, which means you're developing valuable skills.
- It's highly flexible. You can easily control the look and feel of your blog and ensure it works on all devices.
- It's extensible. With plugins, you can turn your blog into an online journal or an e-commerce store.

You can create a blog for free at wordpress.com where everything is done for you. The compromise here is that WordPress reserves the right to display ads on your site (they usually only do this once it's receiving a lot of traffic). There are paid plans that allow you to decline ads and also give you more control.

Alternatively, you can download the WordPress software for free and install it on your own server. I'm guessing you don't have your own web server. In which case, you'll need to find a host. There are many dedicated WordPress hosts and you've probably seen adverts all over the internet. An affordable option is Reclaim Hosting (www.reclaimhosting.com), who specialise in academic sites. They're currently charging $45 per year, which is less than £3 per month. They'll also help you get set up with your own domain name.

Contributing to a Blog

If creating your own blog sounds like a faff, you could contribute to an existing blog instead. There are a few options here:

- **Multi-author blogs** — examples include *The Conversation* (www.theconversation.com), a news site sourced from the academic and research community.

- **Collaborations** — establishing a blog with one or more colleagues, where you all share the work. This might involve holding committee meetings, though, which is nobody's idea of fun.

- **Guest posts** — contributing a one-off post to an existing blog. This is the easiest option, as it's much less work and there's a ready-made audience. The Thesis Whisperer (www.thesiswhisperer.com) is a great example of a blog that benefits from regular guest posts.

As always, consider what's right for you and your overall strategy.

Social Media

Social media isn't just about telling the world what you've had for lunch. It's sometimes an effective way of promoting your research, finding useful information, and building a community. By employing a few simple techniques, you can transform sites like Twitter from a time sink into an essential tool.

Find the Appropriate Social Media Platform

Some publishers are considering the author's Twitter followers when reviewing a proposal. This might seem like a daft metric, but remember: they're in the business of *selling* books and they want to know about potential audiences. You need to hang out wherever your potential readers spend time.

Twitter is arguably still the most popular social medium, even though people complain about it incessantly. Bear in mind, though, that Twitter is blocked in some countries. It's not a good platform if many of your potential readers are based in China, for example.

For visual research, such as art history, Instagram could be a better choice. Audiences tend to engage more with images and it's much harder to get into an argument. Pinterest is a hugely popular platform, too. Although it's perhaps less academic than Instagram, that might help you stand out more. You can use tools like Canva (www.canva.com) to create attractive images in the correct format.

LinkedIn is potentially useful if your research is relevant to industry. Its enormous userbase of 740,000,000 members can help you reach new audiences. Otherwise, although you'll find academics lurking there, it's not designed for this purpose. Personally, I think LinkedIn has become like Facebook, with people mainly showing off and attention-seeking. You might have a better experience than me, though.

If you have the skills to create video, YouTube is a good platform. Users can subscribe to your channel and receive alerts whenever you post new content. You can also then embed those videos in posts for other social media sites. I'm far too old to even describe TikTok — you're on your own with that one.

By the time this book goes to press, there'll be at least a dozen more alternatives. You don't need to be everywhere, though. Just pick one or two platforms and focus your efforts there. Otherwise, you're spreading yourself too thin and won't gain any traction. And don't become one of those annoying people who posts identical content in 10 different places.

Here are three tips for using social media effectively.

1. Engage, Don't Broadcast

It's helpful, if perhaps intimidating, to think of social media as a big party. Unless you were a massive extrovert, you wouldn't attempt to address everyone in a room with a megaphone. Indeed, if you're anything like me, you'd skulk in a corner near the crisps and hope someone nice strikes up a conversation. The key is to engage with a few people, rather than trying to broadcast to everyone.

If you're new to a social media platform, start by liking and responding to other people's posts. This way, you'll start building relationships and trust. Those people are then more likely to pay attention when you post your own content. The 80/20 rule is helpful here, too. Spend 80% of your time engaging with other people, and only 20% talking about yourself. Otherwise, you're just that eejit with the megaphone. Of course, some of the people with the largest followings never engage at all. But you're not Beyoncé.

On most platforms, you can schedule your posts. This is helpful for alerting people to the imminent release or recent launch of your book. With automation in place, you can then spend your time interacting. Don't get carried away with the scheduled posts, though. Nobody wants to be told incessantly about your book. Where possible, include a link to a related digital artefact, such as a blog post, podcast, or video.

That way, you're sharing useful resources, rather than just tooting your own horn.

2. Don't Overdo It

A few years ago, I received a book proposal from an academic with a strong social media presence. Initially, this pleased me, as I knew she'd be effective at promoting her work. When I looked more closely at her Twitter feed, my enthusiasm evaporated. On average, she was tweeting every 4 minutes. And most of these tweets were complaining about impending deadlines and her inability to get anything done.

There are two lessons here. Firstly, publishers will see anything you tweet, so be careful what you say. Secondly, set some clear limits on how much time you're spending on social media. What *feels* like five minutes is usually at least an hour. There are hundreds of well-paid engineers whose job is to keep you in the chair, endlessly clicking. Set a timer (I often use the Pomodoro Technique for this purpose) and definitely get your writing done *first*.

3. Link Between Sites and Profiles

No one social media platform does everything and reaches everybody. Inevitably, you'll need at least two or three profiles and a way of linking them together. One way of doing this is through your own website or blog. Otherwise, make sure you offer a way for people to find out more about your work. Another solution is Linktree (www.linktre.ee), which allows you to connect to multiple sites with one link. You can place this link in your social media bio, giving everyone easy access to your other profiles and sites. This is especially important on sites like Instagram, where you can't add links to individual posts.

If you don't have one already, create your ORCID, or Open Researcher and Contributor ID (www.orcid.org). This is a free scheme for uniquely identifying academic authors and linking together their publications. You add your publications to the ORCID portal, then add your ID (in the form of a link) to CVs, institutional profiles, or social media bios. By using a tool like Linktree on Twitter, you can easily direct followers to your publications, your blog, and other social media accounts.

This is an example of blending social media with academic networking. There are also sites aimed squarely at researchers.

Academic Networking

The simplest form of academic networking is the listserv, or mailing list. Although they seem rather old-fashioned these days, listservs remain popular in some research areas. They're an effective way of finding out about events, sharing ideas, and connecting with people working on similar areas. Naturally, they're also an excellent place to announce your book. You can find listservs by googling, or through directories such as H-Net (www.h-net.org/lists/)

There are also dedicated academic networking sites, which are modelled on platforms like Facebook. Academia.edu and ResearchGate are the most famous. Although these sites offer a convenient way of sharing your work and connecting with your community, read the terms and conditions carefully. What are you giving away? In some cases, you're handing over your intellectual property for a commercial organisation to monetise. Often, too, your content is only visible to subscribers. These sites aren't necessarily great, then, for increasing the visibility and reach of your work.

A more ethical alternative for some researchers is the Humanities Commons (www.hcommons.org), a non-profit project developed by the Modern Language Association (MLA). This online network allows you to share scholarship, build connections, and even create a blog. It's completely free to use and you retain ownership of all your content. Although it's aimed at the humanities, it's highly interdisciplinary, offering a huge range of innovative projects.

If your research involves code or datasets, it's worth investigating Zenodo (www.zenodo.org). This open-access repository is backed by CERN and allows researchers to upload papers, reports, and digital artefacts.

Creating Your Marketing Plan

An appropriate marketing plan is determined by the nature of your book and also your inclination. Here are some suggestions for different stages of your project:

Before Submitting Your Proposal

- Establish (or smarten up) your social media presence. Make sure everything is connected to establish your academic credentials and expertise, e.g. including your ORCID.

- Create a profile on an academic networking site such as Humanities Commons and share existing work, such as conference papers or journal preprints. This helps build credibility with potential publishers.

- If you have time, create a blog on your book topic. Otherwise, investigate the possibility of writing a guest post or contributing to a multi-author platform such as *The Conversation*. You're then visible as someone who knows about this subject.

While You're Writing Your Book

- Keep any social media accounts up-to-date. This is good for sustaining interest in your research and also for creating accountability. You can share your progress and get encouragement.

- Remain alert to forthcoming conferences and other speaking opportunities. By committing your future self to these engagements, you're getting additional accountability. You really want to have that book finished and ideally available for pre-order.

- If you end up with random bits of writing (which you will), save them for blog posts or articles.

Once Your Book is Published

- Include your book title and (importantly) a link in your email signature. Your correspondents probably won't copy and paste the details into a search engine, so make it easy for them by ensuring it's clickable.

- If you're still affiliated with a university, contact their media office to see whether they'll issue a press release. They might at least give you a mention on the website, in a newsletter, or through social media channels. There might also be an alumni office who are interested in your activities. Your department might also put up a poster or send round an email. They'll need your blurb and the link for ordering copies.

- Notify any professional associations of which you're a member.

- Update your social media, academic networking, and institutional profiles. Make sure you include links, ideally to a destination where people can actually buy your book.

- Identify journals that might be interested in reviewing your book. Target Open Access journals, as your review will be more visible and accessible. You can find most of them at www.doaj.org.

- Pitch your book to New Books Network (www.newbooksnetwork.com) to secure a podcast interview.

You'll want to do most of the marketing once the book is available to purchase. We're highly impatient these days — if something piques our curiosity, we want to grab it immediately. We don't want to know something will be available next year. Our brains will be filled with thousands of other books in the meantime.

There are no quick wins. Effective marketing, in any area, is about engaging with your community, not broadcasting to an audience. Nobody wants to think of themselves as an audience member who's patiently sitting there while someone explains the importance of their work or product. We've all got better things to do with our time. Have proper conversations, with real people. If you create a meaningful connection, those individuals will hopefully buy your book, then tell their own connections about it. This is slow, but more effective than broadcasting. Above all, be respectful of people's time and attention — those are the two most valuable commodities in the 21st century.

Everything is changing, too. Don't expect what worked 10 years ago to still be effective now. And there's no foolproof strategy. All the 'Ten Ways to Promote Your Book' listicles are peddling generic advice that works in only limited cases. How much effort you want to put into promotion depends on your motivation (see Chapter One). If you just want the satisfaction or kudos of having published a book, maybe you're not too fussed about the sales. If, though, you're hoping for royalties or a wide readership, you'll need to get yourself a sandwich board.

Summary

Just like those final stages of your PhD, this phase of your book is exhausting. It feels as though you'll never reach the end — there's always one more task to be completed. By working through it systematically, though, you'll stay on track and become a published author. No doubt you'll vow to never write another book. However, you'll have developed a range of valuable skills that'll help you both with future books and in your overall career strategy. For now, focus on this stage of your *publishing strategy*. Fix your eye on the goal and keep pedalling.

Dealing with readers' reports can be dispiriting, but this is an invaluable part of the process. You'll receive comprehensive feedback from at least two people who have read your manuscript in detail. They'll help you see your work from a completely different perspective. While you won't necessarily agree with their suggestions (and you don't need to implement them), this feedback forces you to get out of your own head for a little while. That can be a very welcome excursion.

By involving readers at this stage (and hopefully earlier, too), you'll produce a much better book. And with a better book, you'll be keen to tell the world. As a published author, you'll find all sorts of opportunities available to you. This experience will clarify both your publishing and your career strategies and you'll have a stronger sense of what to do next.

KEY POINTS

- Make a plan for dealing with readers' reports and be selective about what you implement.
- Allow yourself enough time for checking the proofs carefully. And make sure you spot check every version that's sent to you.
- Negotiate on any unrealistic deadlines imposed by your publisher. Work out what's feasible for you.
- If you need to compile your own index, set aside sufficient time to learn the basic principles and do a thorough job.
- Create a marketing plan. And don't just rely on traditional methods for promoting your book. Embrace social media (if you can bear it) and investigate podcasting, blogging, and networking.
- Keep notes on everything you've learned. They'll come in handy for your next book!

We're almost at the end of our publishing adventure. Join me in the conclusion, where we'll review what we've covered and consider your next steps.

TROUBLESHOOTING

My readers are recommending lots of changes and I'm despairing

The key word here is *recommending*. You don't have to implement everything they suggest, although you should *consider* it all. Publishers will understand that you don't have time to completely rewrite your book. Show them you've spent time assessing the feedback and that you've identified what will make the biggest impact. The Pareto Principle probably applies here: 20% of the suggestions will make 80% of the difference. Once you've decided what to implement, break it down into more manageable tasks and set yourself a schedule.

My publisher has given me an impossible deadline for checking proofs

Ideally, your publisher should tell you when to expect the proofs, then you can block out time in your diary. In reality, I've never heard of this happening. There's usually a dreadful silence for months on end, then you're suddenly expected to complete a range of difficult tasks within a week. If this happens, you should negotiate. First, work out how long it'll take you, based on a 500-word sample. Assuming it's 20 hours, for instance, see how that'll fit into your schedule. Remember, you can't really spend an entire day proofreading.

Allow some contingency time, too, as everything always

takes longer than we think. Also, you want to be in a position to haggle. If you ask for three weeks, your publisher might talk you down to two. Start with two, and they might talk you down to one — which would be one hell of a week. If they still want you to do it in less time, explain that you'll have to be less thorough.

Nobody is any taking notice of my book

It takes time. Book reviews in journals are especially slow to emerge, partly because the peer-review process is so protracted. Also, people offer to review books, then it keeps ending up at the bottom of their to-do list. Maybe you can find someone who's already bought or read your book. Would they be prepared to review it on a blog? This is one of the advantages of Twitter. Happy readers will often tweet about the book and tag the author (assuming you're there, of course).

And don't rely on just a couple of promotion methods, either. You'll need to experiment with different platforms and learn what suits both you and your book. There are so many ways to learn about new publications now, including tweets, blog posts, and podcasts. You can't be sure of your audience's preferred channels, so you have to find them.

CONCLUSION

> "Have a bias towards action – let's see something happen now. You can break that big plan into small steps and take the first step right away." –
> Indira Gandhi

Maybe you haven't yet started on your book, but hopefully you're now better prepared for what lies ahead. As you'll have seen, you spend remarkably little time actually writing. Many more months are devoted to planning, revising, and promoting your book. All these stages are necessary to produce a successful monograph. While this might've seemed a Herculean effort, these skills are also transferable to other areas of your work. And once you've published a book, many other feats will seem possible.

By understanding your purpose (Chapter One), you'll ensure this is the right project *and* the right time. As it's such a big challenge, you need to know whether it fits with your career strategy and commitments. Are there other projects that should take priority right now? The planning stage in Chapter Two establishes whether your project is viable. It's much better to discover the problems early on, rather than when you're halfway through writing it. And scoping, mapping, and planning makes that writing stage significantly easier.

If you want someone to spend their time and money on publishing your book, it's vital you understand their perspective (Chapter Three). By appreciating the realities of scholarly publishing and what editors are seeking, you'll produce a more compelling proposal (Chapter Four). And you can save yourself a lot of time and disappointment by identifying the most appropriate presses for your book. It's also crucial for you to understand the rights you are giving up and the potential costs you might incur.

Publishing deadlines are usually tight — many first-time authors assume it's a typo when they read the contract. The only way to stay on track is to think like a professional writer. After all, that's what you are. You'll need to develop a writing process that's effective for you (Chapter Five) and create the right conditions for your book to emerge. By breaking everything down, setting yourself realistic milestones, and getting feedback, you'll reach the finish line.

Then you'll realise that's just the first part of the race. Next, you must turn that baggy first draft into something that looks like a book. While this is a lot of work, you can make it easier by adopting a strategic approach to editing (Chapter Six), rather than going at it in a frenzy. This involves inhabiting the mind of your reader — what will make them happy? And what will make them grumpy?

The most important readers — at least at this stage — are your reviewers. They'll give you invaluable feedback on shaping your final manuscript (Chapter Seven). Once that's done, you can get everything ready for submission. By understanding the publishing process and managing your time effectively, you'll produce a book you'll be proud to promote. You can share all your enthusiasm, expertise, and insights with the world.

Although there's a lot of guff in the media about the 'death of the book' and this being the digital age, we still crave the physical artefact. Indeed, it's become even more important, now that so many formerly tangible objects have become virtual. When lockdown was partially eased here in the UK in April 2021, booksellers reported customers coming in to sniff the books.

You'll understand the excitement of discovering there's a book published on the topic that interests you. Well, you'll be performing that role for someone else. Also, the legal deposit system means your book will be safely stored in six libraries in the UK, ensuring it's available to future scholars. While websites, videos, and podcasts are trendy, they're easily deleted. Publishing a book is the best way of achieving immortality (and it's a lot cheaper than cryonic suspension). As Carl Sagan wrote:

> A book is made from a tree. It is an assemblage of flat, flexible parts (still called "leaves") imprinted with dark pigmented squiggles. One glance at it and you hear the voice of another person, perhaps someone dead for thousands of years. Across the millennia, the author is speaking, clearly and silently, inside your head, directly to you. Writing is perhaps the greatest of human inventions, binding together people, citizens of distant epochs, who never knew one another. Books break the shackles of time — proof that humans can work magic.

And heaven knows we need some magic right now.

Maybe you've also identified some activities you want to pursue professionally? Few people enjoy checking proofs or compiling an index, but there might be other areas that suit you, such as editing or podcasting. This can feed back into your career strategy. Perhaps this experience has convinced you of the merits of self-publishing for your next book. Although you'll have additional skills to learn, you'll have acquired many of the basics and you'll also have a thorough understanding of the publishing process. Take a look at the Resources section for more information on self-publishing. Revisit your sense of purpose (see Chapter One) and decide on your next steps. If you write another book, you'll be much faster and also feel more confident. With one book to your name, there's unequivocal evidence that you're capable of writing another one.

I'd love to hear about your progress. You're welcome to either tweet me @DrCatherinePope or email catherine@phdprogress.com. Thanks so much for reading my book. I hope you found it useful. Wishing you all the best with your publishing adventures, and beyond.

RESOURCES

For further resources and clickable links, visit:

www.howtopublishyourphd.com

Book Resources

H-Net reviews — https://networks.h-net.org/reviews

Library Hub Discover — https://discover.libraryhub.jisc.ac.uk/

Contracts & Royalties

Authors Guild Sample Contract — https://go.authorsguild.org/contract_sections/1

Authors' Licensing and Collecting Society — www.alcs.co.uk

Public Lending Right — www.bl.uk/plr/plr-payments

Textbook & Academic Authors Association — www.taaonline.net)

Writers' and Artists' Yearbook — www.writersandartists.co.uk

Copyright

Copyright User — www.copyrightuser.org

Intellectual Property and Copyright — www.gov.uk/topic/intellectual-property/copyright

PLS Clear — www.plsclear.com

WATCH (Writers and their Copyright Holders) — www.reading.ac.uk/library/about-us/projects/lib-watch.aspx

Editing & Proofreading

Susan Rabiner & Alfred Fortunato, *Thinking Like Your Editor*

Chartered Institute of Editing and Proofreading — www.ciep.uk

Open Access

Directory of Open Access Books — www.doabooks.org

Knowledge Unlatched — www.knowledgeunlatched.org

Open Research Library — www.openresearchlibrary.org

Open Access Scholarly Publishing Association — www.oaspa.org

Open Access Theses and Dissertations — www.oatd.org

The Research Excellence Framework — www.ref.ac.uk

Indexing

Nancy C. Mulvaney, *Indexing Books*

Society of Indexers — www.indexers.org.uk/find-an-indexer/directory/

Journals

JournalSeek — www.journalseek.net

Think Check Submit — www.thinkchecksubmit.org

Academic Networking

Humanities Commons — www.hcommons.org

Listservs — www.h-net.org/lists/

ORCID — www.orcid.org

Zenodo — www.zenodo.org

Blogging

The Conversation — www.theconversation.com

Reclaim Hosting — www.reclaimhosting.com

WordPress — www.wordpress.com

Podcasting

H-Podcast — https://networks.h-net.org/node/84048/pages/114315/academic-podcast-roundup

Pod Academy — www.podacademy.org

Social Media

Canva — www.canva.com

Linktree — www.linktre.ee

Traditional Media

Help a Report Out (HARO) — www.helpareporter.com

Publishers

Association of University Presses — https://aupresses.org/resources/aupresses-subject-area-grid/

Open Book Publishers — www.openbookpublishers.com

Self-Publishing

Joanna Penn — www.thecreativepenn.com

Reedsy — www.reedsy.com

Online Tools

Focusmate — www.focusmate.com

Grammarly — www.grammarly.com

Hemingway Editor — www.hemingwayapp.com

PerfectIt — www.intelligentediting.com

ProWritingAid — www.prowritingaid.com/

QR Code Generator — www.qr-code-generator.com

Writers' Diet — www.writersdiet.com

Time Management
David Allen, *Getting Things Done*

Greg McKeown, *Essentialism*

Brian P. Moran & Michael Lennington, *The 12 Week Year*

Cal Newport, *Deep Work*

Writing
Stephen King, *On Writing*

T J Fitikides, *Common Mistakes in English*

Stephen Pressfield, *Nobody Wants to Read Your Sh*t*

Stephen Pressfield, *The War of Art*

Helen Sword, *Stylish Academic Writing*

Helen Sword, *The Writer's Diet*

Acknowledgements

If you decide to write a book, you'll need some support. This book wouldn't have happened without all these marvellous people. Firstly, the organisers, attendees, and fellow speakers at the Thesis to Monograph event, hosted by the University of Sussex in 2019. On the bottom of my programme, I scribbled a note to myself: "write a book about this". Thanks to COVID-19, I got the time to realise my idea.

Attendees of my Academia on the Side webinars generously shared their experiences and asked excellent questions. Thank you to all of them, and especially to Dr Alison Moulds for supporting and promoting these events.

I would've struggled to finish this book without Focusmate. My regular partners — Aida, Asma, Cheima, Hisae, Nat, and Natasha — provided accountability, energy, and empathy.

Viktoria Doppelstein has encouraged me with my recent writing projects, especially when I've been tempted to pursue the *next* project instead. Debbie Harrison gave me lots of detailed feedback on an early draft and gamely tried the exercises. Philippa St George has been an absolute star. She read the manuscript thoroughly, discussed the concepts repeatedly, and sustained my often flagging enthusiasm. Everyone needs a cheerleader like Philippa.

As I mentioned in Chapter Seven, it's good practice to thank your indexer in the Acknowledgements. Tanya Izzard compiled an exemplary index. She also prepared many meals, supplied treats, and supported me throughout lockdown and this book. I don't think all indexers will cook your dinner, but I have the good fortune to be married to Tanya.

Finally, thanks to you, the reader, for wanting to share your knowledge with the world.

You might also like ...

How to Finish Your PhD

Are you stuck in your PhD? Is progress imperceptible to the naked eye? I'll help you understand *why* you're stuck and what you can do about it. By the end of the book, you'll have the clarity and confidence you need to finish your PhD. Together, we'll create an action plan that's right for you. Each chapter includes activities and downloadable resources.

Getting Started with Zotero

Zotero is a free tool to help you collect, manage, cite, and share your bibliographic information. If you're handling more than a few dozen citations in your research project, Zotero will make life much easier for you. Through tutorials and screenshots, you'll learn how to make the most of its features.

Find out more at:
www.phdprogress.com

Index

A

Academia.edu 312
accessibility 158, 169
accountability 208
acknowledgements 284
  image use 131
adaptation rights 119
advances 41
agents, literary 41
ALCS (Authors' Licensing and Collecting Society) 125
Allen, David 198
Angelou, Maya 189
argument 66, 223
  emphasising 247
  Golden Thread 73
  research questions based on 69
Association of University Presses 147

attention residue 195
audio books 118
audit
  thesis 60–62, 70
  writing 218
authority 158, 169
Authors Guild 116
Authors' Licensing and Collecting Society (ALCS) 125
avoidance
  completion 221
  writing 233
awards 303

B

blogs and blogging 301, 305, 314
blurbs 295

Book Processing Charges (BPC) for Open Access publishing 112, 115, 142
books
  audio books 118
  ebooks 9, 111
  edited collections 45
  formats 111, 118
  mini monographs 42
  prices of 47
  trade 40, 57
brain structure 22, 211, 218
British Library's EThOS database 53

C

career strategy 25, 324
  and journal publication 44
  and publishing expectations 26, 34
  and trade publishing 41
Cartesian Logic 24
chapters 80–81
  edited collections 28, 45
  length of 80
  number of 83
  planning of 154, 163
  standalone publications 80
  subsections in 81
  titles for 82

Cirillo, Francesco 201
citations
  checking 199
  copyright rules for 127, 129
  formatting 269
  over-reliance on 244
  proofreading of 262
clarity, editing for 249–251, 271
clearance readers 284
competitor works 169, 222
comprehensiveness 158, 169
concept of book 66, 223
conclusions 88
  mini 247
conferences
  promotion through 167, 300, 314
  publisher contact at 147
content
  auditing, in thesis 70
  gaps, filling of 64, 104
  reuse of 47, 64, 116
  rewriting of 64
contracts 116–121
  advance/pre-publication 175
  author copies 122
  copyright 121
  deadlines 119, 272

format rights 118
libel 121
media appearances and adaptations 119
proofreading requirements in 121
publishable quality requirement in 120
reuse of content 47, 64, 116
territorial rights 117
translation rights 117
word count in 121
copy-editors 262
copyright
  contracts on 121
  permissions 126
costs 8, 38, 132–134
  editing, professional 261, 262
  editing software 265, 266
  image reproductions 131
  indexing, professional 291
  Open Access (OA) publishing 110, 112, 142
  opportunity 28
  proofreading, professional 260, 263
  publishers' fees 134
  revisions, due to 133
cross-references 248
currency/up-to-dateness 157, 169

D

Darwin Days 201, 225
deadlines 119, 272
deductive reasoning 75
deep work 195–197, 233
developmental editors 261
distractions 195
  removal of 205
  spellchecker as 213
  writing journal articles as 44
drafts 210

E

ebooks 9, 111
edited collections 45, 47
editing 132, 244–246
  checklist for 272
  clarity 249–251, 271
  flow 241–242, 270
  formatting 268
  paragraph-level 241
  proofreading 256–263, 271
  reverse outlining 242–243
  sentence-level 249
  signposting 245–246, 271
  software use in 264
  structure 238, 270
  style 193, 194, 249–251

ambiguity, avoiding 254
consistent word use 255
power verbs 251
simplicity vs. complexity in 250
unnecessary words, eliminating 254
Zombie Nouns/nominalisations 252
time needed for 270
troubleshooting 276
writing, difference from 211, 234
editing and writing cycle 210, 257
editors, professional 260
embargos on thesis publication 139
emotions 22
 and competition 222
 and distractions 196
 and making progress 218
 and procrastination 223
energy
 levels, suiting tasks to 197, 199, 201
 starting/finishing 96
EThOS database, British Library 53
examiners, PhD 31

F

fair dealing/use 127
feedback
 beta readers 227
 evaluating 281
 implementing and responding to 283
 readers' reports 9, 280–281
 viva as source of 31
flow 241, 270
Focusmate 208
formats, of books 111, 118
formatting 262, 268
Fortuna, Alfred 42
freewriting 205, 207, 224

G

Gaiman, Neil 230
goal setting 99
Golden Thread 73
Grammarly (editing software) 265

H

handwriting 213
HARO (Help a Reporter Out) 304

headings for sections/subsections 248
Help a Reporter Out (HARO) 304
Hemingway, Ernest 191
H-Net 302, 312
hooks 78, 85, 89
Humanities Commons 313

I

ideas, surfeit of 104
images
 copyright for 129
 costs of 131
 cover 9
 proposals, detailed in 165
 public domain 132
imposter syndrome 190
income from publishing 123
independent researchers/scholars 27, 35
indexers, professional 290
indexing 133, 289
inductive reasoning 75
interdisciplinarity 67

J

journal articles 28, 43
 accessibility of 47
 predatory journals 44
 promotion through 299
 timescales 299
journal publishing
 timescales 44
JournalSeek 44

K

Kearns, Hugh 91
King, Stephen 193
knowledge gap, creation of 77

L

Lennington, Michael 98
libel 121
libraries 108
 image 130
 income from 125
 self-published books, purchase of 135
line editors 261
links/segues 81, 84, 249
literary agents 41
literary mascots 50

literature reviews 63
Lock, Pam 236
longhand writing 213

M

manuscript
  clarity of 249–251, 271
  drafts 210
  flow of 241, 270
  proofreading 256–263, 271, 277
  proposals 153
  reverse outlining 242–243
  signposting 245–246, 271
  structure of 238, 270
  submission of 18
    checklist 285
mapping
  during editing 238
  during planning 69
  thesis 70
mascots, literary 50
McKeown, Greg 56
media appearances 119, 315
metadata 82, 83, 297
methodology 63
monographs 57
  acknowledgements 284
  conclusions 88
  deciding against 65
  dedications 285
  definitions of 39, 49
  evaluating 52
  introductions 76
  length of 63
  mini 42
  Open Access (OA) 112
  sales figures 107
  series 40
  thesis, difference from 48, 191
  titles for 160
Moran, Brian P. 97
motivation 22, 56
  and career strategy 25, 34
  maintaining 37, 218, 271
multiple discovery 223

N

neuroscience 22, 211, 218
Newport, Cal 195
nominalisations 252
nouns
  verbs, keeping with 255
  Zombie 252

O

Open Access (OA) 110, 115, 142
  journals 315
Open Book Publishers 112
Open Researcher and Contributor ID (ORCID) 312
Open Research Library 51
originality 66, 157, 169, 244
outlines 216, 247
outlining, reverse 242–243

P

paragraphs 241
Pareto Principle 220
Penn, Joanna 119
perfectionism, avoiding 220, 234
PerfectIt (editing software) 266, 277
planning
  concept of book 66
  mapping 69
  point of view 66, 69, 73
  research reading 91
  scope 66
  structure
    chapters 80–81
  chronological 72
  conclusions 88
  Golden Thread 73
  setting limits 90
  thematic 72
  word budgets 90
  subject of book 66
  thesis audit 60–62
  time management 95, 195
  troubleshooting 104
  writing 213
PLR (Public Lending Right) 125
PLS Clear website 128
podcasts 119, 304, 315
point of view 66, 223
  emphasising 247
  Golden Thread 73
  research questions based on 69
Pomodoro Technique 201, 225, 258
Pressfield, Stephen 196, 211, 223
priorities and prioritisation 56, 200
prizes 303
procrastination, overcoming 223
productivity, boosting 195–212

progress
  charts 207
  lack of 234
  maintaining 218
  resistance to 223
  reviewing 225, 234
promotion 320
  academic networking 312, 314
  awards and prizes 303
  blogging 301, 305, 314
  blurbs 295
  book reviews as 301
  by publishers 294
  chapter titles, used in 82
  conferences/talks 167, 300, 314
  interdisciplinary work, effect on 68
  journal articles as 299
  marketing plan 295, 313
  mass media 303
  metadata 82, 83, 297
  podcasts 304, 315
  puffs 302
  social media 308, 314
proofreaders, professional 259–260
proofreading 133
  after typesetting 287, 319
  before submission of manuscript 256–263, 271, 277
  proposals and covering emails 173
proposals
  audience/readership in 165
  image use 165
  informal approaches 152
  length of book 164
  manuscript completion for 153
  marketing plans for 314
  monograph titles, used in 160
  publishers, selecting 144
  publishers' templates 155
  readers' reports, use of 176
  references, academic 172
  rejection 7, 151, 152, 175, 178, 186
  responses to 174
  reviewers, identifying 169
  review timescales 174
  submission 151, 172
  troubleshooting 186
  writing 155
    author biography 168
    chapter plan 163
    competitive analysis 169
    marketing plan 165
    overview statement 157

ProWritingAid (editing software) 265, 276, 277
Public Lending Right (PLR) 125
publishers
  assessing 148
  identifying 17, 146
  interdisciplinarity, views on 67
  promotion by 294
publishing
  academic 107
  and copyright 126
  contracts 116–122, 175
  during PhD 30
  economics of 107
  income from 123
  indexing 289
  Open Access (OA) 110, 115, 142
  process 278
  rights 116–122
  scams 149
  self-publishing 43, 135, 142
  strategy for 28
  timeline 17, 18, 182
  timescales 35, 37, 155, 187
    edited collections 46
    journals 44
  trade 40, 41, 57
  troubleshooting 142, 319

vanity publishing 135
puffs, promotional 302
purpose
  of your book 157
  personal 22, 56
    and career strategy 25, 34
  troubleshooting 56

R

Rabiner, Susan 42
readers
  beta 227
  introductions, curiosity piqued by 77
  proposals, defined in 165
  writing for 213
readers' reports 9, 280–281, 319
  identifying reviewers 169
  implementation and response 283
  interdisciplinary works 68
  proposal submission 176
  self-published works 138
  timing of 37
reading
  like a writer 193
  research 91
  SQ3R (Survey, Question, Read, Recite, Review) 94

Readitis 91
references
  checking 199
  copyright rules for 127, 129
  formatting 269
  proofreading of 262
rejection 7, 151, 152, 175, 178, 186
relevance 61
repositories, university 139
Research Excellence Framework (REF) 115
ResearchGate 312
research questions 69, 74
research reading 91
resources
  Association of University Presses 147
  British Library's EThOS database 53
  contracts 116
  Focusmate 208
  Help a Reporter Out (HARO) 304
  H-Net 302, 312
  JournalSeek 44
  literary mascots 50
  Open Research Library 51
  PLS Clear website 128
  podcasting 304, 315
  Society of Authors 122
  Society of Indexers 291
  Textbook & Academic Authors Association 123
  Think Check Submit 44, 149
  WATCH (Writers and their Copyright Holders) database 128
  Writers' and Artists' Yearbook 42
reverse outlining 242–243
reviews, post-publication
  evaluation through 52
  literature 63
  potential journals for 315
  promotion through 301
rights 116–122, 143
  copyright 121, 126
  format 118
  media appearances and adaptations 119
  territorial 117
  translation 117
routines for writing 196, 204
royalties 123
Rule of Three
  chapter structure 85
  outlines 216
  research reading 92
  sprints 99

S

Sagan, Carl 323
sales figures for monographs 39, 107
schedules, for writing 196, 213
scope 29, 66
screen readers 259
sections/subsections 81, 247, 248
segues/links 81, 84, 249
self-publishing 43, 135
self-sabotage 221
sentences
  editing 249
  length of 250
shutdown routines 206
signposting 245–246, 271
simultaneous invention 223
Sinek, Simon 22
social media
  Instagram 309
  LinkedIn 309
  marketing through 167
  publishers on 147
  Twitter 308
  YouTube 309
Society of Authors 122
Society of Indexers 291
spellchecker 264
  distracting possibilities of 213
sprints, 12-week 97, 197
SQ3R (Survey, Question, Read, Recite, Review) 94
start-up routines 204
storyboarding 215
structure
  chapters 80–81
  chronological 72
  conclusions 88
  editing 238, 270
  Golden Thread 73
  setting limits 90
  thematic 72
  word budgets 90
style 193, 194, 249–251
  ambiguity, avoiding 254
  blurb writing 296
  consistent word use 255
  power verbs 251
  simplicity vs. complexity in 250
  unnecessary words, eliminating 254
  Zombie Nouns/nominalisations 252
subheadings 248

subject, of book 66
subsections 81, 247, 248
Survey, Question, Read, Recite, Review (SQ3R) 94
Sword, Helen 252

T

task selection 198
territorial rights 117
Textbook & Academic Authors Association 123
thesis 12, 62
  audit of 60–62, 61, 70
  book, basis for 29, 32
  definition of 49
  embargo 139
  monograph, difference from 48, 191
  publication of, unchanged 43
Think Check Submit 44, 149
time
  commitments 35, 37
  delays 8
  editing, needed for 270
  ideal, for monograph writing 30
  lack of 56, 105, 272, 276
  proofreading, needed for 257
  scheduled 196, 213

timelines, narrative 73
time management 95
  12-week sprints 97, 197
  deep work 195–197, 233
  energy levels 197, 199, 201
  Pomodoro Technique 201, 225, 258
timescales
  journal publishing 44, 299
  monograph publishing 17, 18, 35, 37, 155, 182, 187
titles
  chapters 82
  monographs 160
  sections/subsections 81, 248
trade publishing 40, 41, 57
troubleshooting
  editing 276
  finding your purpose 56
  planning 104
  proposals 186
  publishing 142, 319
  writing 233

V

verbs
  nouns, keeping with 255
  power 251
viva (PhD examination) 31

W

WATCH (Writers and their Copyright Holders) database 128
why, starting with 22, 84, 157, 224
wireframes 216
word budgets 90
word counts
　contracts on 121
　limits for 90
　tracking, motivation through 219
workspaces
　optimising 205
　tidying 207
Writers' and Artists' Yearbook 42
writer, thinking like a 189
writing
　accountability 207–208
　audit 218
　avoiding finishing 221
　brain structure and 211
　drafts 210
　editing, difference from 211, 234
　feedback on 227
　freewriting 205, 207, 224
　links/segues 81, 84, 249
　longhand 213
　outlines 216
　paragraph-level 241
　perfectionism, avoiding 220, 234
　planning a piece of 213
　procrastination, overcoming 223
　productivity 195–212
　progress, maintaining 218
　progress, reviewing 225, 234
　readers, consideration of 213
　reading like a writer 193
　routines 196
　scheduling time for 196, 213
　sentence-level 249
　shutdown routines 206
　start-up routines 204
　storyboarding 215
　thinking like a writer 189
　troubleshooting 233
　wireframes 216
writing and editing cycle 210, 257
writing fortress 203
writing style 193, 194, 249–251
　ambiguity, avoiding 254
　blurb writing 296
　consistent word use 255

power verbs 251
simplicity vs. complexity in 250
unnecessary words, eliminating 254
Zombie Nouns/nominalisations 252

Z

Zenodo (open-access repository) 313

www.ingramcontent.com/pod-product-compliance
Lightning Source LLC
Chambersburg PA
CBHW071556080526
44588CB00010B/931